PLOTINOS
Complete Works

In Chronological Order, Grouped in Four Periods;

With

BIOGRAPHY by Porphyry, Eunapius, & Suidas,
COMMENTARY by Porphyry,
ILLUSTRATIONS by Jamblichus & Ammonius,
STUDIES in Sources, Development, Influence;
INDEX of Subjects, Thoughts and Words.

by

Kenneth Sylvan Guthrie,

Professor in Extension, University of the South, Sewanee;
A.M., Sewanee, and Harvard; Ph D., Tulane, and Columbia.
M.D., Medico-Chirurgical College, Philadelphia.

PLOTINOS
Complete Works

In Chronological Order, Grouped in Four Periods;

With
BIOGRAPHY by PORPHYRY, EUNAPIUS, & SUIDAS,
COMMENTARY by PORPHYRY,
ILLUSTRATIONS by JAMBLICHUS & AMMONIUS,
STUDIES in Sources, Development, Influence;
INDEX of Subjects, Thoughts and Words.

by
KENNETH SYLVAN GUTHRIE,
Professor in Extension, University of the South, Sewanee;
A.M., Sewanee, and Harvard; Ph.D., Tulane, and Columbia.
M.D., Medico-Chirurgical College, Philadelphia.

Vol. I
Biographies; Amelian Books, 1-21.

WIPF & STOCK · Eugene, Oregon

Wipf and Stock Publishers
199 W 8th Ave, Suite 3
Eugene, OR 97401

Plotinos: Complete Works, Volume 1
In Chronological Order, Grouped in Four Periods
By Guthrie, Kenneth Sylvan
Softcover ISBN-13: 978-1-6667-3391-4
Hardcover ISBN-13: 978-1-6667-2923-8
eBook ISBN-13: 978-1-6667-2924-5
Publication date 8/12/2021
Previously published by Comparative Literature Press, 1918

This edition is a scanned facsimile of
the original edition published in 1918.

FOREWORD

It is only with mixed feelings that such a work can be published. Overshadowing all is the supreme duty to the English-speaking world, and secondarily to the rest of humanity to restore to them in an accessible form their, till now, unexploited spiritual heritage, with its flood of light on the origins of their favorite philosophy. And then comes the contrast—the pitiful accomplishment. Nor could it be otherwise; for there are passages that never can be interpreted perfectly; moreover, the writer would gladly have devoted to it every other leisure moment of his life—but that was impossible. As a matter of fact, he would have made this translation at the beginning of his life, instead of at its end, had it not been for a mistaken sense of modesty; but as no one offered to do it, he had to do it himself. If he had done it earlier, his "Philosophy of Plotinos" would have been a far better work.

Indeed, if it was not for the difficulty and expense of putting it out, the writer would now add to the text an entirely new summary of Plotinos's views. The fairly complete concordance, however, should be of service to the student, and help to rectify the latest German summary of Plotinos, that by Drews, which in its effort to furnish a foundation for Hartmann's philosophy of the unconscious, neglected both origins and spiritual aspects. However, the present genetic

FOREWORD

insight of Plotinos's development should make forever impossible that theory of cast-iron coherence, which is neither historical nor human.

The writer, having no thesis such as Drews' to justify, will welcome all corrections and suggestions. He regrets the inevitable uncertainties of capitalization (as between the supreme One, Intelligence World-Soul and Daemon or guardian, and the lower one, intelligence, soul and demon or guardian); and any other inconsistencies of which he may have been guilty; and he beseeches the mantle of charity in view of the stupendousness of the undertaking, in which he practicaly could get no assistance of any kind, and also in view of the almost insuperable difficulties of his own career. He, however, begs to assure the reader that he did everything "ad majorem Dei gloriam."

INDEX.

PLOTINOS' COMPLETE WORKS.

Preface 1
Concordance of Enneads and Chronological Numbers 2
Concordance of Chronological Numbers and Enneads 3
Biography of Plotinos, by Porphyry 5
Biographies by Eunapius and Suidas 39
Amelian Books, 1-21 40
Amelio-Porphyrian Books, 22-23 283
Porphyrian Books, 34-45 641
Eustochian Books, 46-54 1017

PLOTINIC STUDIES

IN SOURCES, DEVELOPMENT AND INFLUENCE.

1. Development in the Teachings of Plotinos..1269
2. Platonism: Significance, Progress, and Results 1288
3. Plotinos' View of Matter 1296
4. Plotinos' Creation of the Trinity 1300
5. Resemblances to Christianity 1307
6. Indebtedness to Numenius 1313
7. Value of Plotinos 1327

Concordance to Plotinos...................i

An outline of the doctrines of Plotinos is published under the title "The Message of Plotinos."

CONCORDANCE OF ENNEADS AND CHRONOLOGICAL NUMBERS

i.1	53	iii.1	3	v.1	10
i.2	19	iii.2	47	v.2	11
i.3	20	iii.3	48	v.3	49
i.4	46	iii.4	15	v.4	7
i.5	36	iii.5	50	v.5	32
i.6	1	iii.6	26	v.6	24
i.7	54	iii.7	45	v.7	18
i.8	51	iii.8	30	v.8	31
i.9	16	iii.9	13	v.9	5
ii.1	40	iv.1	4	vi.1	42
ii.2	14	iv.2	21	vi.2	43
ii.3	52	iv.3	27	vi.3	44
ii.4	12	iv.4	28	vi.4	22
ii.5	25	iv.5	29	vi.5	23
ii.6	17	iv.6	41	vi.6	34
ii.7	37	iv.7	2	vi.7	38
ii.8	35	iv.8	6	vi.8	39
ii.9	33	iv.9	8	vi.9	9

CONCORDANCE OF CHRONOLOGICAL NUMBERS AND ENNEADS

1	i.6	19	i.2	37	ii.7
2	iv.7	20	i.3	38	vi.7
3	iii.1	21	iv.2	39	vi.8
4	iv.1	22	vi.4	40	ii.1
5	v.9	23	vi.5	41	iv.6
6	iv.8	24	v.6	42	vi.1
7	v.4	25	ii.5	43	vi.2
8	iv.9	26	iii.6	44	vi.3
9	vi.9	27	iv.3	45	iii.7
10	v.1	28	iv.4	46	i.4
11	v.2	29	iv.5	47	iii.2
12	ii.4	30	iii.8	48	iii.3
13	iii.9	31	v.8	49	v.3
14	ii.2	32	v.5	50	iii.5
15	iii.4	33	ii.9	51	i.8
16	i.9	34	vi.6	52	ii.3
17	ii.6	35	ii.8	53	i.1
18	v.7	36	i.5	54	i.7

Life of Plotinos
And Order of His Writings

By PORPHYRY.

(Written when about 70 years of age, see 23.)

I. PLOTINOS, LIKE PORPHYRY, DESPISED HIS PHYSICAL NATURE, BUT A PICTURE OF HIM WAS SECURED.

Plotinos the philosopher, who lived recently, seemed ashamed of having a body. Consequently he never spoke of his family or home (Lycopolis, now Syout, in the Thebaid, in Egypt). He never would permit anybody to perpetuate him in a portrait or statue. One day that Amelius* begged him to allow a painting to be made of him, he said, "Is it not enough for me to have to carry around this image†, in which nature has enclosed us? Must I besides transmit to posterity the image of this image as worthy of attention?" As Amelius never succeeded in getting Plotinos to reconsider his refusal, and to consent to give a sitting, Amelius begged his friend Carterius, the most famous painter of those times, to attend Plotinos's lectures, which were free to all. By dint of gazing at Plotinos, Carterius so filled his own imagination with Plotinos's features that he succeeded in painting them from memory. By his advice, Amelius directed Carterius in these labors, so that this portrait was a very good like-

*See 7.   †See vi, 7, 8.

ness. All this occurred without the knowledge of Plotinos.

II. SICKNESS AND DEATH OF PLOTINOS; HIS BIRTHDAY UNKNOWN.

Plotinos was subject to chronic digestive disorders, nevertheless, he never was willing to take any remedies, on the plea that it was unworthy of a man of his age to relieve himself by such means. Neither did he ever take any of the then popular "wild animal remedy," because, said he, he did not even eat the flesh of domestic animals, let alone that of savage ones. He never bathed, contenting himself with daily massage at home. But when at the period of the plague, which was most virulent,* the man who rubbed him died of it, he gave up the massage. This interruption in his habits brought on him a chronic quinsy, which never became very noticeable, so long as I remained with him; but after I left him, it became aggravated to the point that his voice, formerly sonorous and powerful, became permanently hoarse; besides, his vision became disturbed, and ulcers appeared on his hands and feet. All this I learned on my return, from my friend Eustochius, who remained with him until his end. These inconveniences hindered his friends from seeing him as often as they used to do, though he persisted in his former custom of speaking to each one individually. The only solution of this difficulty was for him to leave Rome. He retired into Campania, on an estate that had belonged to Zethus, one of his friends who had died earlier. All he needed was furnished by the estate itself, or was brought to him from the estate at Minturnae, owned by Castricius (author of a Commentary on Plato's Parmenides, to whom Porphyry dedicated his treatise on Vegetarianism). Eustochius himself told me that he happened to be at Puzzoli at the time

*A. D. 262.

LIFE OF PLOTINOS

of Plotinos's death, and that he was slow in reaching the bedside of Plotinos. The latter then said to him, "I have been waiting for you; I am trying to unite what is divine in us* to that which is divine in the universe." Then a serpent, who happened to be under Plotinos's death-bed slipped into a hole in the wall (as happened at the death of Scipio Africanus, Pliny, Hist. Nat. xv. 44), and Plotinos breathed his last. At that time Plotinos was 66 years old (in 270, born in 205), according to the account of Eustochius. The emperor Claudius II was then finishing the second year of his reign. I was at Lilybaeum; Amelius was at Apamaea in Syria, Castricius in Rome, and Eustochius alone was with Plotinos. If we start from the second year of Claudius II and go back 66 years, we will find that Plotinos's birth falls in the 18th year of Septimus Severus (205). He never would tell the month or day of his birth, because he did not approve of celebrating his birth-day either by sacrifices, or banquets. Still he himself performed a sacrifice, and entertained his friends on the birth-days of Plato and Socrates; and on those days those who could do it had to write essays and read them to the assembled company.

III. PLOTINOS'S EARLY EDUCATION.

This is as much as we learned about him during various interviews with him. At eight years of age he was already under instruction by a grammarian, though the habit of uncovering his nurse's breast to suck her milk, with avidity, still clung to him. One day, however, she so complained of his importunity that he became ashamed of himself, and ceased doing so. At 28 years of age he devoted himself entirely to philosophy. He was introduced to the teachers who at that time were the most famous in Alexandria. He would return from their lectures sad and discouraged.

*See vi. 5, 1.

He communicated the cause of this grief to one of his friends, who led him to Ammonius, with whom Plotinos was not acquainted. As soon as he heard this philosopher, he said to his friend, "This is the man I was looking for!" From that day forwards he remained close to Ammonius. So great a taste for philosophy did he develop, that he made up his mind to study that which was being taught among the Persians, and among the Hindus. When emperor Gordian prepared himself for his expedition against the Persians, Plotinus, then 39 years old, followed in the wake of the army. He had spent between 10 to 11 years near Ammonius. After Gordian was killed in Mesopotamia, Plotinos had considerable trouble saving himself at Antioch. He reached Rome while Philip was emperor, and when he himself was 50 years of age.

THE SCHOOL OF AMMONIUS.

Herennius, (the pagan) Origen, and Plotinos had agreed to keep secret the teachings they had received from Ammonius. Plotinos carried out his agreement. Herennius was the first one to break it, and Origen followed his example. The latter limited himself to writing a book entitled, "Of Daemons;" and, under the reign of Gallienus, he wrote another one to prove that "The Emperor alone is the Only Poet" (if the book was a flattery; which is not likely. Therefore it probably meant: "The King (of the universe, that is, the divine Intelligence), is the only 'demiurgic' Creator.")

PLOTINOS AN UNSYSTEMATIC TEACHER.

For a long period Plotinos did not write anything. He contented himself with teaching orally what he had learned from Ammonius. He thus passed ten whole years teaching a few pupils, without committing anything to writing. However, as he allowed his pupils

LIFE OF PLOTINOS

to question him, it often happened that his school was disorderly, and that there were useless discussions, as I later heard from Amelius.

AMELIUS, PLOTINOS'S FIRST SECRETARY.

Amelius enrolled himself among the pupils of Plotinos during the third year of Plotinos's stay in Rome, which also was the third year of the reign of Claudius II, that is, 24 years. Amelius originally had been a disciple of the Stoic philosopher Lysimachus.* Amelius surpassed all his fellow-pupils by his systematic methods of study. He had copied, gathered, and almost knew by heart all the works of Numenius. He composed a hundred copy-books of notes taken at the courses of Plotinos, and he gave them as a present to his adopted son, Hostilianus Hesychius, of Apamea. (Fragments of Amelius's writings are found scattered in those of Proclus, Stobaeus, Olympiodorus, Damascius, and many of the Church Fathers.)

IV. HOW PORPHYRY CAME TO PLOTINOS. FOR THE FIRST TIME, IN 253.

In the tenth year of the reign of Gallienus, I (then being twenty years of age), left Greece and went to Rome with Antonius of Rhodes. I found there Amelius, who had been following the courses of Plotinos for eighteen years. He had not yet dared to write anything, except a few books of notes, of which there were not yet as many as a hundred. In this tenth year of the reign of Gallienus, Plotinos was fifty-nine years old. When I (for the second, and more important time) joined him, I was thirty years of age. During the first year of Gallienus, Plotinos began to write upon some topics of passing interest, and in the tenth year of Gallienus, when I visited him for the first time, he had written twenty-one books, which had been circulated only among a very small number of friends.

*See 20.

LIFE OF PLOTINOS

They were not given out freely, and it was not easy to go through them. They were communicated to to students only under precautionary measures, and after the judgment of those who received them had been carefully tested.

PLOTINOS'S BOOKS OF THE FIRST PERIOD
(THE AMELIAN PERIOD).

I shall mention the books that Plotinos had already written at that time. As he had prefixed no titles to them, several persons gave them different ones. Here are those that have asserted themselves:

1. Of the Beautiful. i. 6.
2. Of the Immortality of the Soul. iv. 7.
3. Of Fate. iii. 1.
4. Of the Nature of the Soul. iv. 1.
5. Of Intelligence, of Ideas, and of Existence. v. 9.
6. Of the Descent of the Soul into the Body. iv. 8.
7. How does that which is Posterior to the First Proceed from Him? Of the One. v. 4.
8. Do all the Souls form but a Single Soul? iv. 9.
9. Of the Good, or of the One. vi. 9.
10. Of the Three Principal Hypostatic Forms of Existence, v. 1.
11. Of Generation, and of the Order of Things after the First, v. 2.
12. (Of the Two) Matters, (the Sensible and Intelligible). ii. 4.
13. Various Considerations, iii. 9.
14. Of the (Circular) Motion of the Heavens. ii. 2.
15. Of the Daemon Allotted to Us, iii. 4.
16. Of (Reasonable) Suicide, i. 9.
17. Of Quality, ii. 6.
18. Are there Ideas of Individuals? v. 7.
19. Of Virtues. i. 2.
20. Of Dialectics. i. 3
21. (How does the Soul keep the Mean between Indivisible Nature and Divisible Nature?) iv. 2

LIFE OF PLOTINOS

These twenty-one books were already written when I visited Plotinos; he was then in the fifty-ninth year of his age.

V. HOW PORPHYRY CAME TO PLOTINOS FOR THE SECOND TIME (A. D. 263-269).

I remained with him this year, and the five following ones. I had already visited Rome ten years previously; but at that time Plotinos spent his summers in vacation, and contented himself with instructing his visitors orally.

During the above-mentioned six years, as several questions had been cleared up in the lectures of Plotinos, and at the urgent request of Amelius and myself that he write them down, he wrote two books to prove that

PLOTINOS'S BOOKS OF THE SECOND PERIOD (THE PORPHRYRIAN PERIOD).

22. The One and Identical Existence is Everywhere Entire, I, vi. 4.
23. Second Part Thereof. vi. 5.

Then he wrote the book entitled:

24. The Superessential Transcendent Principle Does Not Think. Which is the First Thinking Principle? And Which is the Second? v. 6.

He also wrote the following books:

25. Of Potentiality and Actualization. ii. 5.
26. Of the Impassibility of Incorporeal Entities. iii. 6.
27. Of the Soul, First Part. iv. 3.
28. Of the Soul, Second Part. iv. 4.
29. (Of the Soul, Third; or, How do We See?) iv. 5.
30. Of Contemplation. iii. 8.
31. Of Intelligible Beauty. v. 8.
32. The Intelligible Entities are not Outside of Intelligence. Of Intelligence and of Soul. v. 5.
33. Against the Gnostics. ii. 9.

(To be continued.)

34.	Of Numbers.	vi. 6.
35.	Why do Distant Objects Seem Small?	ii. 8.
36.	Does Happiness (Consist in Duration?)	i. 5.
37.	Of the Mixture with Total Penetration.	ii. 7.
38.	Of the Multitude of Ideas; Of the Good.	vi. 7.
39.	Of the Will.	vi. 8.
40.	(Of the World).	ii. 1.
41.	Of Sensation, and of Memory.	iv. 6.
42.	Of the Kinds of Existence, First.	vi. 1.
43.	Of the Kinds of Existence, Second.	vi. 2.
44.	Of the Kinds of Existence, Third.	vi. 3.
45.	Of Eternity and Time.	iii. 7.

Plotinos wrote these twenty-four books during the six years I spent with him; as subjects he would take the problems that happened to come up, and which we have indicated by the titles of these books. These twenty-four books, joined to the twenty-one Plotinos had written before I came to him, make forty-five.

VI. PLOTINOS'S BOOKS OF THE THIRD PERIOD (THE EUSTOCHIAN PERIOD).

While I was in Sicily, where I went in the fifteenth year of the reign of Gallienus, he wrote five new books that he sent me:

46.	Of Happiness.	i. 4.
47.	Of Providence, First.	iii. 2.
48.	Of Providence, Second.	iii. 3.
49.	Of the Hypostases that Act as Means of Knowledge, and of the Transcendent.	v. 3.
50.	Of Love.	iii. 5.

These books he sent me in the last year of the reign of Claudius II, and at the beginning of the second.

Shortly before dying, he sent me the following four books:

(To be continued.)

51.	Of the Nature of Evils.	i. 8.
52.	Of the Influence of the Stars.	ii. 3.
53.	What is the Animal? What is Man?	i. 1.
54.	Of the First Good (or, of Happiness).	i. 7.

These nine books, with the forty-five previously written, make in all fifty-four.

Some were composed during the youth of the author, others when in his bloom, and finally the last, when his body was already seriously weakened; and they betray his condition while writing them. The twenty-one first books seem to indicate a spirit which does not yet possess all its vigor and firmness. Those that he wrote during the middle of his life, show that his genius was then in its full form. These twenty-four books may be considered to be perfect, with the exception of a few passages. The last nine are less powerful than the others; and of these nine, the last four are the weakest.

VII. VARIOUS DISCIPLES OF PLOTINOS.

Plotinos had a great number of auditors and disciples, who were attracted to his courses by love of philosophy.

Among this number was Amelius of Etruria, whose true name was Gentilianus. He did indeed insist that in his name the letter "l" should be replaced by "r," so that his name should read "Amerius," from "ameria" (meaning indivisibility, though Suidas states that it was derived from the town of Ameria, in the province of Umbria), and not Amelius, from "amellia" (negligence).

A very zealous disciple of Plotinos was a physician from Scythopolis (or, Bethshean, in Palestine), named Paulinus, whose mind was full of ill-digested information, and whom Amelius used to call Mikkalos (the tiny).

Eustochius of Alexandria, also a physician, knew Plotinos at the end of his life, and remained with him until his death, to care for him. Exclusively occupied with the teachings of Plotinos, he himself became a genuine philosopher.

Zoticus, also, attached himself to Plotinos. He was both critic and poet; he corrected the works of Antimachus, and beautifully versified the fable of the Atlantidae. His sight gave out, however, and he died shortly before Plotinos. Paulinus also, died before Plotinos.

Zethus was one of the disciples of Plotinos. He was a native of Arabia, and had married the daughter of Theodosius, friend of Ammonius. He was a physician, and much beloved by Plotinos, who sought to lead him to withdraw from public affairs, for which he had considerable aptitude; and with which he occupied himself with zeal. Plotinos lived in very close relations with him; he even retired to the country estate of Zethus, distant six miles from Minturnae.

Castricius, surnamed Firmus, had once owned this estate. Nobody, in our times, loved virtue more than Firmus. He held Plotinos in the deepest veneration. He rendered Amelius the same services that might have been rendered by a good servant, he displayed for me the attentions natural towards a brother. Nevertheless this man, who was so attached to Plotinos, remained engaged in public affairs.

Several senators, also, came to listen to Plotinos. Marcellus, Orontius, Sabinillus and Rogatianus applied themselves, under Plotinos, to the study of philosophy.

The latter, who also was a member of the senate, had so detached himself from the affairs of life, that he had abandoned all his possessions, dismissed all his attendants, and renounced all his dignities. On being appointed praetor, at the moment of being inaugurated, while the lictors were already waiting for him, he refused to sally forth, and carry out any of the functions of this dignity. He even failed to dwell in his own house (to avoid needless pomp); he visited his friends, boarding and sleeping there; he took food only every other day; and by this dieting, after having been afflicted with gout to the point of having to be carried around in a litter, he recovered his strength, and stretched out his hands as easily as any artisan, though formerly his hands had been incapacitated. Plotinos was very partial to him; he used to praise him publicly, and pointed him out as a model to all who desired to become philosophers.

Another disciple of Plotinos was Serapion of Alexandria. At first he had been a rhetorician, and only later applied himself to philosophy. Nevertheless he never was able to cure himself of fondness for riches, or usury.

Me also, Porphyry, a native of Tyre, Plotinos admitted to the circle of his intimate friends, and he charged me to give the final revision to his works.

VIII. PERSONAL CHARACTERISTICS OF PLOTINOS.

Once Plotinos had written something, he could neither retouch, nor even re-read what he had done, because his weak eyesight made any reading very painful. His penmanship was poor. He did not separate words, and his spelling was defective; he was chiefly occupied with ideas. Until his death he continuously persisted in this habit, which was for us all a subject of surprise. When he had finished composing something in his head, and when he then wrote what he had meditated on, it seemed as if he copied a book. Neither in conversation nor in discussion did he allow himself to be distracted from the purpose of his thoughts, so that he was able at the same time to attend to the needs of conversation, while pursuing the meditation of the subject which busied him. When the person who had been talking with him went away, he did not re-read what he had written before the interruption, which, as has been mentioned above, was to save his eyesight; he could, later on, take up the thread of his composition as if the conversation had been no obstacle to his attention. He therefore was able simultaneously to live with others and with himself. He never seemed to need recuperation from this interior attention, which hardly ceased during his slumbers, which, however, were troubled both by the insufficiency of food, for sometimes he did not even eat bread, and by this continuous concentration of his mind.

IX. PLOTINOS AS GUARDIAN AND ARBITRATOR.

There were women who were very much attached to him. There was his boarding house keeper Gemina, and her daughter, also called Gemina; there was also Amphiclea, wife of Aristo, son of Jamblichus, all three of whom were very fond of philosophy. Several men and women of substance, being on the point of death, entrusted him with their boys and girls, and all their possessions, as being an irreproachable trustee; and the result was that his house was filled with young boys and girls. Among these was Polemo, whom Plotinos educated carefully; and Plotinos enjoyed hearing Polemo recite original verses (?). He used to go through the accounts of the managers with care, and saw to their economy; he used to say that until these young people devoted themselves entirely to philosophy, their possessions should be preserved intact, and see that they enjoyed their full incomes. The obligation of attending to the needs of so many wards did not, however, hinder him from devoting to intellectual concerns a continuous attention during the nights. His disposition was gentle, and he was very approachable by all who dwelt with him. Consequently, although he dwelt full twenty-six years in Rome, and though he was often chosen as arbitrator in disputes, never did he offend any public personage.

X. HOW PLOTINOS TREATED HIS ADVERSARY, OLYMPIUS.

Among those who pretended to be philosophers, there was a certain man named Olympius. He lived in Alexandria, and for some time had been a disciple of Ammonius. As he desired to succeed better than Plotinos, he treated Plotinos with scorn, and developed sufficient personal animosity against Plotinos to try to bewitch him by magical operations. However, Olympius noticed that this enterprise was really turning against himself, and he acknowledged to his friends that the soul of Plotinos must be very powerful, since it was able to throw back upon his enemies the evil practices directed against him. The first time that Olympius attempted to harm him, Plotinos having noticed it, said, "At this very moment the body of Olympius is undergoing convulsions, and is contracting like a purse." As Olympius several times felt himself undergoing the very ills he was trying to get Plotinos to undergo, he finally ceased his practices.

HOMAGE TO PLOTINOS FROM A VISITING EGYPTIAN PRIEST.

Plotinos showed a natural superiority to other men. An Egyptian priest, visiting Rome, was introduced to him by a mutual friend. Having decided to show some samples of his mystic attainments, he begged Plotinos to come and witness the apparition of a familiar spirit who obeyed him on being evoked. The evocation was to occur in a chapel of Isis, as the Egyptian claimed that he had not been able to discover any other place pure enough in Rome. He therefore evoked Plotinos's guardian spirit. But instead of the spirit appeared a divinity of an order superior to that of guardians, which event led the Egyptian to say to Plotinos, "You are indeed fortunate, O Plotinos, that your guardian spirit is a divinity, instead of a being of a lower order." The divinity that appeared could not be questioned or seen for as long a period as they would have liked, as a friend who was watching over the sacrificed birds choked them, either out of jealousy, or fear.

PLOTINOS'S ATTITUDE TOWARDS THE PUBLIC MYSTERIES.

As Plotinos's guardian spirit was a divinity, Plotinos kept the eyes of his own spirit directed on that divine guardian. That was the motive of his writing his book* that bears the title "Of the Guardian Allotted to Us." In it he tries to explain the differences between the various spirits that watch over mankind. Amelius, who was very scrupulous in his sacrifices, and who carefully celebrated the Festivals of the New Moon (as Numenius used to do?) (on the Calends of each month), one day besought Plotinos to come and take part in a function of that kind. Plotinos, however, answered him, "It is the business of those divinities to come and visit me, and not mine to attend on them." We could not understand why he should make an utterance that revealed so much pride, but we dared not question the matter.

XI. PLOTINOS AS DETECTIVE AND AS PROPHET; PORPHYRY SAVED FROM SUICIDE.

So perfectly did he understand the character of men, and their methods of thought, that he could discover stolen objects, and foresaw what those who resided with him should some day become. A magnificent necklace had been stolen from Chione, an estimable widow, who resided with him and the children (as matron?). All the slaves were summoned, and Plotinos examined them all. Then, pointing out one of them, he said, "This is the culprit." He was put to

*iii. 4

LIFE OF PLOTINOS

the torture. For a long while, he denied the deed; but later acknowledged it, and returned the necklace. Plotinos used to predict what each of the young people who were in touch with him was to become. He insisted that Polemo would be disposed to amorous relations, and would not live long; which also occurred. As to me, he noticed that I was meditating suicide. He came and sought me, in his house, where I was staying. He told me that this project indicated an unsound mind, and that it was the result of a melancholy disposition. He advised me to travel. I obeyed him. I went to Sicily,* to study under Probus, a celebrated philosopher, who dwelt in Lilybaeum. I was thus cured of the desire to die; but I was deprived of the happiness of residing with Plotinos until his death.

XII. THE PROJECT OF A PLATONOPOLIS COMES TO NAUGHT.

The emperor Gallienus and the empress Salonina, his wife, held Plotinos in high regard. Counting on their good will, he besought them to have a ruined town in Campania rebuilt, to give it with all its territory to him, that its inhabitants might be ruled by the laws of Plato. Plotinos intended to have it named Platonopolis, and to go and reside there with his disciples. This request would easily have been granted but that some of the emperor's courtiers opposed this project, either from spite, jealousy, or other unworthy motive.

XIII. PERSONAL CHARACTERISTICS OF PLOTINOS'S DELIVERY

In his lectures his delivery was very good; he knew how to make immediate apposite replies. Nevertheless, his language was not correct. For instance, he used to say "anamnemisketai" for "anamimnesketai"; and he made similar blunders in writing. But when he would speak, his intelligence seemed to shine in his face, and

*See above, 6.

20 LIFE OF PLOTINOS

to illuminate it with its rays. He grew especially handsome in discussions; a light dew of perspiration appeared on his forehead, gentleness radiated in his countenance, he answered kindly, but satisfactorily. For three days I had to question him, to learn from him his opinions about the union of the body with the soul; he spent all that time in explaining to me what I wanted to know.* A cerain Thaumasius, who had entered into the school, said that he wanted to take down the arguments of the discussion in writing, and hear Plotinos himself speak; but that he would not stand Porphyry's answering and questioning. "Nevertheless," answered Plotinos, "if Porphyry does not, by his questions, bring up the difficulties that we should solve (notice, in the course of the Enneads, the continual objections), we would have nothing to write."

XIV. PHILOSOPHICAL RELATIONS OF PLOTINOS.

The style of Plotinos is vigorous and substantial, containing more thoughts than words, and is often full of enthusiasm and emotion. He follows his own inspirations rather than ideas transmitted by tradition. The teachings of the Stoics and Peripatetics are secretly mingled among his works; the whole of Aristotle's Metaphysics is therein condensed. Plotinos was fully up to the times in geometry, arithmetic, mechanics, optics and music, although he did not take an overweening interest in these sciences. At his lectures were read the Commentaries of Severus, of Cronius;† of Numenius,‡ of Gaius and Atticus (Platonic Philosophers, the latter, setting forth the differences between Plato and Aristotle);|| there were also readings of the works of the Peripatetics, of Aspasius, of Alexander (of Aphrodisia, whose theory of Mixture in the Universe

*See iv. 2.
†Often quoted by Porphyry in his Cave of the Nymphs.
‡See 3. ||Euseb. Prep. Ev. xi. 2; xv. 4-9, 12-13.

LIFE OF PLOTINOS

Plotinos studies several times), of Adrastus, and other philosophers of the day. None of them, however, was exclusively admired by Plotinos. In his speculations he revealed an original and independent disposition. In all his researches he displayed the spirit of Ammonius. He could readily assimilate (what he read); then, in a few words, he summarized the ideas aroused in him by profound meditation thereon. One day Longinus's book "On the Principles," and his "On Antiquarians" were read. Plotinos said, "Longinus is a literary man, but not a philosopher." Origen (the Pagan*) once came among his audience; Plotinos blushed, and started to rise. Origen, however, besought him to continue. Plotinos, however, answered that it was only natural for lecturers to cease talking when they were aware of the presence, in the audience, of people who already knew what was to be said. Then, after having spoken a little longer, he rose.

XV. PORPHYRY EARNED RECOGNITION AT THE SCHOOL OF PLOTINOS.

At a celebration of Plato's birthday I was reading a poem about the "Mystic Marriage" (of the Soul) when somebody doubted my sanity, because it contained both enthusiasm and mysticism. Plotinos spoke up, and said to me, loud enough to be heard by everybody, "You have just proved to us that you are at the same time poet, philosopher, and hierophant." On this occasion the rhetorician Diophanes read an apology on the utterances of Alcibiades in Plato's "Banquet," and he sought to prove that a disciple who seeks to exercise himself in virtue should show unlimited "complaisance" for his teacher, even in case the latter were in love with him. Plotinos rose several times, as if he wanted to leave the assembly; nevertheless, he restrained himself, and after the audience

*See 3.

had dispersed, he asked me to refute the paper. As Diophanes would not communicate it to me, I recalled his arguments, and refuted them; and then I read my paper before the same auditors as those who had heard what had been said by Diophanes. I pleased Plotinos so much, that several times he interrupted me by the words, "Strike that way, and you will become the light of men!" When Eubulus, who was teaching Platonism at Athens, sent to Plotinos some papers on Platonic subjects, Plotinos had them given to me to examine them and report to him about them. He also studied the laws of astronomy, but not as a mathematician would have done; he carefully studied astrology; but realizing that no confidence could be placed in its predictions, he took the trouble to refute them several times, in his work.*

XVI. PLOTINOS'S POLEMIC AGAINST THE GNOSTICS.

At that time there were many Christians, among whom were prominent sectarians who had given up the ancient philosophy (of Plato and Pythagoras), such as Adelphius and Aquilinus. They esteemed and possessed the greater part of the works of Alexander of Lybia, of Philocomus, of Demostrates and of Lydus. They advertised the Revelations of Zoroaster, of Zostrian, of Nicotheus, of Allogenes, of Mesus, and of several others. These sectarians deceived a great number of people, and even deceived themselves, insisting that Plato had not exhausted the depths of intelligible "being," or essence. That is why Plotinos refuted them at length in his lectures, and wrote the book that we have named "Against the Gnostics." The est (of their books) he left me to investigate. Amelius wrote as much as forty books to refute the work of Zostrian; and as to me, I demonstrated by numerous

*See ii. 3; iii. 1, 2, 4.

LIFE OF PLOTINOS 23

proofs that this alleged Zoroastrian book was apocryphal, and had only recently been written by those of that ilk who wished to make people believe that their doctrines had been taught by Zoroaster.

XVII. START OF THE AMELIO-PORPHYRIAN CONTROVERSY, OVER NUMENIUS.

The Greeks insisted that Plotinos had appropriated the teachings of Numenius. Trypho, who was both a Stoic and a Platonist, insisted on this to Amelius, who wrote a book that we have entitled, "On the Difference Between the Teachings of Plotinos and Numenius." He dedicated it to me under the title, "To Basil" (the King, recently used as a name, "Royal"). That was my name before I was called "Porphyry," the "Purple One." In my own home language (Phoenician) I used to be called "Malchus"; that was my father's name, and in Greek "Malchus" is translated by "Basileus" (Basil, or King). Indeed, Longinus, who dedicated his book "On Instinct" to Cleodamus, and me jointly, there calls me "Malchus"; and Amelius has translated this name in Greek, just as Numenius translated "Maximus" (from Latin into Greek by) "Megaos" (the great one). (I will quote the letter in full).

"Greetings from Amelius to Basil (Royal, or Purple One):

"You may be sure that I did not have the least inclination even to mention some otherwise respectable people who, to the point of deafening you, insist that the doctrines of our friend (Plotinos) are none other than those of Numenius of Apamea. It is evident enough that these reproaches are entirely due to their desire to advertise their oratorical abilities. Possessed with the desire to rend Plotinos to pieces, they dare to σo as far as to assert that he is no more than a babbler, a forger, and that his opinions are impossible. But since you think that it would be well for us to seize the occasion to recall to the public the teachings of which we approve (in Plotinos's system of philosophy), and in order to honor so great a man as our friend Plotinos by spreading his teachings—although this really is needless, inasmuch as they have long since become celebrated—I comply with your request, and, in accordance with my promise, I am hereby inscribing to you this work which, as you well know, I threw together in three days. You will not find in it that system and judiciousness natural to a book composed with care; they are only reflections suggested by the lectures (received from Plotinos), and arranged as they happened to come to mind. I, therefore, throw myself on your indulgence, especially as the thought of (Plotinos, that) philosopher whom some people are slandering to us, is not easy to grasp, because he expresses the same ideas in different manners in accordance with the exigencies of the occasion. I am sure you will have the goodness to correct me, if I happen to stray from the opinions of Plotinos. As the tragic poet says somewhere, being overwhelmed with the pressure of duties, I find myself compelled to submit to criticism and correction if I am discovered in altering the doctrines of our leader. You see how anxious I am to please you. Farewell!"

XVIII. POLEMIC BETWEEN AMELIUS AND PORPHYRY; AMELIUS TEACHES PORPHYRY.

I have quoted this letter in full to show that, even in the times of Plotinos himself, it was claimed that Plotinos had borrowed and advertised as his own teachings of Numenius; also that he was called a trifler, and in short that he was scorned—which happened chiefly because he was not understood. Plotinos was far from the display and vanity of the Sophists. When lecturing, he seemed to be holding a conversation with his pupils. He did not try to convince you by a formal argument. This I realized from the first, when attending his courses. I wished to make him explain himself more clearly by writing against him a work to prove that the intelligible entities subsist outside of intelligence.* Plotinos had Amelius read it to him; and after the reading he laughingly said to him, "It would be well for you to solve these difficulties that Porphyry has advanced against me, because he does not clearly understand my teachings." Amelius indeed wrote a rather voluminous work to answer my objections.† In turn, I responded. Amelius wrote again. This third work at last made me understand, but not without difficulty, the thought of Plotinos; and I changed my views, reading my retraction at a meeting. Since that time, I have had complete confidence in the teachings of Plotinos. I begged him to polish his writings, and to explain his system to me more at length. I also prevailed upon Amelius to write some works.

XIX. HOW THE WORKS OF PLOTINOS WERE PUT INTO SHAPE.

You may judge of the high opinion of Plotinos held by Longinus, from a part of a letter he addressed to me. I was in Sicily; he wished me to visit him in Phoenicia, and desired me to bring him a copy of the works of that philosopher. This is what he wrote to me about the matter:

"Please send me the works; or rather, bring them with you; for I shall never cease begging you to travel in this one of all other countries, were it only because of our ancient friendship, and of the sweetness of the air, which would so well suit your ruined health;‡ for you must not expect to find any new knowledge here when you visit us. Whatever your expectations may be,

*See v 5.
†This suggests that Suidas was right in claiming that Amelius was the teacher of Porphyry. ‡See 11.

do not expect to find anything new here, nor even the ancient works (of myself, Longinus?) that you say are lost. There is such a scarcity of copyists here, that since I have been here I have hardly been able to get what I lacked of Plotinos here, by inducing my copyist to abandon his usual occupations to devote himself exclusively to this work. Now that I have those works of Plotinos you sent me, I think I have them all, but these that I have are imperfect, being full of errors. I had supposed that our friend Amelius had corrected the errors of the copyist; but his occupations have been too pressing to allow of his attending to this. However passionately I desire to examine what Plotinos has written about the soul, and about existence, I do not know what use to make of his writings; these are precisely those of his works that have been most miswritten by the copyists. That is why I wish you would send them to me transcribed exactly; I would compare the copies and return them promptly. I repeat that I beg you not to send them, but to bring them yourself with the other works of Plotinos, which might have escaped Amelius. All those he brought here I have had transcribed exactly; for why should I not most zealously seek works so precious? I have often told you, both when we were together, and apart, and when you were at Tyre, that Plotinos's works contained reasonings of which I did not approve, but that I liked and admired his method of writing; his concise and forceful style, and the genuinely philosophical arrangement of his discussions. I am persuaded that those who seek the truth must place the works of Plotinos among the most learned."

XX. OPINION OF LONGINUS, THE GREAT CRITIC, ABOUT PLOTINOS.

I have made this rather long quotation only to show what was thought of Plotinos by the greatest critic of our days, the man who had examined all the works of his time. At first Longinus had scorned Plotinos, because he had relied on the reports of people ignorant (of philosophy). Moreover, Longinus supposed that the copy of the works of Plotinos he had received from Amelius was defective, because he was not yet accustomed to the style of Plotinos. Nevertheless, if any one had the works of Plotinos in their purity, it was certainly Amelius, who possessed a copy made upon the originals themselves. I will further add what was written by Longinus about Plotinos, Amelius, and the other philosophers of his time, so that the reader may better appreciate this great critic's high opinion of them. This book, directed against Plotinos and Gentilianus Amelius, is entitled "Of the Limit (of Good and Evil?)" and begins as follows:

"There were, O Marcellus Orontius* many philosophers in our time, and especially in the first years of our childhood—for it is useless to complain of their rarity at the present; but when I was still a youth, there were still a rather goodly number of men celebrated as philosophers. I was fortunate enough to get acquainted with all of them, because I traveled early with our parents in many countries. Visiting many nations and towns, I entered into personal relations with such of these men as were still alive. Among these philosophers, some committed their teachings to writings, with the purpose of being useful to posterity, while others thought that it was sufficient for them to explain their opinions to their disciples. Among the former are the Platonists Euclides, Democritus (who wrote Commentaries on the Alcibiades, on the Phaedo, and on the Metaphysics of Aristotle), Proclinus, who dwelt in the Troad, Plotinos and his disciple Gentilianus Amelius, who are at present teaching at Rome; the Stoics Themistocles, Phebion, and both Annius and

*See 7.

Medius, who were much talked of only recently, and the Peripatetician Heliodorus of Alexandria. Among those who did not write their teachings are the Platonists Ammonius (Saccas) and (the pagan) Origen,* who lived with him for a long while, and who excelled among the philosophers of that period; also Theodotus and Eubulus, who taught at Athens. Of course, they did write a little; Origen, for instance, wrote about "The Guardian Spirits"; and Eubulus wrote Commentaries on the Philebus, and on the Gorgias, and "Observations on Arsitotle's Objections against Plato's Republic." However, these works are not considerable enough to rank their authors among those who have seriously treated of philosophy; for these little works were by them written only incidentally, and they did not make writing their principal occupation. The Stoics Herminus, Lysimachus,† Athenaeus and Musonius (author of "Memorable Events," translated in Greek by Claudius Pollio), who lived at Athens. The Peripateticians Ammonius and Ptolemy, who were the most learned of their contemporaries, especially Ammonius, whose erudition was unequalled, none of these philosophers wrote any important work; they limited themselves to writing poems, or festal orations, which have been preserved in spite of them. I doubt very much that they wished to be known by posterity merely by books so small (and unrepresentative), since they had neglected to acquaint us with their teachings in more significant works. Among those who have left written works, some have done no more than gather or transcribe what has been left to us from the ancient (philosophers); among these are Euclides, Democritus and Proclinus. Others limited themselves to recalling some details extracted from ancient histories, and they tried to compose books with the same materials as their predecessors, as did Annius, Medius, and Phebio;

*See 3. †See 3.

LIFE OF PLOTINOS

the latter one trying to make himself famous by style, rather than by thought. To these we might add Heliodorus, who has put in his writings nothing that had not been said by the ancients, without adding any philosophical explanation. But Plotinos and Gentilianus Amelius, have shown that they really made a profession of being writers, both by the great number of questions they treated, and by the originality of their doctrines. Plotinos explained the principles of Pythagoras and Plato more clearly than his predecessors; for neither Numenius, nor Cronius, nor Moderatus,* nor Thrasyllus,‡ come anywhere near the precision of Plotinos when they touch on the same topics. Amelius tried to follow in his footsteps, and adopted the greater part of his ideas; but differs from him in the verbosity of his demonstrations, and the diffusion of his style. The writings of these two men alone deserve special consideration; for what is the use of criticizing the works of imitators; had we not better study the authors whose works they copied, without any additions, either in essential points, or in argumentation, doing no more than choosing out the best? This has been our method of procedure in our controversy with Gentilianus Amelius's strictures on justice, in Plato's works; and in my examination of Plotinos's books on the Ideas.§ So when our mutual friends Basil of Tyre, (Porphyry||), who has written much on the lines of Plotinos, having even preferred the teachings of Plotinos to my own (as he had been my pupil), undertook to demonstrate that Plotinos's views about the Ideas were better than my own, I have fully refuted his contentions, proving that he was wrong in changing his views on the subject.¶ Besides, I have criticized several opinions of

*Mentioned in Porphyry's Life of Pythagoras, 48, living under Nero.
‡Living under Tiberius, see Suetonius, Life of Tiberius, 14.
§See vi. 5. ||See 17.   ¶See 18.

Gentilianus Amelius and Plotinos, as for instance in the "Letter to Amelius" which is long enough to form a whole book. I wrote it to answer a letter sent me from Rome by Amelius, which was entitled "The Characteristics of the Philosophy of Plotinos."* I, however, limited myself to entitling my little work, "A Letter to Amelius."

XXI. RESULTS OF LONGINUS'S CRITICISM AND VINDICATION OF PLOTINOS'S ORIGINALITY.

From the above it will be seen that Plotinos and Amelius are superior to all their contemporaries by the great number of questions they consider, and by the originality of their system; that Plotinos had not appropriated the opinions of Numenius, and that he did not even follow them; that he had really profited by the opinions of the Pythagoreans (and of Plato); further, that he was more precise than Numenius, Cronius, and Thrasyllus. After having said that Amelius followed in the footsteps of Plotinos, but that he was prolix and diffuse in his expositions, which characteristic forms the difference between their styles, he speaks of me, who at that time had known Plotinos for only a short time, and says, "Our mutual friends, Basil (King) of Tyre (Porphyry), who has written much, taking Plotinos as his model." By that he means that I have avoided the rather unphilosophical diffuseness of Amelius, and have imitated the (concise) style of Plotinos. The quotation of the judgment of this famous man, the first critic of his day, should decide of the reverence due to our philosopher, Plotinos. If I had been able to visit Longinus when he begged me to do so, he would not have undertaken the refutation he wrote, before having clearly understood Plotinos's system.

*See 17.

LIFE OF PLOTINOS

XXII. THE APOLLONIAN ORACLE ABOUT PLOTINOS.

(But when I have a long oracle of Apollo to quote, why should I delay over a letter of Longinus's, or, in the words of the proverb, quoted in Iliad xxii. 126 and Hesiod Theogony 35), "Why should I dally near the oak-trees, or the rock?" If the testimony of the wise is to be adduced, who is wiser than Apollo, a deity who said of himself, "I know the number of the grains of sand, and the extent of the ocean; I understand the dust, and I hear him who does not speak!" This was the divinity who had said that Socrates was the wisest of men; and on being consulted by Amelius to discover what had become of the soul of Plotinos, said:

"Let me sing an immortal hymn to my dear friend!
Drawing my golden bow, I will elicit melodious sounds
    from my lyre.
I also invoke the symphonic voice of the choir of
    Muses,
Whose harmonious power raises exultant paeans,
As they once sang in chorus in praise of Achilles,
A Homeric song in divine inspiration.
Sacred choir of Muses, let us together celebrate this
    man,
For long-haired Apollo is among you!
  "O Deity, who formerly wert a man, but now approachest
The divine host of guardian spirits, delivered from the
    narrowing bonds of necessity
That enchains man (while in the body), and from the
    tumult caused by the
Confusing whirlwind of the passions of the body,
Sustained by the vigor of thy mind, thou hastenest to
    swim
(And like the sage Ulysses in Phaeacia), to land on a
    shore not submerged by the waves,
With vigorous stroke, far from the impious crowds.

Persistently following the straightening path of the purified soul,
Where the splendor of the divinity surrounds you, the home of justice,
Far from contamination, in the holy sanctuary of initiation,
When in the past you struggled to escape the bitter waves,*
When blood-stained life eddied around you with repulsive currents,
In the midst of the waters dazed by frightening tumult,
Even then the divinities often showed you your end;†
And often, when your spirit was about to stray from the right path,
The immortals beckoned you back to the real end; the eternal path,
Enlightening your eyes with radiant beams in the midst of gloomy darkness.
No deep slumber closed your eyelids, and when shaken by the eddies (of matter),
You sought to withdraw your eyes from the night that pressed down upon them;
You beheld beauties hidden from any who devote themselves to the study of wisdom.
"Now that you have discarded your cloak of mortality, and ascended
Climbing out from the tombs of your angelic soul,
You have entered the choir of divinities, where breathes a gentle zephyr.
There dwell friendship, and delightful desire, ever accompanied by pure joy;
There may one quench one's thirst with divine ambrosia;
There bound by the ties of love, one breathes a gentle air, under a tranquil sky.

*See ii. 3. 17.
†See 23.

LIFE OF PLOTINOS 33

There dwell the sons of Jupiter, who lived in the golden age;
The brothers Minos and Rhadamanthus, the just Aeacus,
The divine Plato, the virtuous Pythagoras,
And all those who formed the band of immortal love,
And who by birth belong to the most blessed of divinities.
Their soul tastes continual joy amidst perpetual feasts!
And you, blessed man, after having fought many a valiant fight,
In the midst of chaste angels, you have achieved eternal Felicity.
  "Here, O Muses, let us close this hymn in honor of Plotinos;
Cease the mazes of the dancing of the graceful choir;
This is what my golden lyre had to say of this eternally blessed man!"

XXIII. PERSONAL CHARACTERISTICS OF PLOTINOS; THE ECSTATIC TRANCES.

This oracle (pieced out of numerous quotations) says (in some now lost lines, perhaps) that Plotinos was kindly, affable, indulgent, gentle, such as, indeed we knew him in personal intercourse. It also mentions that this philosopher slept little, that his soul was pure, ever aspiring to the divinity that he loved wholeheartedly, and that he did his utmost to liberate himself (from terrestrial domination) "to escape the bitter waves of this cruel life."

That is how this divine man, who by his thoughts often aspired to the first (principle), to the divinity superior (to intelligence), climbing the degrees indicated by Plato (in his Banquet), beheld the vision of the formless divinity, which is not merely an idea, being founded on intelligence and the whole intelligible world. I, myself, had the blessed privilege of approaching this divinity, uniting myself to him, when I was about sixty-eight years of age.

That is how "the goal (that Plotinos sought to achieve) seemed to him located near him." Indeed, his goal, his purpose, his end was to approach the supreme divinity, and to unite himself with the divinity. While I dwelt with him, he had four times the bliss of reaching that goal, not merely potentially, but by a real and unspeakable experience. The oracle adds that the divinities frequently restored Plotinos to the right path when he strayed from it, "enlightening his eyes by radiant splendor." That is why it may truthfully be said that Plotinos composed his works while in contemplation of the divinities, and enjoying that vision. "Thanks to this sight that your 'vigilant' eyes had of both interior and exterior things, you have," in the words of the oracle, "gazed at many beauties that would hardly be granted to many of those who study philosophy." Indeed, the contemplation of men may be superior to human contemplation; but, compared to divine knowledge, if it be of any value whatever, it, nevertheless, could not penetrate the depths reached by the glances of the divinities.

Till here the oarcle had limited itself to indicating what Plotinos had accomplished while enclosed in the vesture of the body. It then proceeds to say that he arrived at the assembly of the divinities where dwell friendship, delightful desire, joy, and love communing with the divinity, where the sons of God, Minos, Rhadamanthus, and Aeacus are established as the judges of souls. Plotinos joined them, not to be judged, but to enjoy their intimacy, as did the higher divinities. There indeed dwell Plato, Pythagoras, and the other sages who formed the choir of immortal love. Reunited with their families, the blessed angels spend their life "in continued festivals and joys," enjoying the perpetual beatitude granted them by divine goodness.

LIFE OF PLOTINOS

XXIV. CONTENTS OF THE VARIOUS ENNEADS.

This is what I have to relate of the life of Plotinos, He had, however, asked me to arrange and revise his works. I promised both him and his friends to work on them. I did not judge it wise to arrange them in confusion chronologically. So I imitated Apollodorus of Athens, and Andronicus the Peripatetician, the former collecting in ten volumes the comedies of Epicharmus, and the latter dividing into treatises the works of Aristotle and Theophrastus, gathering together the writings that referred to the same subject. Likewise, I grouped the fifty-four books of Plotinos into six groups of nine (Enneads), in honor of the perfect numbers six and nine. Into each Ennead I have gathered the books that treat of the same matter, in each case prefixing the most important ones.

The First Ennead contains the writings that treat of Morals. They are:

1.	What is an Animal? What is a Man?	53.
2.	Of the Virtues,	19.
3.	Of Dialectics,	20.
4.	Of Happiness,	46.
5.	Does Happiness (consist in Duration)?	36.
6.	Of Beauty,	1.
7.	Of the First Good, and of the Other Goods,	54.
8.	Of the Origin of Evils,	51.
9.	Of (Reasonable) Suicide,	16.

Such are the topics considered in the First Ennead; which thus contains what relates to morals.

In the Second Ennead are grouped the writings that treat of Physics, of the World, and of all that it contains. They are:

1.	(Of the World).	40.
2.	Of the (Circular) Motion (of the Heavens),	14.
3.	Of the Influence of the Stars,	52.

LIFE OF PLOTINOS

4. (Of both Matters) (Sensible and Intelligible), 12.
5. Of Potentiality and Actuality, 25.
6. Of Quality (and of Form), 17.
7. Of Mixture, Where there is Total Penetration, 37.
8. Of Vision. Why do Distant Objects Seem Smaller? 35.
9. (Against Those Who say that the Demiurgic Creator is Evil, as well as The World Itself), Against the Gnostics, 33.

The Third Ennead, which also relates to the world, contains the different speculations referring thereto. Here are its component writings:

1. Of Destiny, 3.
2. Of Providence, the First, 47.
3. Of Providence, the Second, 48.
4. Of the Guardian Spirit who was Allotted to Us, 15.
5. Of Love, 50.
6. Of the Impassibility of Incorporeal Things, 26.
7. Of Eternity of Time, 45.
8. Of Nature, of Contemplation, and of the One, 30.
9. Different Speculations, 13.

We have gathered these three Enneads into one single body. We have assigned the book on the Guardian Spirit Who has been Allotted to Us, in the Third Ennead, because this is treated in a general manner, and because it refers to the examination of conditions characteristic of the production of man. For the same reason the book on Love was assigned to the First Ennead. The same place has been assigned to the book on Eternity and Time, because of the observations which, in this Ennead, refer to their nature. Because of its title, we have put in the same group the book on Nature, Contemplation, and the One.

LIFE OF PLOTINOS

After the books that treat of the world, the Fourth Ennead contains those that refer to the soul. They are:

1. Of the Nature of the Soul, the First, 4.
2. Of the Nature of the Soul, the Second, 21.
3. Problems about the Soul, the First, 27.
4. Problems about the Soul, the Second, 28.
5. (Problems about the Soul, the Third, or) Of Vision, 29.
6. Of Sensation, of Memory, 41.
7. Of the Immortality of the Soul, 2.
8. Of the Descent of the Soul into the Body, 6.
9. Do not all Souls form a Single Soul? 8.

The Fourth Ennead, therefore, contains all that relates to Psychology.

The Fifth Ennead treats of Intelligence. Each book in it also contains something about the principle superior to intelligence, and also about the intelligence characteristic of the soul, and about Ideas.

1. About the three Principal Hypostatic Forms of Existence, 10.
2. Of Generation, and of the Order of Things Posterior to the First, 11.
3. Of the Hypostatic Forms of Existence that Transmit Knowledge, and of the Superior Principle, 49.
4. How that which is Posterior to the First Proceeds from it? Of the One, 7.
5. The Intelligibles are not Outside of Intelligence. Of the Good, 32.
6. The Super-essential Principle Does Not Think. Which is the First Thinking Principle? Which is the Second? 24.
7. Are there Ideas of Individuals? 18.
8. Of Intelligible Beauty, 31.
9. Of Intelligence, of Ideas, and of Existence, 5.

LIFE OF PLOTINOS

We have gathered the Fourth and Fifth Ennead into a single volume. Of the Sixth Ennead, we have formed a separate volume, so that all the writings of Plotinos might be divided into three parts, of which the first contains three Enneads, the second two; and the third, a single Ennead.

Here are the books that belong to the Sixth Ennead, and to the Third Volume.

1. Of the Kinds of Existence, the First, 42.
2. Of the Kinds of Existence, the Second, 43.
3. Of the Kinds of Existence, the Third, 44.
4. The One Single Existence is everywhere Present in its Entirety, First, 22.
5. The One Single Existence is everywhere Present in its Entirety, Second, 23.
6. Of Numbers, 34
7. Of the Multitude of Ideas. Of the Good, 38.
8. Of the Will, and of the Liberty of the One, 39.
9. Of the Good, or of the One, 9.

This is how we have distributed into six Enneads the fifty-four books of Plotinos. We have added to several of them, Commentaries, without following any regular order, to satisfy our friends who desired to have explanations of several points. We have also made headings of each book, following the chronological order, with the exception of the book on The Beautiful, whose date of composition we do not know. Besides, we have not only written up separate summaries for each book, but also Arguments, which are contained among the summaries.*

Now we shall try to punctuate each book, and to correct the mistakes. Whatever else we may have to do besides, will easily be recognized by a reading of these books.

*The fragments of all this are probably the Principles of the Theory of the Intelligibles, by Porphyry.

LIFE OF PLOTINOS, BY EUNAPIUS.

The philosopher Plotinos came from Egypt; to be accurate, I will add that his home was Lycopolis. This fact was not set down by the divine Porphyry, though he himself, as he reports, was a student of Plotinos, and had spent a great part of his life near him.

The altars dedicated to Plotinos are not yet cold; and not only are his books read by the learned more than are even those of Plato, but even the multitude, though incapable of clearly understanding his doctrine, nevertheless conforms its conduct of life to his suggestions.

Porphyry has set down all the details of the life of this philosopher, so that little can be added thereto; besides Porphyry seems to have clearly expounded many of Plotinos's writings.

LIFE OF PLOTINOS, BY SUIDAS.

Plotinos of Lycopolis, philosopher, disciple of that Ammonius who had once been a porter, was the teacher of Amelius, who himself had Porphyry as pupil; the latter formed Jamblichus, and Jamblichus Sopater. Plotinos prolonged his life till the seventh year of the reign of Gallienus. He composed fifty-four books, which are grouped in six enneads. His constitution was weakened by the effects of the sacred disease (epilepsy), He wrote besides other works,

FIRST ENNEAD, BOOK SIXTH.

Of Beauty.

REVIEW OF BEAUTY OF DAILY LIFE.

1. Beauty chiefly affects the sense of sight. Still, the ear perceives it also, both in the harmony of words, and in the different kinds of music; for songs and verses are equally beautiful. On rising from the domain of the senses to a superior region, we also discover beauty in occupations, actions, habits, sciences and virtues. Whether there exists a type of beauty still higher, will have to be ascertained by discussion.

PROBLEMS CONCERNING HIGHER BEAUTY

What is the cause that certain bodies seem beautiful, that our ears listen with pleasure to rhythms judged beautiful, and that we love the purely moral beauties? Does the beauty of all these objects derive from some unique, immutable principle, or will we recognize some one principle of beauty for the body, and some other for something else? What then are these principles, if there are several? Or which is this principle, if there is but one?

WHAT IS THE PRINCIPLE BY PARTICIPATION IN
WHICH THE BODY IS BEAUTIFUL?

First, there are certain objects, such as bodies, whose beauty exists only by participation, instead of being inherent in the very essence of the subject. Such are beautiful in themselves, as is, for example, virtue. Indeed, the same bodies seem beautiful at one time, while at another they lack beauty; consequently, there is a great difference between being a body and being beautiful. What then is the principle whose presence in a body produces beauty therein? What is that element in the bodies which moves the spectator, and which attracts, fixes and charms his glances? This is the first problem to solve; for, on finding this principle, we shall use it as a means to resolve other questions.

POLEMIC AGAINST SYMMETRY, THE STOIC DEFINITION OF BEAUTY.

(The Stoics), like almost everybody, insist that visual beauty consists in the proportion of the parts relatively to each other and to the whole, joined to the grace of colors. If then, as in this case, the beauty of bodies in general consists in the symmetry and just proportion of their parts, beauty could not consist of anything simple, and necessarily could not appear in anything but what was compound. Only the totality will be beautiful; the parts by themselves will possess no beauty; they will be beautiful only by their relation with the totality. Nevertheless, if the totality is beautiful, it would seem also necessary that the parts be beautiful; for indeed beauty could never result from the assemblage of ugly things. Beauty must therefore be spread among all the parts. According to the same doctrine, the colors which, like sunlight, are beautiful, are beautiful but simple, and those whose beauty is not derived from proportion, will also be excluded from the domain of beauty. According to this hypothesis, how will gold be beautiful? The brilliant lightning in the night, even the stars, would not be beautiful to contemplate. In the sphere of sounds, also, it would be necessary to insist that what is simple possesses no beauty. Still, in a beautiful harmony, every sound, even when isolated, is beautiful. While preserving the same proportions, the same countenance seems at one time beautiful, and at another ugly. Evidently, there is but one conclusion: namely, that proportion is not beauty itself, but that it derives its beauty from some superior principle. (This will appear more clearly from further examples). Let us examine occupations and utterances. If also their beauty depended on proportion, what would be the function of proportion when considering occupations, laws, studies and sciences? Relations of proportion could not obtain in scientific speculations; no, nor even in the mutual agreement of these speculations. On the other hand, even bad things may show a certain mutual agreement and harmony; as, for instance, were we to assert that wisdom is softening of the brain, and that justice is a generous folly. Here we have two revoltingly absurd statements, which agree perfectly, and harmonize mutually. Further, every virtue is a soul-beauty far truer than any that we have till now examined; yet it could not admit of proportion, as it involves neither size nor number. Again, granting that the soul is divided into several faculties, who will undertake to decide which combination of these faculties, or of the speculations to which the soul devotes itself, will produce beauty? Moreover (if beauty is but proportion), what beauty could be predicated of pure intelligence?

BEAUTY CONSISTS IN KINSHIP TO THE SOUL.

2. Returning to our first consideration, we shall examine the nature of the element of beauty in bodies. It is something perceivable at the very first glance, something which the soul recognizes as kindred, and sympathetic to her own nature, which she welcomes and assimilates. But as soon as she meets an ugly object, she recoils, repudiates it, and rejects it as something foreign, towards which her real nature feels antipathy. That is the reason why the soul, being such as it is, namely, of an essence superior to all other

beings, when she perceives an object kindred to her own nature, or which reveals only some traces of it, rejoices, is transported, compares this object with her own nature, thinks of herself, and of her intimate being as it would be impossible to fail to perceive this resemblance.

BEAUTY CONSISTS IN PARTICIPATION IN A FORM.

How can both sensible and intelligible objects be beautiful? Because, as we said, sensible objects participate in a form. While a shapeless object, by nature capable of receiving shape (physical) and form (intelligible), remains without reason or form, it is ugly. That which remains completely foreign to all divine reason (a reason proceeding from the universal Soul), is absolute ugliness. Any object should be considered ugly which is not entirely molded by informing reason, the matter, not being able to receive perfectly the form (which the Soul gives it). On joining matter, form co-ordinates the different parts which are to compose unity, combines them, and by their harmony produces something which is a unit. Since (form) is one, that which it fashions will also have to be one, as far as a composite object can be one. When such an object has arrived at unity, beauty resides in it, and it communicates itself to the parts as well as to the whole. When it meets a whole, the parts of which are perfectly similar, it interpenetrates it evenly. Thus it would show itself now in an entire building, then in a single stone, later in art-products as well as in the works of nature. Thus bodies become beautiful by communion with (or, participation in) a reason descending upon it from the divine (universal Soul).

THE SOUL APPRECIATES THE BEAUTIFUL BY AN AESTHETIC SENSE.

3. The soul appreciates beauty by an especially ordered faculty, whose sole function it is to appreciate

all that concerns beauty, even when the other faculties take part in this judgment. Often the soul makes her (aesthetic) decisions by comparison with the form of the beautiful which is within her, using this form as a standard by which to judge. But what agreement can anything corporeal have with what is incorporeal? For example, how can an architect judge a building placed before him as beautiful, by comparing it with the Idea which he has within himself? The only explanation can be that, on abstracting the stones, the exterior object is nothing but the interior form, no doubt divided within the extent of the matter, but still one, though manifested in the manifold? When the senses perceive in an object the form which combines, unites and dominates a substance which lacks shape, and therefore is of a contrary nature; and if they also perceive a shape which distinguishes itself from the other shapes by its elegance, then the soul, uniting these multiple elements, fuses them, comparing them to the indivisible form which she bears within herself, then she pronounces their agreement, kinship and harmony with that interior type.

INSTANCES OF CORRESPONDENCE OF OUTER SENSE BEAUTY WITH ITS IDEA.

Thus a worthy man, perceiving in a youth the character of virtue, is agreeably impressed, because he observes that the youth harmonizes with the true type of virtue which he bears within himself. Thus also the beauty of color, though simple in form, reduces under its sway that obscurity of matter, by the presence of the light, which is something incorporeal, a reason, and a form. Likewise, fire surpasses all other bodies in beauty, because it stands to all other elements in the relation of a form; it occupies the highest regions;* it is the subtlest of bodies because it most approaches the

*See ii. 1.

incorporeal beings; without permitting itself to be penetrated by other bodies, it penetrates them all; without itself cooling, it communicates to them its heat, by its own essence it possesses color, and communicates it to others; it shines and coruscates, because it is a form. The body in which it does not dominate, shows but a discolored hue, and ceases being beautiful, merely because it does not participate in the whole form of color. Once more, thus do the hidden harmonies of sound produce audible harmonies, and also yield to the soul the idea of beauty, though showing it in another order of things. Audible harmonies can be expressed in numbers; not indeed in any kind of numbers, but only in such as can serve to produce form, and to make it dominate.

TRANSITION FROM SENSE BEAUTY TO INTELLECTUAL BEAUTY.

So much then for sense-beauties which, descending on matter like images and shadows, beautify it and thereby compel our admiration. 4. Now we shall leave the senses in their lower sphere, and we shall rise to the contemplation of the beauties of a superior order, of which the senses have no intuition, but which the soul perceives and expresses.

INTERIOR BEAUTIES COULD NOT BE APPRECIATED WITHOUT AN INTERIOR MODEL.

Just as we could not have spoken of sense-beauties if we had never seen them, nor recognized them as such, if, in respect to them, we had been similar to persons born blind, likewise we would not know enough to say anything about the beauty either of the arts or sciences, or of anything of the kind, if we were not already in possession of this kind of beauty; nor of the splendor of virtue, if we had not contemplated the ("golden) face of Justice," and of temperance, before whose splendor the morning and evening stars grow pale.

MORAL BEAUTIES MORE DELIGHTFUL THAN SENSE-BEAUTIES.

To see these beauties, they must be contemplated by the faculty our soul has received; then, while contemplating them, we shall experience far more pleasure, astonishment and admiration, than in contemplation of the sense-beauties, because we will have the intuition of veritable beauties. The sentiments inspired by beauty are admiration, a gentle charm, desire, love, and a pleasurable impulse.

THEY WHO FEEL THESE SENTIMENTS MOST KEENLY ARE CALLED LOVERS.

Such are the sentiments for invisible beauties which should be felt, and indeed are experienced by all souls, but especially by the most loving. In the presence of beautiful bodies, all indeed see them; but not all are equally moved. Those who are most moved are designated "lovers."*

THE CAUSE OF THESE EMOTIONS IS THE INVISIBLE SOUL.

5. Let us now propound a question about experiences to these men who feel love for incorporeal beauties. What do you feel in presence of the noble occupations, the good morals, the habits of temperance, and in general of virtuous acts and sentiments, and of all that constitutes the beauty of souls? What do you feel when you contemplate your inner beauty? What is the source of your ecstasies, or your enthusiasms? Whence come your desires to unite yourselves to your real selves, and to refresh yourselves by retirement from your bodies? Such indeed are the experiences of those who love genuinely. What then is the object which causes these, your emotions? It is neither a figure, nor a color, nor any size; it is that (colorless)

*See i. 3.

invisible soul, which possesses a wisdom equally invisible; this soul in which may be seen shining the splendor of all the virtues, when one discovers in oneself, or contemplates in others, the greatness of character, the justice of the heart, the pure temperance, the imposing countenance of valor, dignity and modesty, proceeding alone firmly, calmly, and imperturbably; and above all, intelligence, resembling the divinity, by its brilliant light. What is the reason that we declare these objects to be beautiful, when we are transported with admiration and love for them? They exist, they manifest themselves, and whoever beholds them will never be able to restrain himself from confessing them to be veritable beings. Now what are these genuine beings? They are beautiful.

LOVE OF BEAUTY EXPLAINED BY AVERSION FOR OPPOSITE.

But reason is not yet satisfied; reason wonders why these veritable beings give the soul which experiences them the property of exciting love, from which proceeds this halo of light which, so to speak, crowns all virtues. Consider the things contrary to these beautiful objects, and with them compare what may be ugly in the soul. If we can discover of what ugliness consists, and what is its cause, we shall have achieved an important element of the solution we are seeking. Let us picture to ourselves an ugly soul; she will be given up to intemperance; and be unjust, abandoned to a host of passions, troubled, full of fears caused by her cowardliness, and of envy by her degradation; she will be longing only for vile and perishable things; she will be entirely depraved, will love nothing but impure wishes, will have no life but the sensual, and will take pleasure in her turpitude. Would we not explain such a state by saying that under the very mask of beauty turpitude had invaded this soul, brutalized her, soiled her with all kinds of vices, rendering her incapable of a pure life, and pure sentiments, and had reduced her to an existence obscure, infected with evil, poisoned by lethal germs; that it had hindered her from contemplating anything she should, forcing her to remain solitary, because it misled her out from herself towards inferior and gloomy regions? The soul fallen into this state of impurity, seized with an irresistible inclination towards the things of sense, absorbed by her intercourse with the body, sunk into matter, and having even received it within herself, has changed form by her admixture with an inferior nature. Not otherwise would be a man fallen into slimy mud, who no longer would present to view his primitive beauty, and would exhibit only the appearance of the mud that had defiled him; his ugliness would be derived from something foreign; and to recover his pristine beauty he would have to wash off his defilement, and by purification be restored to what he once was.

UGLINESS IS ONLY A FOREIGN ACCRETION.

We have the right to say that the soul becomes ugly by mingling with the body, confusing herself with it, by inclining herself towards it. For a soul, ugliness consists in being impure, no longer unmingled, like gold tarnished by particles of earth. As soon as this dross is removed, and nothing but gold remains, then again it is beautiful, because separated from every foreign body, and is restored to its unique nature. Likewise the soul, released from the passions begotten by her intercourse with the body when she yields herself too much to it, delivered from exterior impressions, purified from the blemishes contracted from her alliance with the body—that is, reduced to herself, she lays aside that ugliness which is derived from a nature foreign to her.

VIRTUES ARE ONLY PURIFICATIONS.

6. Thus, according to the ancient (Platonic or Empedoclean) maxim, "courage, temperance, all the virtues, nay, even prudence, are but purifications." The mysteries were therefore wise in teaching that the man who has not been purified will, in hell, dwell at the bottom of a swamp; for everything that is not pure, because of its very perversity, delights in mud, just as we see the impure swine wallow in the mud with delight. And indeed, what would real temperance consist of, if it be not to avoid attaching oneself to the pleasures of the body, and to flee from them as impure, and as only proper for an impure being? What else is courage, unless no longer to fear death, which is mere separation of the soul from the body? Whoever therefore is willing to withdraw from the body could surely not fear death. Magnanimity is nothing but scorn of things here below. Last, prudence is the thought which, detached from the earth, raises the soul to the intelligible world. The purified soul, therefore, becomes a form, a reason, an incorporeal and intellectual essence; she belongs entirely to the divinity, in whom resides the source of the beautiful, and of all the qualities which have affinity with it.

THE SOUL'S WELFARE IS TO RESEMBLE THE DIVINITY.

Restored to intelligence, the soul sees her own beauty increase; indeed, her own beauty consists of the intelligence with its ideas; only when united to intelligence is the soul really isolated from all the remainder. That is the reason that it is right to say that "the soul's welfare and beauty lie in assimilating herself to the divinity," because it is the principle of beauty and of the essences; or rather, being is beauty, while the other nature (non-being, matter), is ugliness. This is the First Evil, evil in itself, just as that one (the First

Principle) is the good and the beautiful; for good and beauty are identical. Consequently, beauty or good, and evil or ugliness, are to be studied by the same methods. The first rank is to be assigned to beauty, which is identical with the good, and from which is derived the intelligence which is beautiful by itself. The soul is beautiful by intelligence, then, the other things, like actions, and studies, are beautiful by the soul which gives them a form. It is still the soul which beautifies the bodies to which is ascribed this perfection; being a divine essence, and participating in beauty, when she seizes an object, or subjects it to her dominion, she gives to it the beauty that the nature of this object enables it to receive.

APPROACH TO THE GOOD CONSISTS IN SIMPLIFICATION.

We must still ascend to the Good to which every soul aspires. Whoever has seen it knows what I still have to say, and knows the beauty of the Good. Indeed, the Good is desirable for its own sake; it is the goal of our desires. To attain it, we have to ascend to the higher regions, turn towards them, and lay aside the garment which we put on when descending here below; just as, in the (Eleusynian, or Isiac) mysteries, those who are admitted to penetrate into the recesses of the sanctuary, after having purified themselves, lay aside every garment, and advance stark naked.

THE SUPREME PURPOSE OF LIFE IS THE ECSTATICAL VISION OF GOD.

7. Thus, in her ascension towards divinity, the soul advances until, having risen above everything that is foreign to her, she alone with Him who is alone, beholds, in all His simplicity and purity, Him from whom all depends, to whom all aspires, from whom every-

thing draws its existence, life and thought. He who beholds him is overwhelmed with love; with ardor desiring to unite himself with Him, entranced with ecstasy. Men who have not yet seen Him desire Him as the Good; those who have, admire Him as sovereign beauty, struck simultaneously with stupor and pleasure, thrilling in a painless orgiasm, loving with a genuine emotion, with an ardor without equal, scorning all other affections, and disdaining those things which formerly they characterized as beautiful. This is the experience of those to whom divinities and guardians have appeared; they reck no longer of the beauty of other bodies. Imagine, if you can, the experiences of those who behold Beauty itself, the pure Beauty, which, because of its very purity, is fleshless and bodiless, outside of earth and heaven. All these things, indeed are contingent and composite, they are not principles, they are derived from Him. What beauty could one still wish to see after having arrived at vision of Him who gives perfection to all beings, though himself remains unmoved, without receiving anything; after finding rest in this contemplation, and enjoying it by becoming assimilated to Him? Being supreme beauty, and the first beauty, He beautifies those who love Him, and thereby they become worthy of love. This is the great, the supreme goal of souls; this is the goal which arouses all their efforts, if they do not wish to be disinherited of that sublime contemplation the enjoyment of which confers blessedness, and privation of which is the greatest of earthly misfortunes. Real misfortune is not to lack beautiful colors, nor beautiful bodies, nor power, nor domination, nor royalty. It is quite sufficient to see oneself excluded from no more than possession of beauty. This possession is precious enough to render worthless domination of a kingdom, if not of the whole earth, of the sea, or even of the heavens—if indeed it were possible, while abandoning and scorning all that (natural beauty), to succeed in contemplating beauty face to face.

THE METHOD TO ACHIEVE ECSTASY IS TO CLOSE THE EYES OF THE BODY.

8. How shall we start, and later arrive at the contemplation of this ineffable beauty which, like the divinity in the mysteries, remains hidden in the recesses of a sanctuary, and does not show itself outside, where it might be perceived by the profane? We must advance into this sanctuary, penetrating into it, if we have the strength to do so, closing our eyes to the spectacle of terrestrial things, without throwing a backward glance on the bodies whose graces formerly charmed us. If we do still see corporeal beauties, we must no longer rush at them, but, knowing that they are only images, traces and adumbrations of a superior principle, we will flee from them, to approach Him of whom they are merely the reflections. Whoever would let himeslf be misled by the pursuit of those vain shadows, mistaking them for realities, would grasp only an image as fugitive as the fluctuating form reflected by the waters, and would resemble that senseless (Narcissus) who, wishing to grasp that image himself, according to the fable, disappeared, carried away by the current. Likewise he would wish to embrace corporeal beauties, and not release them, would plunge, not his body, but his soul into the gloomy abysses, so repugnant to intelligence; he would be condemned to total blindness; and on this earth, as well as in hell, he would see naught but mendacious shades.

HOW TO FLY TO OUR FATHERLAND.

This indeed is the occasion to quote (from Homer) with peculiar force, "Let us fly unto our dear fatherland!" But how shall we fly? How escape from here? is the question Ulysses asks himself in that allegory which represents him trying to escape from the magic sway of Circe or Calypso, where neither the pleasure of the eyes, nor the view of fleshly beauty were able to hold him in those enchanted places. Our fatherland is the region whence we descend here below. It is there that dwells our Father. But how shall we return thither? What means shall be employed to return us thither? Not our feet, indeed; all they could do would be to move us from one place of the earth to another. Neither is it a chariot, nor ship which need be prepared. All these vain helps must be left aside, and not even considered. We must close the eyes of the body, to open another vision, which indeed all possess, but very few employ.

HOW TO TRAIN THIS INTERIOR VISION.

9. But how shall we train this interior vision? At the moment of its (first) awakening, it cannot contemplate beauties too dazzling. Your soul must then first be accustomed to contemplate the noblest occupations of man, and then the beautiful deeds, not indeed those performed by artists, but those (good deeds) done by virtuous men. Later contemplate the souls of those who perform these beautiful actions. Nevertheless, how will you discover the beauty which their excellent soul possesses? Withdraw within yourself, and examine yourself. If you do not yet therein discover beauty, do as the artist, who cuts off, polishes, purifies until he has adorned his statue with all the marks of beauty. Remove from your soul, therefore, all that is superfluous, straighten out all that is crooked, purify and illuminate what is obscure, and do not cease perfecting your statue until the divine resplendence of virtue shines forth upon your sight, until you see temperance in its holy purity seated in your breast. When you shall have acquired this perfection; when you will see it in yourself; when you will purely dwell

within yourself; when you will cease to meet within yourself any obstacle to unity; when nothing foreign will any more, by its admixture, alter the simplicity of your interior essence; when within your whole being you will be a veritable light, immeasurable in size, uncircumscribed by any figure within narrow boundaries, unincreasable because reaching out to infinity, and entirely incommensurable because it transcends all measure and quantity; when you shall have become such, then, having become sight itself, you may have confidence in yourself, for you will no longer need any guide. Then must you observe carefully, for it is only by the eye that then will open itself within you that you will be able to perceive supreme Beauty. But if you try to fix on it an eye soiled by vice, an eye that is impure, or weak, so as not to be able to support the splendor of so brilliant an object, that eye will see nothing, not even if it were shown a sight easy to grasp. The organ of vision will first have to be rendered analogous and similar to the object it is to contemplate. Never would the eye have seen the sun unless first it had assumed its form; likewise, the soul could never see beauty, unless she herself first became beautiful. To obtain the view of the beautiful, and of the divinity, every man must begin by rendering himself beautiful and divine.

THE LANDMARKS OF THE PATH TO ECSTASY.

Thus he will first rise to intelligence, and he will there contemplate beauty, and declare that all this beauty resides in the Ideas. Indeed, in them everything is beautiful, because they are the daughters and the very essence of Intelligence.

Above intelligence, he will meet Him whom we call the nature of the Good, and who causes beauty to radiate around Him; so that, to repeat, the first thing that is met is beauty. If a distinction is to be established among the intelligibles, we might say that intelligible beauty is the locus of ideas, and that the Good, which is located above the Beautiful, is its source and principle. If, however, we desire to locate the Good and the Beautiful within one single principle, we might regard this one principle first as Good, and only afterwards, as Beauty.

REFERENCES.

Page 40, line 4, Equally Beautiful, Phaedrus p 250, Cary 63-65; Hippias Major, 295, Cary 44; Philebus p 17, Cary 20, 21.
Page 41, line 11, Stoic definition, Cicero, Tusculans, iv. 13
Page 44, line 30, Obscurity of Matter, Timaeus, p. 31, Cary 11; Philebus, p 29, Cary 52.
Page 45, line 22, Superior Order, Banquet 210, Cary 34; Timaeus, p 31, Cary 11
Page 45, line 35, Golden Face of Justice, Athenaeus, Deipnosophistae, xii 546
Page 46, line 10, Pleasurable Impulse, Banquet, p 191, Cary 17, 18, Cratylos, p 420, Cary 78-80
Page 47, line 5, Justice of the Heart, Banquet, p 209, Cary 33, Republic, iii. 402, Cary 12
Page 48, line 23, Ugliness, Banquet, p 215-217, Cary 39, 40; Philebus, p 66, Cary 158 159
Page 49, line 4, Purifications, Phaedo, p 69, Cary 37.
Page 49, line 32, Assimilating to Divinity, Republic x. p. 613, Cary 12.
Page 50, line 1, Good and Beautiful, Timaeus, p 35, Cary 12
Page 50, line 5, Identical with Good, Philebus, p 64, Cary 153-155; First Alcibiades, p. 115, Cary 23, 24.
Page 51, line 1, 2, He who Beholds, Phaedrus, p 278, Cary 145.
Page 51, line 8, Ardor without Equal; line 15, Very Purity, Banquet, p 210, 211; Cary 34, 35
Page 51, line 29, Confers Blessedness, Phaedrus, p 250, Cary 64.
Page 53, line 16, Interior Vision, Republic, x, p 533, Cary 13.
Page 53, line 34, Temperance Seated, Phaedrus, p 279, Cary 147.
Page 54, line 19, Organ of Vision, Timaeus, p. 45, Cary 19
Page 54, line 23, Assumed its form, Republic, vi., p. 508, Cary 19.
Page 54, line 29, Rise to Intelligence Philebus, p. 64, Cary 153-155.

FOURTH ENNEAD, BOOK SEVEN.

Of the Immortality of the Soul: Polemic Against Materialism.

IS THE SOUL IMMORTAL?

1. Are we immortal, or does all of us die? (Another possibility would be that) of the two parts of which we are composed, the one might be fated to be dissolved and perish, while the other, that constitutes our very personality, might subsist perpetually. These problems must be solved by a study of our nature.

THE BODY AS THE INSTRUMENT OF THE SOUL.

Man is not a simple being; he contains a soul and a body, which is united to this soul, either as tool, or in some other manner.* This is how we must distinguish the soul from the body, and determine the nature and manner of existence ("being") of each of them.

THE BODY IS COMPOSITE, AND THEREFORE PERISHABLE.

As the nature of the body is composite, reason convinces us that it cannot last perpetually, and our senses show it to us dissolved, destroyed, and decayed, because the elements that compose it return to join the elements of the same nature, altering, destroying them and each other, especially when this chaos is abandoned to the soul, which alone keeps her parts combined. Even if a body were taken alone, it would not be a unity; it may be analyzed into form and matter, prin-

*As pilot, perhaps, iv. 3. 21.

ciples that are necessary to the constitution of all bodies, even of those that are simple.* Besides, as they contain extension, the bodies can be cut, divided into infinitely small parts, and thus perish.† Therefore if our body is a part of ourselves,‡ not all of us is immortal; if the body is only the instrument of the soul, as the body is given to the soul only for a definite period, it still is by nature perishable.

THE SOUL IS THE INDIVIDUALITY, AS ITS FORM, AND AS A SKILLED WORKMAN.

The soul, which is the principal part of man, and which constitutes man himself,§ should bear to the body the relation of form to matter, or of a workman to his tool;|| in both cases the soul is the man himself.

IF THE SOUL IS INCORPOREAL, WE MUST STUDY INCORPOREALITY.

2. What then is the nature of the soul? If she is a body, she can be decomposed, as every body is a composite. If, on the contrary, she is not a body, if hers is a different nature, the latter must be examined; either in the same way that we have examined the body, or in some other way.

A.—THE SOUL IS NOT CORPOREAL (AS THE STOICS THOUGHT).

(a.) (Neither a material molecule, nor a material aggregation of material atoms could possess life and intelligence.) First, let us consider the nature of this alleged soul-body. As every soul necessarily possesses life, and as the body, considered as being the soul, must obtain at least two molecules, if not more (there are three possibilities): either only one of them possesses life, or all of them possess it, or none of them. If one

*See ii., 4. 6. †See ii. 7 1. ‡See i. 1. 10.
§See i. 9. 8. 10. ||See iv. 3. 20, 21.

molecule alone possesses life, it alone will be the soul. Of what nature will be that molecule supposed to possess life by itself? Will it be water (Hippo), air (Anaximenes, Archelaus, and Diogenes), earth, or fire (Heraclitus, Stobaeus?*) But those are elements that are inanimate by themselves, and which, even when they are animated, possess but a borrowed life. Still there is no other kind of body. Even those (philosophers, like the Pythagoreans) who posited elements other (than water, air, earth and fire) still considered them to be bodies, and not souls, not even attributing souls to them. The theory that life results from the union of molecules of which, nevertheless, none by itself possesses life, is an absurd hypothesis. If further any molecule possesses life, then a single one would be sufficient.

NEITHER MIXTURE NOR ITS PRINCIPLE WILL EXPLAIN LIFE AS A BODY.

The most irrational theory of all is that an aggregation of molecules should produce life, that elements without intelligence should beget intelligence. Others (like Alexander of Aphrodisia) insist that to produce life these elements must be mingled in a certain manner. That would, however, imply (as thought Galien and Hippocrates,†) the existence of a principle which produces order, and which should be the cause of mixture or, temperament,‡ and that should alone deserve being considered as soul. No simple bodies could exist, much less composite bodies, unless there was a soul in the universe; for it is (seminal) reason which, in adding itself to matter, produces body.§ But surely a (seminal) reason could proceed from nowhere except a soul.

*Ecl. Phys., p. 797, Heeren and Aristotle, de Anima, i. 2.
†See Nemesius, de Nat. Hom. 2.
‡See ii. 7, 1.
§See ii. 7, 3.

NO ATOMIC AGGREGATION COULD PRODUCE A SELF-HARMONIZING UNITY.

3. (b.) (No aggregation of atoms could form a whole that would be one and sympathetic with itself.) Others, on the contrary, insist that the soul is constituted by the union of atoms or indivisibles (as thought Leucippus, Democritus and Epicurus.*) To refute this error, we have to examine the nature of sympathy (or community of affection, a Stoic characteristic of a living being,†) and juxtaposition.‡ On the one hand an aggregation of corporeal molecules which are incapable of being united, and which do not feel cannot form a single sympathetic whole such as is the soul, which is sympathetic with herself. On the other hand, how could a body or extension be constituted by (a juxtaposition of) atoms?

SOUL IS A SIMPLE SUBSTANCE, WHILE EVERY BODY IS COMPOSED OF MATTER AND FORM.

(c.) (Every body is a composite of matter and form, while the soul is a simple substance.) Inasmuch as matter possesses no quality,§ the matter of no simple body will be said to possess life in itself. That which imparts life to it must then be its form. If form is a "being," the soul cannot simultaneously be matter and form; it will be only matter or form. Consequently, the soul will not be the body, since the body is not constituted by matter exclusively, as could be proved analytically, if necessary.

IF SOUL IS ONLY AN AFFECTION OF MATTER, WHENCE THAT AFFECTION?

(d.) (The soul is not a simple manner of being of matter, because matter could not give itself a form.) Some Stoics might deny that form was a "being," asserting the soul to be a mere affection (or, manner of

*Stob. Ecl. Phys. 797. †See ii 3, 5.
‡See ii 7, 1. §ii. 4, 7.

being) of matter.* From whence then did matter acquire this affection and animating life? Surely matter itself could not endow itself with a form and a soul. That which endows matter or any body with life must then be some principle alien and superior to corporeal nature.

NO BODY COULD SUBSIST WITHOUT THE POWER OF THE UNIVERSAL SOUL.

(e.) (No body could subsist without the power of the universal soul.) Besides no body could subsist without the power of the universal Soul (from Numenius†), Every body, indeed, is in a perpetual flow and movement (as thought Heraclitus, in Plato, Cratylus§), and the world would soon perish if it contained nothing but bodies, even if some one of them were to be called soul; for such a soul, being composed of the same matter as the other bodies, would undergo the same fate that they do; or rather, there would not even be any body, everything would remain in the condition of shapeless matter, since there would exist no principle to fashion it. Why, there would not even be any matter, and the universe would be annihilated to nothingness, if the care of keeping its parts united were entrusted to some body which would have nothing but the name of soul, as for instance, to air, or a breath without cohesion,‡ which could not be one, by itself. As all bodies are divisible, if the universe depended on a body, it would be deprived of intelligence and given up to chance. How, indeed, could there be any order in a spirit which itself would need to receive order from a soul? How could this spirit contain reason and intelligence? On the hypothesis of the existence of the soul, all these elements serve to constitute the body of the world, and of every animal,

*See iv. 7, 8. †Euseb., Prep. Ev. xv. 17.
‡Cicero, Tusculans, i. 9. §p. 54, Cousin.

because all different bodies together work for the end of all; but without the soul, there is no order, and even nothing exists any more.

IF THE SOUL IS NOT SIMPLE MATTER, SHE MUST BE A SUBSTANTIAL FORM.

4. (f) (If the soul is anything but simple matter, she must be constituted by a substantial form.) Those who claim that the soul is a body are, by the very force of the truth, forced to recognize the existence, before and above them, of a form proper to the soul; for they acknowledge the existence of an intelligent spirit, and an intellectual fire (as do the Stoics, following in the footsteps of Heraclitus, Stobaeus*). According to them, it seems that, without spirit or fire, there canot be any superior nature in the order of beings, and that the soul needs a location where she may be built up. On the contrary, it is bodies alone that need to be built up on something, and indeed, they are founded on the powers of the soul. If really we do believe that the soul and life are no more than a spirit, why add the qualification "of a certain characteristic,"† a meaningless term employed when forced to admit an active nature superior to that of bodies. As there are thousands of inanimate spirits, not every spirit is a soul. If only that spirit is a soul which possesses that "special characteristic," this "special characteristic" and this "manner of being" will either be something real, or will be nothing. If they are nothing, there will be nothing real but spirit, and this alleged "manner of being" is nothing more than a word. In that system, therefore, nothing but matter really exists. God, the soul, and all other things are no more than a word; the body alone really subsists. If, on the contrary, that "manner of being" is something real, if it is anything else than substrate or

*Ecl. Phys. 797, Cicero, de Nat. Deor. iii. 14.
†See ii. 4, 1. 'pôs echon.' of Dikearchus and Aristoxenus.

matter, if it resides in matter without being material or composed of matter, it must then be a nature different from the body, namely, a reason (by a pun).*

THE BODY EXERTS A UNIFORM ACTION, WHILE THE SOUL EXERTS A VARIED ONE.

(g.) (The body exerts an uniform action, while the soul exerts a very diverse action.) The following considerations further demonstrate the impossibility of the soul being a body. A body must be hot or cold, hard or soft, liquid or solid, black or white, or qualities differing according to its nature. If it is only hot or cold, light or heavy, black or white, it communicates its only quality to what comes close to it; for fire could not cool, nor ice heat. Nevertheless, the soul produces not only different effects in different animals, but contrary effects even in the same being; she makes certain things solid, dense, black, light; and certain others liquid, sparse, white, or heavy. According to the different quality of the body, and according to its color, she should produce but a single effect; nevertheless, she exerts a very diverse action.

THREE MORE PROOFS OF THE INCORPOREITY OF THE SOUL.

5. (h.) (The body has but a single kind of motion, while the soul has different ones.) If the soul is a body, how does it happen that she has different kinds of motion instead of a single one, as is the case with the body? Will these movements be explained by voluntary determinations, and by (seminal) reasons? In this case neither the voluntary determinations, nor these reasons, which differ from each other, can belong to a single and simple body; such a body does not participate in any particular reason except by the principle that made it hot or cold.

*See ii. 6, on 'logos.'

BODIES CAN LOSE PARTS, NOT SO THE SOUL.

(i.) (Souls cannot, as do bodies, lose or gain parts, ever remaining identical.) The body has the faculty of making its organs grow within a definite time and in fixed proportions. From where could the soul derive them? Its function is to grow, not to cause growth, unless the principle of growth be comprehended within its material mass. If the soul that makes the body grow was herself a body, she should, on uniting with molecules of a nature similar to hers, develop a growth proportional to that of the organs. In this case, the molecules that will come to add themselves to the soul will be either animate or inanimate; if they are animate, how could they have become such, and from whom will they have received that characteristic? If they are not animate, how will they become such, and how will agreement between them and the first soul arise? How will they form but a single unity with her, and how will they agree with her? Will they not constitute a soul that will remain foreign to the former, who will not possess her requirements of knowledge? This aggregation of molecules that would thus be called soul will resemble the aggregation of molecules that form our body. She would lose parts, she would acquire new ones; she will not be identical. But if we had a soul that was not identical, memory and self-consciousness of our own faculties would be impossible.

THE SOUL IS EVERYWHERE ENTIRE; THAT IS NOT THE CASE WITH THE BODY.

(j.) (The soul, being one and simple, is everywhere entire, and has parts that are identical to the whole; this is not the case with the body.) If the soul is a body, she will have parts that are not identical with the whole, as every body is by nature divisible. If then the soul has a definite magnitude of which she cannot lose anything without ceasing to be a soul, she will by losing her parts, change her nature, as happens to every quantity. If, on losing some part of its magnitude, a body, notwithstanding, remains identical in respect to quality, it does not nevertheless become different from what it was, in respect to quantity, and it remains identical only in respect to quality, which differs from quantity. What shall we answer to those who insist that the soul is a body? Will they say that, in the same body, each part possesses the same quality as the total soul, and that the case is similar with the part of a part? Then quantity is no longer essential to the nature of the soul; which contradicts the hypothesis that the soul needed to possess a definite magnitude. Besides the soul is everywhere entire; now it is impossible for a body to be entire in several places simultaneously, or have parts identical to the whole. If we refuse the name of soul to each part, the soul is then composed of inanimate parts. Besides, if the soul is a definite magnitude, she cannot increase or diminish without ceasing to be a soul; but it often happens that from a single conception or from a single germ are born two or more beings, as is seen in certain animals in whom the germs divide;* in this case, each part is equal to the whole. However superficially considered, this fact demonstrates that the principle in which the part is equal to the whole is essentially superior to quantity, and must necessarily lack any kind of quantity. On this condition alone can the soul remain identical when the body loses its quantity, because she has need of no mass, no quantity, and because her essence is of an entirely different nature. The soul and the (seminal) reasons therefore possess no extension.

THE BODY COULD NOT POSSESS SENSATION.

6. (k.) (The body could not possess either sensation, thought, or virtue.) If the soul were a body, she

*See v. 7, 3.

would not possess either sensation, thought, science, virtue, nor any of the perfections that render her more beautiful. Here follows the proof.

IMPOSSIBILITY FOR THE BODY TO HAVE SENSATION.

The subject that perceives a sense-object must itself be single, and grasp this object in its totality, by one and the same power. This happens when by several organs we perceive several qualities of a single object, or when, by a single organ, we embrace a single complex object in its totality, as, for instance, a face. It is not one principle that sees the face, and another one that sees the eyes; it is the "same principle" which embraces everything at once. Doubtless we do receive a sense-impression by the eyes, and another by the ears; but both of them must end in some single principle. How, indeed, could any decision be reached about the difference of sense-impressions unless they all converged toward the same principle? The latter is like a centre, and the individual sensations are like radii which from the circumference radiate towards the centre of a circle. This central principle is essentially single. If it was divisible, and if sense-impressions were directed towards two points at a distance from each other, such as the extremities of the same line, they would either still converge towards one and the same point, as, for instance, the middle (of the line), or one part would feel one thing, and another something else. It would be absolutely as if I felt one thing, and you felt another, when placed in the presence of one and the same thing (as thought Aristotle, de Anima*). Facts, therefore, demonstrate that sensations centre in one and the same principle; as visible images are centred in the pupil of the eye; otherwise how could we, through the pupil, see the greatest objects? So much the more, there-

*iii. 2.

fore, must the sensations that centre in the (Stoic) "directing principle"* resemble indivisible intuitions and be perceived by an indivisible principle. If the latter possessed extension, it could, like the sense-object, be divided; each of its parts would thus perceive one of the parts of the sense-object, and nothing within us would grasp the object in its totality. The subject that perceives must then be entirely one; otherwise, how could it be divided? In that case it could not be made to coincide with the sense-object, as two equal figures superimposed on each other, because the directing principle does not have an extension equal to that of the sense-object. How then will we carry out the division? Must the subject that feels contain as many parts as there are in the sense-object? Will each part of the soul, in its turn, feel by its own parts, or will (we decide that) the parts of parts will not feel? Neither is that likely. If, on the other hand, each part feels the entire object, and if each magnitude is divisible to infinity, the result is that, for a single object, there will be an infinity of sensations in each part of the soul; and, so much the more, an infinity of images in the principle that directs us. (This, however, is the opposite of the actual state of affairs.)

AGAINST THE STOICS, SENSATIONS ARE NOT IMPRESSIONS OF A SEAL ON WAX.

Besides, if the principle that feels were corporeal, it could feel only so long as exterior objects produced in the blood or in the air some impression similar to that of a seal on wax.† If they impressed their images on wet substances, as is no doubt supposed, these impressions would become confused as images in water, and memory would not occur. If, however, these impressions persisted, they would either form an obstacle to subsequent ones, and no further sensation would occur;

*See iv. 2, 2   †iv 2, 1.

or they would be effaced by the new ones, which would destroy memory. If then the soul is capable of recalling earlier sensations, and having new ones, to which the former would form no obstacle, it is because she is not corporeal.

SENSATION CANNOT BE RELAYED FROM SENSE-ORGAN TO DIRECTING PRINCIPLE.

7. The same reflections may be made about pain, and one's feeling of it. When a man's finger is said to give him pain, this, no doubt, is a recognition that the seat of the pain is in the finger, and that the feeling of pain is experienced by the directing principle. Consequently, when a part of the spirit suffers, this suffering is felt by the directing principle, and shared by the whole soul.* How can this sympathy be explained? By relay transmission, (the Stoic) will answer; the sense-impression is felt first by the animal spirit that is in the finger, and then transmitted to the neighboring part, and so on till it reaches the directing part. Necessarily, if the pain is felt by the first part that experiences it, it will also be felt by the second part to which it is transmitted; then by the third, and so on, until the one pain would have caused an infinite number of sensations. Last the directing principle will perceive all these sensations, adding thereto its own sensation. Speaking strictly, however, each of these sensations will not transmit the suffering of the finger, but the suffering of one of the intermediate parts. For instance, the second sensation will relay the suffering of the hand. The third, that of the arm, and so on, until there will be an infinity of sensations. The directing principle, for its part, will not feel the pain of the finger, but its own; it will know none but that, it will

*Plutarch, de Placitis Philosoph, iii 8. The Stoic definition of sensation being that senses are spirits stretched (by relays with "tension") from the directing principle to the organs.

pay no attention to the rest, because it will ignore the pain suffered by the finger. Therefore, relayed sensation is an impossibility, nor could one part of the body perceive the suffering felt by another part; for the body has extension, and, in every extension, parts are foreign to each other (the opposite of the opinion of Cleanthes, Nemesius).* Consequently, the principle that feels must everywhere be identical with itself; and among all beings, the body is that which is least suitable to this identity.

THE BODY CANNOT THINK.

8. If, in any sense whatever, the soul were a body, we could not think. Here is the proof. If feeling† is explained as the soul's laying hold of perceptible things by making use of the body, thinking cannot also of making use of the body. Otherwise, thinking and feeling would be identical. Thus, thinking must consist in perceiving without the help of the body (as thought Aristotle‡). So much the more, the thinking principle cannot be corporeal. Since it is sensation that grasps sense-objects, it must likewise be thought, or intellection, that grasps intelligible objects. Though this should be denied, it will be admitted that we think certain intelligibles entities, and that we perceive entities that have no extension. How could an entity that had extension think one that had no extension? Or a divisible entity, think an indivisible one? Could this take place by an indivisible part? In this case, the thinking subject will not be corporeal; for there is no need that the whole subject be in contact with the object; it would suffice if one of its parts reached the object (as Aristotle said against Plato).§

*de Nat. Hom. 2.
†See iv. 4, 23. In the words of Zeno, as, for the Stoics, the principal act of the intelligence was comprehensive vision, "phantasia kataleptike."
‡de Anima, iii. 4, 5.   §de Anima, 1. 3.

If then this truth be granted, that the highest thoughts must have incorporeal objects, the latter can be cognized only by a thinking principle that either is, or becomes independent of body. Even the objection that the object of thought is constituted by the forms inherent in matter, implies that these forces cannot be thought unless, by intelligence, they are separated from matter. It is not by means of the carnal mass of the body, nor generally by matter, that we can effect the abstraction of triangle, circle, line or point. To succeed in this abstraction, the soul must separate from the body, and consequently, the soul cannot be corporeal.

THE BODY CANNOT POSSESS VIRTUE.

Neither do beauty or justice possess extension, I suppose; and their conception must be similar. These things can be cognized or retained only by the indivisible part of the soul. If the latter were corporeal, where indeed could virtues, prudence, justice and courage exist? In this case, virtues (as Critias thought),* would be no more than a certain disposition of the spirit, or blood (as Empedocles also thought).† For instance, courage and temperance would respectively be no more than a certain irritability, and a fortunate temperament of the spirit; beauty would consist in the agreeable shape of outlines, which cause persons, in whom they occur, to be called elegant and handsome. Under this hypothesis, indeed, the types of spirit might possess vigor and beauty. But what need would it have of temperance? On the contrary, the spirit would seek to be agreeably affected by the things it touches and embraces, to enjoy a moderate heat, a gentle coolness, and to be in contact only with sweet, tender, and smooth entities. What incentive would the spirit have to apportion rewards to those who had deserved them?

*de Anim. Arist. i. 2. †Cicero, Tusculans, i. 9.

IF VIRTUE WERE CORPOREAL IT WOULD BE PERISHABLE.

Are the notions of virtue, and other intelligible entities by the soul thought eternal, or does virtue arise and perish? If so, by what being, and how will it be formed? It is the same problem that remains to be solved. Intelligible entities must therefore be eternal and immutable, like geometrical notions, and consequently cannot be corporeal. Further, the subject in whom they exist must be of a nature similar to theirs, and therefore not be corporeal; for the nature of body is not to remain immutable, but to be in a perpetual flow.

BODIES ARE ACTIVE ONLY BY MEANS OF INCORPOREAL POWERS.

(9.) There are men who locate the soul in the body, so as to give her a foundation in some sphere of activity, to account for the various phenomena in the body, such as getting hot or cold, pushing on or stopping, (and the like). They evidently do not realize that bodies produce these effects only through incorporeal powers, and that those are not the powers that we attribute to the soul, which are thought, sensation, reasoning, desire, judiciousness, propriety and wisdom, all of them entities that cannot possible be attributes of a corporeal entity. Consequently, those (materialists) attribute to the body all the faculties of incorporeal essences, and leave nothing for the latter.

WHY BODIES ARE ACTIVATED BY INCORPOREAL POWERS.

The proof that bodies are activated only by incorporeal faculties may be proved as follows: Quantity and quality are two different things. Every body has a quantity, but not always a quality, as in the case of matter, (according to the Stoic definition, that it was a body without quality, but possessing magnitude*). Granting this, (you Stoic) will also be forced to admit that as quality is something different from quantity, it must consequently be different from the body. Since then every body has a quantity, how could quality, which is no quantity, be a body? Besides, as we said above,† every body and mass is altered by division; nevertheless, when a body is cut into pieces, every part preserves the entire quality without undergoing alteration. For instance, every molecule of honey, possesses the quality of sweetness as much as all the molecules taken together; consequently that sweetness cannot be corporeal; and other qualities must be in a similar case. Moreover, if the active powers were corporeal, they would have to have a material mass proportional to their strength or weakness. Now there are great masses that have little force, and small ones that have great force; demonstrating that power does not depend on extension, and should be attributed to some (substance) without extension. Finally, you may say that matter is identical with body, and produces different beings only by receiving different qualities (the Stoics considering that even the divinity was no more than modified matter, their two principles being matter and quality;‡ the latter, however, was also considered as body). How do you (Stoics) not see that qualities thus added to matter are reasons, that are primary and immaterial? Do not object that when the spirit (breath) and blood abandon animals, they cease to live; for if these things are necessary to life, there are for our life many other necessities, even during the presence of the soul (as thought Nemesius).§ Besides, neither spirit nor blood are distributed to every part of the body.

*See ii. 4, 1.
†See iv. 7, 5.
‡See ii. 4, 1.
§de Nat. Hom. 2.

THE SOUL CAN PENETRATE THE BODY; BUT TWO BODIES CANNOT PENETRATE EACH OTHER.

(10). The soul penetrates the whole body, while an entire body cannot penetrate another entire body. Further, if the soul is corporeal, and pervades the whole body, she will, with the body, form (as Alexander of Aphrodisia pointed out) a mixture,* similar to the other bodies (that are consititued by a mixture of matter and quality, as the Stoics taught). Now as none of the bodies that enter into a mixture is in actualization† the soul, instead of being in actualization in the bodies, would be in them only potentially; consequently, she would cease to be a soul, as the sweet ceases to be sweet when mingled with the bitter; we would, therefore, have no soul left. If, when one body forms a mixture with another body, total penetration occurs, so that each molecule contains equal parts of two bodies and that each body be distributed equally in the whole space occupied by the mass of the other, without any increase of volume, nothing that is not divided will remain. Indeed, mixture operates not only between the larger parts (which would be no more than a simple juxtaposition); but the two bodies must penetrate each other mutually, even if smaller—it would indeed be impossible for the smaller to equal the greater; still, when the smaller penetrates the larger it must divide it entirely. If the mixture operates in this manner in every part, and if no undivided part of the mass remain, the body must be divided into points, which is impossible. Indeed, were this division pushed to infinity, since every body is fully divisible, bodies will have to be infinite not only potentially, but also in actuality. It is therefore impossible for one entire body to penetrate another in its entirety. Now as the soul penetrates the entire body, the soul must be incorporeal (as thought Nemesius).‡

*See ii. 7.   †See ii. 7, 1.   ‡Nat. Hom. 2.

THE STOIC DEVELOPMENT FROM HABIT TO SOUL AND INTELLIGENCE WOULD MAKE THE PERFECT ARISE FROM THE IMPERFECT, AN IMPOSSIBILITY.

(11). (If, as Stoics claim, man first was a certain nature called habit,* then a soul, and last an intelligence, the perfect would have arisen from the imperfect, which is impossible). To say that the first nature of the soul is to be a spirit, and that this spirit became soul only after having been exposed to cold, and as it were became soaked by its contact, because the cold subtilized it;‡ this is an absurd hypothesis. Many animals are born in warm places, and do not have their soul exposed to action of cold. Under this hypothesis, the primary nature of the soul would have been made dependent on the concourse of exterior circumstances. The Stoics, therefore, posit as principle that which is less perfect (the soul), and trace it to a still less perfect earlier thing called habit (or form of inorganic things).† Intelligence, therefore, is posited in the last rank since it is alleged to be born of the soul, while, on the contrary, the first rank should be assigned to intelligence, the second to the soul, the third to nature, and, following natural order, consider that which is less perfect as the posterior element. In this system the divinity, by the mere fact of his possessing intelligence, is posterior and begotten, possessing only an incidental intelligence. The result would, therefore, be that there was neither soul, nor intelligence, nor divinity; for never can that which is potential pass to the condition of actualization, without the prior existence of some actualized principle. If what is potential were to transform itself into actualization—which is absurd— its passage into actualization will have to involve at the

---
*See ii. 4, 16. †See ii. 4, 16.
‡As thought Chrysippus, in Plutarch, de Stoic. Repugnant.

very least a contemplation of something which is not merely potential, but actualized. Nevertheless, on the hypothesis that what is potential can permanently remain identical, it will of itself pass into actualization, and will be superior to the being which is potential only because it will be the object of the aspiration of such a being. We must, therefore, assign the first rank to the being that has a perfect and incorporeal nature, which is always in actualization. Thus intelligence and soul are prior to nature; the soul, therefore, is not a spirit, and consequently no body. Other reasons for the incorporeality of the soul have been advanced; but the above suffices (as thought Aristotle).*

II. THE SOUL IS NEITHER THE HARMONY NOR ENTELECHY OF THE BODY—THE SOUL IS THE HARMONY OF THE BODY; AGAINST THE PYTHAGOREANS.

(12). a. Since the soul is not corporeal, its real nature must be ascertained. Shall we assert that she is something distinct from the body, but dependent thereon, as, for instance, a harmony? Pythagoras, indeed, used this word in a technical sense; and after him the harmony of the body has been thought to be something similar to the harmony of a lyre. As tension produces in the lyre-strings an affection (or, manner of being, or state) that is called harmony, likewise, as contrary elements are mingled in our body, an individual mixture produces life and soul, which, therefore, is only an individual affection of this mixture.

WHY THE SOUL IS NOT A HARMONY

As has already been said above† this hypothesis is inadmissible for several reasons. To begin with, the soul is prior (to the body), and the harmony is pos-

*Met. xii 6; see ii. 5, 3.
†iv. 7, 3.

terior thereto. Then the soul dominates the body, governs it, and often even resists it, which would be impossible if the soul were only a harmony. The soul, indeed, is a "being," which harmony is not. When the corporeal principles of which we are composed are mingled in just proportions, their temperament constitutes health (but not a "being," such as the soul). Besides, every part of the body being mingled in a different manner should form (a different harmony, and consequently) a different soul, so that there would be several of them. The decisive argument, however, is that this soul (that constitutes a harmony) presupposes another soul which would produce this harmony, as a lyre needs a musician who would produce harmonic vibrations in the strings, because he possesses within himself the reason according to which he produces the harmony. The strings of the lyre do not vibrate of themselves, and the elements of our body cannot harmonize themselves. Nevertheless, under this hypothesis, animated and orderly "being" would have been made up out of inanimate and disordered entities; and these orderly "beings" would owe their order and existence to chance. That is as impossible for parts as for the whole. The soul, therefore, is no harmony.

THE SOUL IS NOT THE ENTELECHY OF THE BODY (POLEMIC AGAINST ARISTOTLE) ARISTOTLE'S STATEMENT OF THE PROBLEM.*

(13). b. Now let us examine the opinion of those who call the soul an entelechy. They say that, in the composite, the soul plays the part of form in respect to matter, in the body the soul animates. The soul, however, is not said to be the form of any body, nor of the body as such; but of the natural body, that is organized, and which possesses life potentially.†

*From end of iv. 2. 3.   †Aristotle, de Anima, ii. 1.

IF THE SOUL IS AN ENTELECHY, SHE IS A DIFFERENT ONE THAN ARISTOTLE'S.

If the soul's relation to the body is the same as that of the statue to the metal, the soul will be divided with the body, and on cutting a member a portion of the soul would be cut along with it. According to this teaching, the soul separates from the body only during sleep, since she must inhere in the body of which she is the entelechy, in which case sleep would become entirely inexplicable. If the soul be an entelechy, the struggle of reason against the passions would become entirely impossible. The entire human being will experience but one single sentiment, and never be in disagreement with itself. If the soul be an entelechy, there will perhaps still be sensations, but mere sensations; pure thoughts will have become impossible. Consequently the Peripateticians themselves are obliged to introduce (into human nature) another soul, namely, the pure intelligence, which they consider immortal.*
The rational soul, therefore, would have to be an entelechy in a manner different from their definition thereof, if indeed this name is at all to be used.

IF AN ENTELECHY BE GRANTED, IT IS INSEPARABLE FROM THE BODY.

The sense-soul, which preserves the forms of sense-objects previously perceived, must preserve them without the body. Otherwise, these forms would inhere in the body like figures and corporeal shapes. Now, if the forms inhered in the sense-soul in this manner, they could not be received therein otherwise (than as corporeal impressions). That is why, if we do grant the existence of an entelechy, it must be inseparable from the body. Even the faculty of appetite, not indeed that which makes us feel the need of eating and drinking,

*Arist. de Anima, ii. 2; iii. 5.

but that which desires things that are independent of the body, could not either be an entelechy.*

NEITHER COULD THE SOUL OF GROWTH BE AN ENTELECHY.

The soul's faculty of growth remains to be considered. This at least might be thought an inseparable entelechy. But neither does that suit her nature. For if the principle of every plant is in its root, and if growth takes place around and beneath it,† as occurs in many plants, it is evident that the soul's faculty of growth, abandoning all the other parts, has concentrated in the root alone; it, therefore, was not distributed all around the soul, like an inseparable entelechy. Add that this soul, before the plant grows, is already contained in the small body (of the seed). If then, after having vivified a great plant, the soul's faculty of growth can condense into a small space, and if later it can, from this small space, again spread over a whole plant, it is evidently entirely separable from the (plant's) matter.

THE ENTELECHY IS NOT A FORM OF THE BODY, AS THE SOUL TRANSMIGRATES.

Besides, as the soul is indivisible, the entelechy of the divisible body could not become divisible as is the body. Besides, the same soul passes from the body of one animal into the body of some other. How could the soul of the first become that of the second, if she were only the entelechy of a single one? The example of animals that metamorphose demonstrates the impossibility of this theory. The soul, therefore, is not the simple form of a body; she is a genuine "being," which does not owe its existence merely to her being founded on the body, but which, on the contrary, exists before having become the soul of some

*See Aristotle, de Anima, i. 5.
†See Aristotle, de Anima, ii. 2.

individual animal. It is, therefore, not the body that begets the soul.

THE SOUL IS AN INCORPOREAL AND IMMORTAL ESSENCE. THE SOUL BEING NONE OF CORPOREAL POSSIBILITIES, MUST BE INCORPOREAL.

c. What then can be the nature of the soul, if she is neither a body, nor a corporeal affection, while, nevertheless, all the active force, the productive power and the other faculties reside in her, or come from her? What sort of a "being," indeed, is this (soul) that has an existence independent of the body? She must evidently be a veritable "being." Indeed, everything corporeal must be classified as generated, and excluded from genuine "being," because it is born, and perishes, never really exists, and owes its salvation exclusively to participation in the genuine existence, and that only in the measure of its participation therein.

THE PERSISTENCE OF THE CHANGEABLE IMPLIES THE ETERNAL IN THE BACKGROUND.*

9. (14). It is absolutely necessary to postulate the existence of a nature different from bodies, by itself fully possessing genuine existence, which can neither be born nor perish. Otherwise, all other things would hopelessly disappear, as a result of the destruction of the existence which preserves both the individuals and the universe, as their beauty and salvation. The soul, indeed, is the principle of movement (as Plato thought, in the Phraedrus); it is the soul that imparts movement to everything else; the soul moves herself. She imparts life to the body she animates; but alone she possesses life, without ever being subject to losing it, because she possesses it by herself. All beings, indeed,

*Here we resume Ennead IV. Book 7. The bracketed numbers are those of the Teubner text; the unbracketed those of the Didot edition.

live only by a borrowed life; otherwise, we would have to proceed from cause to cause unto infinity. There must, therefore, exist a nature that is primarily alive, necessarily incorruptible and immortal because it is the principle of life for everything else. It is thereon that must be founded all that is divine and blessed, that lives and exists by itself, that lives and exists supremely, which is immutable in its essence, and which can neither be born nor perish. How indeed could existence be born or perish? If the name of "existence" really suited it, it must exist forever, just as whiteness is not alternately black and white. If whiteness were existence itself, it would, with its "being" (or nature) (which is, to be whiteness), possess an eternal existence; but, in reality, it is no more than whiteness. Therefore, the principle that possesses existence in itself and in a supreme degree will always exist. Now this primary and eternal existence can not be anything dead like a stone, or a piece of wood. It must live, and live with a pure life, as long as it exists within itself. If something of it mingles with what is inferior, this part meets obstacles in its aspiration to the good; but it does not lose its nature, and resumes its former condition on returning to a suitable condition (as thought Plato, in his Phaedo*).

THE SOUL IS INCORPOREAL BECAUSE OF HER KINSHIP WITH THE DIVINE.

10. (15). The soul has affinities with the divine and eternal nature. This is evident, because, as we have demonstrated it, she is not a body, has neither figure nor color, and is impalpable. Consider the following demonstration. It is generally granted that everything that is divine and that possesses genuine existence enjoys a happy and wise life. Now let us consider the nature of our soul, in connection with that of the divine. Let us take a soul, not one inside of a body, which is

*Page 299, Cousin.

undergoing the irrational motions of appetite and anger, and the other affections born of the body, but a soul that has eliminated all that, and which, so far as possible, had no intercourse with the body. Such a soul would show us that vices are something foreign to the nature of the soul, and come to her from elsewhere, and that, inasmuch as she is purified, she in her own right possesses the most eminent qualities, wisdom, and the other virtues (as thought Plato*). If the soul, when re-entering into herself, is such, how could she not participate in this nature that we have acknowledged to be suitable to every thing that is eternal and divine? As wisdom and real virtue are divine things, they could not dwell in a vile and mortal entity; the existence that receives them is necessarily divine, since it participates in divine things by their mutual affinity and community. Anyone who thus possesses wisdom and virtue in his soul differs little from the superior beings; he is inferior to them only by the fact of his having a body. If all men, or at least, if many of them held their soul in this disposition, no one would be sceptic enough to refuse to believe that the soul is immortal. But as we consider the soul in her present condition of being soiled by vices, no one imagines that her nature is divine and immortal.

THE SOUL, LIKE OTHER THINGS, SHOULD BE JUDGED IN HER PUREST CONDITION

Now when we consider the nature of some being, it should be studied in its rarest condition, since extraneous additions hinder it from being rightly judged. The soul must be therefore considered only after abstraction of foreign things, or rather, he who makes this abstraction should observe himself in that condition. He then will not doubt that he is immortal, when he sees himself in the pure world of intelligence. He

*Quoted in i. 1, 12, in Republic x.

will see his intelligence occupied, not in the observation of some sense-object that is mortal, but in thinking the eternal by an equally eternal faculty.* He will see all the entities in the intelligible world, and he will see himself become intelligible, radiant, and illuminated by the truth emanating from the Good, which sheds the light of truth on all intelligible entities.† Then (like Empedocles, in Diog. Laertes‡), he will have the right to say:

"Farewell, I am now an immortal divinity."

For he has ascended to the divinity, and has become assimilated thereto. As purification permits one to know the better things, so the notions we have within us, and which constitute real science, are made clear. Indeed, it is not by an excursion among external objects that the soul attains the intuition of wisdom and virtue, but by re-entering into herself, in thinking herself in her primitive condition. Then she clears up and recognizes in herself the divine statues, soiled by the rust of time. Likewise, if a piece of gold were animated and released itself from the earth by which it was covered, after first having been ignorant of its real nature because it did not see its own splendor, it would admire itself when considering itself in its purity; it would find that it had no need of a borrowed beauty, and would consider itself happy to remain isolated from everything else.§

EVEN ON THE STOIC HYPOTHESIS THE SOUL MUST BE IMMORTAL.

11. (16). What sensible man, after having thus considered the nature of the soul, could still doubt of the immortality of a principle which derives life from naught but itself, and which cannot lose it? How could the soul lose life, since she did not borrow it from elsewhere, and since she does not possess it as fire possesses heat? For, without being an accident of

*See i. 1, 11.   †See i. 6, 9.   ‡See viii. 62.   §See i. 6, 5.

fire, the heat, nevertheless, is an accident of its matter; for fire can perish. But, in the soul, life is not an accident that comes to add itself to a material subject to constitute a soul. In fact, there is here an alternative: either life is a genuine "being," which is alive by itself; in which case this "being" is the soul that we are seeking to discover, and immortality cannot be refused her; or the soul is a composite, and she must be decomposed until we arrive at something immortal which moves by itself; and such a principle could not be subject to death. Further, when (Stoics) say that life is only an accidental modification of matter, they are thereby forced to acknowledge that the principle that imparted this modification to matter is immortal, and incapable of admitting anything contrary to what it communicates (that is, life, as said Plato, in his Phaedo*), but there is only a single nature that possesses life in actualization.

THERE IS NO CONCEIVABLE WAY IN WHICH SOUL COULD PERISH.

12. (17). (The Stoics), indeed, claim that every soul is perishable. In this case, everything should long since have been destroyed. Others might say that our soul were mortal, while the universal Soul were immortal. On them, however, is the burden of proof of a difference between the individual and universal souls. Both of them, indeed, are a principle of movement; both live by themselves; both grasp the same object by the same faculty, either by thinking the things contained in heaven, or by considering the nature ("being") of each being, ascending unto the first principle. Since our soul thinks absolute essences either by the notions she finds within herself, or by reminiscence, she evidently is prior to the body. Possessing knowledge of eternal entities, she herself must be eternal. All that dissolves, existing only by its compositeness, can naturally dis-

*Page 297, Cousin

solve in the same manner that it became composite. But the soul is a single, simple actualization, whose essence is life; not in this manner therefore can the soul perish. Neither could the soul perish by division into a number of parts; for, as we have shown, the soul is neither a mass nor a quantity. As little could the soul perish by alteration; for when alteration destroys anything, it may remove its form, but leaves its matter; alteration, therefore, is a characteristic of something composite. Consequently as the soul cannot perish in any of these ways, she is imperishable.

DESCENT INTO THE BODY NEED NOT CONFLICT WITH THE ETERNITY OF SOUL.

13. (18). If intelligible entities are separated from sense objects, how does it happen that the soul descends into a body? * So long as the soul is a pure and impassible intelligence, so long as she enjoys a purely intellectual life like the other intelligible beings, she dwells among them; for she has neither appetite nor desire. But that part which is inferior to intelligence and which is capable of desires, follows their impulsion, "proceeds" and withdraws from the intelligible world. Wishing to ornament matter on the model of the Ideas she contemplated in Intelligence, in haste to exhibit her fruitfulness, and to manifest the germs she bears within her (as said Plato, in the Banquet†), the soul applies herself to produce and create, and, as result of this application, she is, as it were, orientated (or, in "tension") towards sense-objects. With the universal Soul, the human soul shares the administration of the whole world, without, however, entering it; then, desiring to administer some portion of the world on her own responsibility, she separates from the universal Soul, and passes into a body. But even when she is present with the body, the soul does not devote herself entirely to

*See iv. 8, 5. †Pages 206, 312, 313, Cousin.

it, as some part of her always remains outside of it; that is how her intelligence remains impassible.*

THE SOUL AS THE ARTIST OF THE UNIVERSE.

The soul is present in the body at some times, and at other times, is outside of it. When, indeed, following her own inclination, she descends from first-rank entities (that is, intelligible entities) to third-rank entities (that is, earthly entities), she "proceeds" by virtue of the actualization of intelligence, which, remaining within herself, embellishes everything by the ministration of the soul, and which, itself being immortal, ordains everything with immortal power; for intelligence exists continuously by a continuous actualization.†

ALL SOULS HAVE IMMORTALITY, EVEN IF SUNK INTO ANIMALS OR PLANTS.

14. (19). What about the souls of animals inferior to man? The (rational) souls that have strayed so far as to descend into the bodies of animals are nevertheless still immortal.‡ Souls of a kind other (than rational souls), cannot proceed from anything else than the living nature (of the universal Soul); and they necessarily are the principles of life for all animals. The case is the same with the souls that inhere in plants. Indeed, all souls have issued from the same principle (the universal Soul), all have an individual life, and are indivisible and incorporeal essences ("beings").

EVEN IF THE SOUL HAS DIFFERENT PARTS, THE ORIGINAL PARTS SURVIVE.

To the objection that the human soul must decompose because she contains three parts, it may be answered that, when souls issue from here below, those that are purified leave what had been added to them in

*See iv. 8, 8.   †See iv. 8, 6, 7.   ‡See i. 1, 11.

generation (the irrational soul,*) while the other non-purified souls do free themselves therefrom with time. Besides, this lower part of the soul does not itself perish, for it exists as long as the principle from which it proceeds. Indeed, nothing that exists is annihilated.

THE HISTORIC EVIDENCE FOR IMMORTALITY OF THE SOUL.

15. (20). This, then, is our answer to those who seek a philosophical demonstration. Those who are satisfied with the testimony of faith and sense, may be referred to those extracts from history which furnish numerous proofs thereof.† We may also refer to the oracles given by the divinities who order an appeasement of the souls who were victims of some injustice, and to honor the dead,** and to the rites observed by all towards those who live no more;‡ which presupposes that their souls are still conscious beyond. Even after leaving their bodies, many souls who lived on the earth have continued to grant benefits to men.§ By revelation of the future;|| and rendering other services, they themselves prove that the other souls cannot have perished.

*See iv. 5, 7.
†Cicero, Tusculans, i. 12-16.
‡Plato, in Diog, Laert, iii 83
§Cicero, Tusculans, i. 18, 37
||Cicero, Tusculans, i. 12, 18; de Divinat, i 58
**Such as Porphyry's "Philosophy derived from Oracles."

As the first book was evidently Platonic, the second seems Numenian, reminding us of the latter's book on the Immortality of the Soul, one of the arguments from which we find in 3 E.

THIRD ENNEAD, BOOK FIRST.

Concerning Fate.

POSSIBLE THEORIES ABOUT FATE.

1. The first possibility is that there is a cause both for the things that become, and those that are; the cause of the former being their becoming, and that of the latter, their existence. Again, neither of them may have a cause. Or, in both cases, some may have a cause, and some not. Further, those that become might have a cause, while, of these that exist, some might partly have a cause. Contrariwise, all things that exist may have a cause, while of those that become, parts may have a cause, and part not. Last, none of the things that become might have any cause.

EXCEPT THE FIRST, ALL THINGS ARE CAUSED.

Speaking of eternal things, the first cannot be derived from other causes, just because they are first. Things dependent from the first, however, may indeed thence derive their being. To each thing we should also attribute the resultant action; for a thing's being is constituted by its displayed energy.

STOIC AND EPICUREAN CAUSELESS ORIGIN REALLY
THE UTMOST DETERMINISM.

Now among the things that become, or among those that although perpetually existent do not always result in the same actions, it may be boldly asserted that everything has a cause. We should not admit (the Stoic contention*) that something happens without a cause, nor accept the (Epicurean†) arbitrary convergence of the atoms, nor believe that any body initiates a movement suddenly and without determining reason, nor suppose (with Epicurus again‡) that the soul undertakes some action by a blind impulse, without any motive. Thus to suppose that a thing does not belong to itself, that it could be carried away by involuntary movements, and act without motive, would be to subject it to the most crushing determinism. The will must be excited, or the desire awakened by some interior or exterior stimulus. No determination (is possible) without motive.

EVERY GOOD THING HAS SOME CAUSE; NATURE BEING THE ULTIMATE CAUSE.

If everything that happens has a cause, it is possible to discover such fact's proximate causes, and to them refer this fact. People go downtown, for example, to see a person, or collect a bill. In all cases it is a matter of choice, followed by decision, and the determination to carry it out. There are, indeed, certain facts usually derived from the arts; as for instance the re-establishment of health may be referred to medicine and the physician. Again, when a man has become rich, this is due to his finding some treasure, or receiving some donation, to working, or exercising some lucrative profession. The birth of a child depends on its father, and the concourse of exterior circumstances, which, by the concatenation of causes and effects, favored his procreation; for example, right food, or even a still more distant cause, the fertility of the mother, or, still more generally, of nature (or, in general, it is usual to assign natural causes).

*Chrysippus, in Cicero, de Fato, 10.
†Cicero, de Finibus, i. 6.   ‡Cicero, de Natura Deorum, i. 25.

PROXIMATE CAUSES ARE UNSATISFACTORY; WE MUST SEEK THE ULTIMATE ONES.

2. To stop, on arriving at these causes, and to refuse further analysis, is to exhibit superficiality. This is against the advice of the sages, who advise ascending to the primary causes, to the supreme principles. For example, why, during the full moon, should the one man steal, and the other one not steal? Or, why, under the same influence of the heavens, has the one, and not the other, been sick? Why, by use of the same means, has the one become rich, and the other poor? The difference of dispositions, characters, and fortunes force us to seek ulterior causes, as indeed the sages have always done.

MATERIALISTS SUPPORT DETERMINISM.

Those sages who (like Leucippus, Democritus and Epicurus) assumed material principles such as the atoms, and who explain everything by their motion, their shock and combinations, pretend that everything existent and occurring is caused by the agency of these atoms, their "actions and reactions." This includes, according to them, our appetites and dispositions. The necessity residing in the nature of these principles, and in their effects, is therefore, by these sages, extended to everything that exists. As to the (Ionic Hylicists), who assume other physical (ultimate) principles, referring everything to them, they thus also subject all beings to necessity.

HERACLITUS, THOUGH MORE SPIRITUAL, IS ALSO DETERMINIST.

There are others (such as Heraclitus*), who, seeking the (supreme) principle of the universe, refer everything to it; saying that this principle penetrates, moves,

*Stobeus, Ecl. Phys. i. 6, p. 178

and produces everything. This they call Fate, and the Supreme Cause. From it they derive everything; its motions are said to give rise not only to the things that are occurring, but even our thought. That is how the members of an animal do not move themselves, but receive the stimulus from the "governing principle" within them.

THE ASTROLOGERS MAKE COSMIC DEDUCTIONS FROM PROGNOSTICATION.

Some (of the astrologers) explain everything by the circular motion of the heavens, by the relative positions of the planets and stars, and by their mutual aspects (or, relations). They base this (principle) on the prevalent habit of deducing therefrom conjectures about futurity.

THE STOIC DETERMINISM IS BASED ON VARIOUS THEORIES

Others (like the Stoic Chrysippus*) define Fate otherwise: it is "the concatenation of causes" in "their connection towards the infinite," by which every posterior fact is the consequence of an anterior one. Thus the things that follow relate to the things that precede, and, as their effects, necessarily depend thereupon. Amidst these (Stoic) philosophers there are two conceptions of Fate: some consider that everything depends from a single principle, while others do not. These views we shall study later.

We shall first examine the system with which we began; later we shall review the others.

THE PHYSICAL THEORIES ARE ABSURD.

3. To refer everything to physical causes, whether you call them atoms or elements, and from their dis-

*Aulus Gellius, Noctes Atticæ, vi. 2.

ordered motion to deduce order, reason and the soul that directs (the body), is absurd and impossible; nevertheless, to deduce everything from atoms, is, if possible, still more impossible; and consequently many valid objections have been raised against this theory.

THE STOIC POLEMIC AGAINST THE EPICUREANS.

To begin with, even if we do admit such atomic principles, their existence does not in any way inevitably lead to either the necessity of all things, or fatality. Let us, indeed, grant the existence of atoms; now some will move downwards—that is, if there is an up and down in the universe—others obliquely, by chance, in various directions. As there will be no order, there will be nothing determinate. Only what will be born of the atoms will be determinate. It will therefore be impossible to guess or predict events, whether by art—and indeed, how could there be any art in the midst of orderless things?—or by enthusiasm, or divine inspiration; for prediction implies that the future is determined. True, bodies will obey the impulses necessarily communicated to them by the atoms; but how could you explain the operations and affections of the soul by movements of atoms? How could atomic shock, whether vertical or oblique, produce in the soul these our reasonings, or appetites, whether necessarily, or in any other way? What explanation could they give of the soul's resistance to the impulsions of the body? By what concourse of atoms will one man become a geometrician, another become a mathematician and astronomer, and the other a philosopher? For, according to that doctrine we no longer produce any act for which we are responsible, we are even no longer living beings, since we undergo the impulsion of bodies that affect us just as they do inanimate things.

APPLICATION OF THIS POLEMIC TO THE PHYSICISTS.

The same objections apply to the doctrine of the philosophers who explain everything by other physical causes (such as "elements"). Principles of inferior nature might well warm us, cool us, or even make us perish; but they could not beget any of the operations which the soul produces; these have an entirely different cause.

RESTATEMENT OF HERACLITUS'S POSITION.

4. But might (Heraclitus) suppose that a single Soul interpenetrating the universe produces everything, and by supplying the universe with motion supplies it simultaneously to all its constituent beings, so that from this primary cause, would necessarily flow all secondary causes, whose sequence and connection would constitute Fate? Similarly, in a plant, for instance, the plant's fate might be constituted by the ("governing") principle which, from the root, administers its other parts, and which organizes into a single system their "actions" and "reactions."*

THIS WOULD INTERFERE WITH SELF-CONSCIOUSNESS AND RESPONSIBILITY.

To begin with, this Necessity and Fate would by their excess destroy themselves, and render impossible the sequence and concatenation of the causes. It is, indeed, absurd to insist that our members are moved by Fate when they are set in motion, or innervated, by the "governing principle." It is a mistake to suppose that there is a part which imparts motion, and on the other hand, a part which receives it from the former; it is the governing principle that moves the leg, as it would any other part. Likewise, if in the universe exists but a single principle which "acts and reacts," if things derive from each other by a series of causes each

*As thought the Stoics, Cicero, de Nat. Deor. ii 11

of which refers to the preceding one, it will no longer be possible to say truly that all things arise through causes, for their totality will constitute but a single being. In that case, we are no longer ourselves; actions are no longer ours; it is no longer we who reason; it is a foreign principle which reasons, wills, and acts in us, just as it is not our feet that walk, but we who walk by the agency of our feet. On the contrary, common sense admits that every person lives, thinks, and acts by his own individual, proper life, thought and action; to each must be left the responsibility of his actions, good or evil, and not attribute shameful deeds to the universal cause.

RESTATEMENT OF THE ASTROLOGICAL THEORY OF FATE.

5. Others, again, insist that this is not the state of affairs. Their disposition depends on the circular movement of the heaven which governs everything, on the course of the stars, of their mutual relative position at the time of their rising, of their setting, of their zenith, or of their conjunction. Indeed, such are the signs on which are founded prognostications and predictions of what is to happen, not only to the universe, but also to each individual, both as to his fortunes and his thought. It is noticed that the other animals and vegetables increase or decrease according to the kind of sympathy existing between them and the stars, that all other things experience their influence, that various regions of the earth differ according to their adjustment with the stars, and especially the sun; that from the nature of these regions depend not only the character of the plants and animals, but also human forms, size, color, affections, passions, tastes, and customs. In this system, therefore, the course of the stars is the absolute cause of everything.

REFUTATION OF THE ASTROLOGICAL SYSTEM

To this we answer that our astrologer attributes indirectly to the stars all our characteristics: will, passions, vices and appetites; he allows us no rôle other than to turn like mills, instead of responsibility, as befits men, producing actions that suit our nature. On the contrary, we should be left in possession of what belongs to us by the observation that the universe limits itself to exercising some influence on what we possess already thanks to ourselves, and which is really characteristic of us. Moreover, one should distinguish the deeds in which we are "active," from those in which we are necessarily "passive," and not deduce everything from the stars. Nobody, indeed, doubts that the differences of place and climate exert an influence over us, imparting to us, for instance, a cool or warm-hearted disposition. Heredity also should be considered; for children usually resemble their parents by their features, form, and some affections of the irrational soul. Nevertheless, even though they resemble them by their facial features, because they are born in the same place, they may differ in habits and thoughts, because these things depend on an entirely different principle. In addition, we can adduce to the support of this truth the resistance which the soul offers to the temperament and to the appetites. As to the claim that the stars are the causes of everything, because one can predict what is to happen to each man from a consideration of their positions, it would be just as reasonable to assert that the birds and the other beings which the augurs consult as omens produce the events of which they are the signs.

HOROSCOPES QUESTIONED; THEY DO NOT ACCOUNT FOR SIMULTANEOUS DIFFERENCES.

This leads us to consider, more in detail, what sort of facts may be predicted according to the inspection of the positions occupied by the stars presiding over the birth of a man. They who, from the assertion that the stars indicate a man's future, draw the consequence that the stars produce them, are in error. In some person's horoscope which indicates birth from noble parents, on either maternal or paternal side, this nobility of birth cannot be attributed to the stars, as this nobility subsisted already in the parents before the stars had taken the position according to which the horoscope is cast. Besides, astrologers pretend they can discover the parent's fortune from the birth of their children, and from the condition of the parents the disposition and fate of the unborn offspring. From a child's horoscope, they announce his brother's death; and from a woman's horoscope, the fortunes of her husband, and conversely. It is unreasonable to refer to the stars things which evidently are necessary consequences of parental conditions. We then reach a dilemma: the cause lies either in these antecedent conditions, or in the stars. The beauty and ugliness of children, when they resemble their parents, must evidently be derived from them, and not from the course of the stars. Moreover, it is probable that at any one moment are born a crowd of human and animal young; now, inasmuch as they are born under the same star, they all ought to have the same nature. How does it then happen that, in the same positions, stars produce men and other beings simultaneously (as Cicero asks*)?

HEREDITY MORE IMPORTANT THAN STAR-INFLUENCE; CONTINUATION.

6. Each being derives his character from his nature. One being is a horse because he is born from a mare, while another is human, because born from a human mother; and more: he is that particular horse, and that particular man because he is born from such and such a horse, or woman. Doubtless, the course of the stars

*Cicero, de Divinatione, ii. 44.

may modify the result, but the greatest part of the influence must be allowed to heredity.

STARS AFFECT THE PHYSICAL, NOT THE MENTAL BEING.

The stars act on the body only in a physical way, and thus impart to them heat, cold, and the variety of temperament which results therefrom. But how could they endow the man with habits, tastes, and inclinations which do not seem to depend on the temperament, such as the avocation of a surveyor, a grammarian, a gambler, or an inventor?

IRRATIONAL CLAIMS OF ASTROLOGERS.

Besides, nobody would admit that perversity could come from beings who are divinities. How could one believe that they are the authors of the evils attributed to them, and that they themselves become evil because they set or pass under the earth, as if they could possibly be affected by the fact that, in regard to us, they seem to set; as if they did not continue to wander around the heavenly sphere, and remained in the same relation to the earth? Besides it is incredible that because a star is in such or such a position in respect of another star, it becomes better or worse, and that it affects us with goodness when it is well disposed, and evil in the contrary case.

STARS SERVE AS LETTERS IN WHICH TO READ NATURE.

We grant that by their movement the stars co-operate in the conservation of the universe, and that they simultaneously play in it another part. They serve as letters for those skilled in deciphering this kind of writing; and who, by the observation of the figures formed by the stars, read into them future events according to the laws of analogy, as for instance, if one presaged high deeds from seeing a bird fly high.

RESTATEMENT OF THE STOIC DOCTRINE, AND THE HERACLITIAN.

7. There remains to be considered the (Stoic) doctrine which, concatenating and interrelating all things among each other, establishes "a single cause which produces everything through seminal reasons." This doctrine reattaches itself to (Heraclitus's) which deduces from the action of the universal Soul the constitution and the movements of the individuals as well as those of the universe.

ALEXANDER OF APHRODISIA'S POLEMIC AGAINST THE STOICS.

In this case, even if we possessed the power of doing something by ourselves, we would not be any the less than the remainder of the universe subjected to necessity, because Fate, containing the whole series of causes, necessarily determines each event. Now since Fate includes all causes, there is nothing which could hinder the occurrence of that event, or alter it. If then everything obeys the impulsion of a single principle, nothing is left to us but to follow it. Indeed, in this case, the fancies of our imagination would result from anterior facts, and would in turn determine our appetites; our liberty would then have become a mere word; nor would we gain any advantage from obeying our appetites, since our appetites themselves will be determined by anterior facts. We would have no more liberty than the other animals, than children, or the insane, who run hither and yon, driven by blind appetites; for they also obey their appetites, as fire would do, and as all the things which fatally follow the dispositions of their nature. These objections will be decisive for those capable of apprehending them; and in the search for other causes of our appetites they will not content themselves with the principles which we have examined.

THE HUMAN SOUL AS AN INDEPENDENT PRINCIPLE.

8. What other cause, besides the preceding, will we have to invoke so as to let nothing occur without a cause, to maintain order and interdependence of things in the world, and in order to preserve the possibility of predictions and omens without destroying our personality?

We shall have to introduce among the number of beings another principle, namely: the soul; and not only the World-soul, but even the individual soul of every person. In the universal concatenation of causes and effects, this soul is a principle of no little importance, because, instead of, like all other things, being born of a "seminal reason," it constitutes a "primary cause." Outside of a body, she remains absolute mistress of herself, free and independent of the cause which administers the world. As soon as she has descended into a body, she is no longer so independent, for she then forms part of the order to which all things are subjected. Now, inasmuch as the accidents of fortune, that is to say, the surrounding circumstances, determine many events, the soul alternately yields to the influence of external circumstances, and then again she dominates them, and does what she pleases. This she does more or less, according as she is good or evil. When she yields to the corporeal temperament, she is necessarily subjected to desire or anger, discouraged in poverty, or proud in prosperity, as well as tyrannical in the exercise of power. But she can resist all these evil tendencies if her disposition is good; she modifies her surroundings more than she is affected by them; some things she changes, others she tolerates without herself incurring guilt.

THE SOUL IS FREE WHEN FOLLOWING REASON.

9. All things therefore, which result either from a choice by the soul, or from exterior circumstances, are

"necessary," or determined by a cause. Could anything, indeed, be found outside of these causes? If we gather into one glance all the causes we admit, we find the principles that produce everything, provided we count, amidst external causes, the influence exercised by the course of the stars. When a soul makes a decision, and carries it out because she is impelled thereto by external things, and yields to a blind impulse, we should not consider her determination and action to be free. The soul is not free when, perverting herself, she does not make decisions which direct her in the straight path. On the contrary, when she follows her own guide, pure and impassible reason, her determination is really voluntary, free and independent, and the deed she performs is really her own work, and not the consequence of an exterior impulse; she derives it from her inner power, her pure being, from the primary and sovereign principle which directs her, being deceived by no ignorance, nor vanquished by the power of appetites; for when the appetites invade the soul, and subdue her, they drag her with them by their violence. and she is rather "passive" than "active" in what she does.

THE SOUL OBEYS FATE ONLY WHEN EVIL.

10. The conclusion of our discussion is that while everything is indicated and produced by causes, these are of two kinds: first the human soul, and then only exterior circumstances. When the soul acts "conformably to right reason" she acts freely. Otherwise, she is tangled up in her deeds, and she is rather "passive" than "active." Therefore, whenever she lacks prudence, the exterior circumstances are the causes of her actions; one then has good reason to say that she obeys Fate, especially if Fate is here considered as an exterior cause. On the contrary, virtuous actions are derived from ourselves; for, when we are independent, it is

natural for us to produce them. Virtuous men act, and do good freely. Others do good only in breathing-spells left them in between by their passions. If, during these intervals, they practice the precepts of wisdom, it is not because they receive them from some other being, it is merely because their passions do not hinder them from listening to the voice of reason.

As the first book seemed Platonic, and the second Numenian, so this third one seems called forth by the practical opposition of astrologers or Gnostics Later in life, his thirty-third book, ii 9, was to take up again this polemic in more extended form This chronologic arrangement of Plotinos's first three books reveals his three chief sources of interest—devotion to Plato, reliance on Numenius, and opposition to the Gnostics and astrologers.

FOURTH ENNEAD, BOOK FIRST.

Of the Being of the Soul.

It is in the intelligible world that dwells veritable being. Intelligence is the best that there is on high; but there are also souls; for it is thence that they descended thither. Only, souls have no bodies, while here below they inhabit bodies and are divided there. On high, all the intelligences exist together, without separation or division; all the souls exist equally together in that world which is one, and there is no local distance between them. Intelligence therefore ever remains inseparable and indivisible; but the soul, inseparable so long as she resides on high, nevertheless possesses a divisible nature. For her "dividing herself" consists in departing from the intelligible world, and uniting herself to bodies; it might therefore be reasonably said that she becomes divisible in passing into bodies, since she thus separates from the intelligible world, and divides herself somewhat. In what way is she also indivisible? In that she does not separate herself entirely from the intelligible world, ever residing there by her highest part, whose nature it is to be indivisible. To say then that the soul is composed of indivisible (essence) and of (essence) divisible in bodies means then no more than that the soul has an (essence) which dwells partly in the intelligible world, and partly descends into the sense-world, which is suspended from the first and extends downwards to the second, as the ray goes from the centre to the circumference. When the soul descended here below, it is by her superior part that she contemplates the intelligible world, as it is thereby that she preserves the nature of the all (of the universal Soul). For here below she is not only divisible, but also indivisible; her divisible part is divided in a somewhat indivisible manner; she is indeed entirely present in the whole body in an indivisible manner, and nevertheless she is said to divide herself because she spreads out entirely in the whole body.

FIFTH ENNEAD, BOOK NINE.

Of Intelligence, Ideas and Essence.

THE SENSUAL MAN, THE MORAL, AND THE SPIRITUAL.

1. From their birth, men exercise their senses, earlier than their intelligence,[1] and they are by necessity forced to direct their attention to sense-objects. Some stop there, and spend their life without progressing further. They consider suffering as evil, and pleasure as the good, judging it to be their business to avoid the one and encompass the other. That is the content of wisdom for those of them that pride themselves on being reasonable; like those heavy birds who, having weighted themselves down by picking up too much from the earth, cannot take flight, though by nature provided with wings. There are others who have raised themselves a little above earthly objects because their soul, endowed with a better nature, withdraws from pleasures to seek something higher;[2] but as they are not capable of arriving at contemplation of the intelligible, and as, after having left our lower region here, they do not know where to lodge, they return to a conception of morality which considers virtue to consist in these common-place actions and occupations whose narrow sphere they had at first attempted to leave behind. Finally a third kind is that of those divine men who are endowed with a piercing vision, and whose penetrating glance contemplates the splendor of the intelligible world, and rise unto it,

OF INTELLIGENCE, IDEAS, ESSENCE

taking their flight above the clouds and darkness of this world. Then, full of scorn for terrestrial things, they remain up there, and reside in their true fatherland with the unspeakable bliss of the man who, after long journeys, is at last repatriated.

THE HIGHER REGION REACHED ONLY BY THOSE WHO ARE BORN PHILOSOPHERS.

2. Which is this higher region? What must be done to reach it? One must be naturally disposed to love, and be really a born philosopher.[3] In the presence of beauty, the lover feels something similar to the pains of childbirth; but far from halting at bodily beauty, he rises to that aroused in the soul by virtue, duties, science and laws. Then he follows them up to the cause of their beauty, and in this ascending progress stops only when he has reached the Principle that occupies the first rank, that which is beautiful in itself.[4] Then only does he cease being driven by this torment that we compare to the pains of childbirth.

LOVE IS TRANSFORMED INTO PROGRESSIVELY HIGHER STAGES.

But how does he rise up thither? How does he have the power to do so? How does he learn to love? Here it is. The beauty seen in bodies is incidental; it consists in the shapes of which the bodies are the matter.[5] Consequently the substance changes, and it is seen changing from beauty to ugliness. The body has only a borrowed beauty. Who imparted that beauty to the body? On the one hand, the presence of beauty; on the other, the actualization of the soul which fashioned the body, and which gave it the shape it possesses. But is the soul, by herself, absolute beauty? No, since some souls are wise and beautiful, while some others are foolish and ugly. It is therefore only by wisdom that the soul is beautiful. But from what is her wisdom derivied? Necessarily from intelligence; not from the intelligence that is intelligent at some time, though not at others, but from the genuine Intelligence, which is beautiful on that very account.[6] Shall we stop at Intelligence, as a first principle? Or shall we on the contrary still rise above it? Surely so, for Intelligence presents itself to us before the first Principle only because it is, so to speak, located in the antechamber of the Good.[7] It bears all things within itself, and manifests them, so that it displays the image of the Good in manifoldness, while the Good itself remains in an absolute simple unity.

PROOFS FOR THE EXISTENCE AND NATURE OF INTELLIGENCE.

3. Let us now consider the Intelligence which reason tells us is absolute essence and genuine "being," and whose existence we have already established in a different manner. It would seem ridiculous to inquire whether Intelligence form part of the scale of beings; but there are men who doubt it, or who at least are disposed to ask for a demonstration that Intelligence possesses the nature we predicate of it, that it is separated (from matter), that it is identical with the essences, and that it contains the ideas. This is our task.

IN THE HUMAN WORLD EVERYTHING IS A COMPOSITE OF FORM AND MATTER.

All things that we consider to be essences are composites; nothing is simple or single, either in works of art, or in the products of nature.[8] Works of art, indeed, contain metal, wood, stone, and are derived from these substances only by the labor of the artist, who, by giving matter its form makes of it a statue, or bed, or house. Among the products of nature, those that

v.9]   OF INTELLIGENCE, IDEAS, ESSENCE   105

are compounds or mixtures may be analyzed into the form impressed on the elements of the compound; so, for instance, we may in a man, distinguish a soul and body, and in the body four elements. Since the very matter of the elements, taken in itself, has no form, every object seems composed of matter and of some principle that supplies it with form.[9] So we are led to ask whence matter derives its form, and to seek whether the soul is simple, or whether it contains two parts, one of which plays the parts of matter, and the other of form,[10] so that the first part would be similar to the form received by the metal of a statue, and the latter to the principle which produces the form itself.

THE WORLD-SOUL ALSO IS A COMPOUND OF FORM AND MATTER.

Applying this conception to the universe, we rise to Intelligence, recognizing therein the demiurgic creator of the world. It was in receiving from it its shapes by the intermediation of another principle, the universal Soul, that the (material) substances became water, air, earth and fire. On the one hand, the Soul shapes the four elements of the world;[11] on the other, she receives from Intelligence the (seminal) reasons,[12] as the souls of the artists themselves receive from the arts the reasons which they work out.[13] In Intelligence, therefore, there is a part which is the form of the soul; it is intelligence considered as shape. There is another which imparts shape, like the sculptor who gives the metal the shape of the statue, and which in itself possesses all it gives.[14] Now the (shapes) which the Intelligence imparts to the soul connect with the truth as closely as possible, while those which the soul imparts to the body are only images and appearances.[15]

WHY OUR ASCENT CANNOT STOP WITH THE SOUL.

4. Why should we not, on arriving at the Soul, stop there, and consider her the first principle? Because Intelligence is a power different from the Soul, and better than the Soul; and what is better must, by its very nature, precede (the worst). The Stoics[16] are wrong in thinking that it is the Soul which, on reaching her perfection, begets Intelligence. How could that which is potential pass into actualization unless there were some principle that effected that transition? If this transition were due to chance, it could not have occurred at all. The first rank must therefore be assigned to that which is in actualization, which needs nothing, which is perfect, while imperfect things must be assigned to the second rank. These may be perfected by the principles that begat them, which, in respect to them, play a paternal part, perfecting what they had originally produced that was imperfect. What is thus produced is matter, as regards the creating principle, and then becomes perfect, on receiving its form from it. Besides, the Soul is (often) affected; and we need to discover some thing that is impassible, without which everything is dissolved by time; therefore there is need of some principle prior to the soul. Further, the Soul is in the world; now there must be something that resides outside of the world, and which consequently would be superior to the Soul; for since that which inheres in the world resides within the body, or matter, if nothing existed outside of the world, nothing would remain permanent. In this case, the (seminal) reason of man, and all the other reasons could be neither permanent nor eternal. The result of all these considerations, as well as of many others that we could add thereto, is the necessary assertion of the existence of Intelligence beyond the Soul.

OF INTELLIGENCE, IDEAS, ESSENCE

INTELLIGENCE IS IN ACTUALIZATION BECAUSE ITS THOUGHT IS IDENTICAL WITH ITS ESSENCE OR EXISTENCE.

5. Taking it in its genuine sense, Intelligence is not only potential, arriving at being intelligent after having been unintelligent—for otherwise, we would be forced to seek out some still higher principle—but is in actualization, and is eternal. As it is intelligent by itself, it is by itself that it thinks what it thinks, and that it possesses what is possesses. Now since it thinks of itself and by itself, it itself is what it thinks. If we could distinguish between its exitsence and its thought, its "being" would be unintelligent; it would be potential, not in actualization. Thought, therefore, must not be separated from its object, although, from sense-objects, we have become accustomed to conceive of intelligible entities as distinct from each other.

REASONS, AS ARCHETYPES, MUST HAVE EXISTED BEFORE STOIC "HABIT," NATURE OR SOUL.

Which then is the principle that acts, that thinks, and what is the actualization and thought of Intelligence, necessary to justify the assertion that it is what it thinks? Evidently Intelligence, by its mere real existence, thinks beings, and makes them exist; it therefore is the beings. Indeed, the beings will either exist outside of it, or within it; and in the latter case they would have to be identical with it. That they should exist outside of Intelligence, is unthinkable; for where would they be located? They must therefore exist within it, and be identical with it. They could not be in sense-objects, as common people think, because sense-objects could not be the first in any genus. The form which inheres in their matter is only the representation of existence; now a form which exists in anything other than itself is put in it by a superior principle, and is its image. Further, if Intelligence must be the creative power of the universe, it could not, while creating the universe, think beings as existent in what does not yet exist. Intelligible entities, therefore, must exist before the world, and cannot be images of sense-objects, being on the contrary, their archetypes, and constituting the "being" of Intelligence. It might be objected that the (seminal) reasons might suffice. These reasons are, no doubt, eternal; and, if they be eternal and impassible, they must exist within the Intelligence whose characteristics we have described, the Intelligence which precedes the "habit,"[17] nature,[18] and the soul,[19] because here these entities are potential.[20]

INTELLIGENCE IS POSTULATED BY THE GENERAL NECESSITIES OF THE WORLD.

Intelligence, therefore, essentially constitutes all beings; and when Intelligence thinks them, they are not outside of Intelligence, and neither precede nor follow it. Intelligence is the first legislator, or rather, it is the very law of existence. Parmenides[21] therefore was right in saying, "Thought is identical with existence." The knowledge of immaterial things is therefore identical with those things themselves. That is why I recognize myself as a being, and why I have reminiscences of intelligible entities. Indeed, none of those beings is outside of Intelligence, nor is contained in any location; all of them subsist in themselves as immutable and indestructible. That is why they really are beings. If they were born, or perished, they would possess existence only in an incidental manner, they would no longer be beings; it would be the existence they possessed which would be essence. It is only by participation that sense-things are what they are said to be; the nature that constitutes their substance derives its shape from elsewhere, as the metal receives its shape from the sculptor, and wood from the carpenter; while the image of art penetrates into the matter, the art itself remains in its identity, and within itself possesses the genuine existence of the statue or of the bed. That is how the bodies' general necessity of participating in images shows that they are different from the beings; for they change, while the entities are immutable, possess within themselves their own foundation, and have no need of existing in any location, since they have no extension, and since they subsist in an intellectual and absolute existence. Again,[22] the existence of the bodies needs to be guarded[23] by some other principle, while intelligence, which furnishes the existence for objects in themselves perishable, has need of nothing to make itself subsist.

INTELLIGENCE CONTAINS ALL BEINGS GENERATIVELY.

6. Thus Intelligence actually constitutes all beings; it contains them all, but not locally; it contains them as it possesses itself; it is identical with them. All entities are simultaneously contained within it, and in it remain distinct, as many kinds of knowledge may exist within the soul without their number causing any confusion; each of them appears when needed, without involving the others. If in the soul each thought be an actualization independent of other thoughts, so much the more must Intelligence be all things simultaneously, with this restriction, however, that each of them is a special power. Considered in its universality, Intelligence contains all entities as the genus contains all species, as the whole contains all parts. Even the seminal powers bear the impress of this universality. Each one, considered in its totality, is a centre which contains all the parts of the organism in an undivided condition; nevertheless in it the reason of the eyes differs from that of the hands, and this diversity is manifested by that of the organs begotten (there-

from).[24] Each of the powers of the seed, therefore, is the total unity of the seminal reason when this power is united to the others which are implied therein. What in the seed is corporeal contains matter, as, for instance, humidity; but the seminal reason is the entire form; it is identical with the generative power, a power which itself is the image of a superior power of the soul. This generative power contained in seeds is[25] usually called "nature." Proceeding from the superior powers as light radiates from the fire, it tames and fashions matter, imparting thereto the seminal reason[26] without pushing it, or moving it as by levers.

THERE ARE SCIENTIFIC NOTIONS THAT ARE POSTERIOR, BUT SOME THAT ARE PRIOR.

7. The scientific notions that the soul forms of sense-objects, by discursive reason, and which should rather be called opinions,[27] are posterior to the objects (they deal with); and consequently, are no more than images of them. But true scientific notions received from intelligence by discursive reasons do not contain any sense-cenceptions. So far as they are scientific notions, they are the very things of which they are the conceptions; they reveal the intimate union of intelligence and thought. Interior Intelligence, which consists of the primary (natures) possesses itself intimately, resides within itself since all eternity, and is an actualization. It does not direct its glances outside of itself, because it possesses everything within itself; it does not acquire, and does not reason to discover things that may not be present to them. Those are operations characteristic of the soul. Intelligence, remaining fixed within itself, is all things simultaneously. Nevertheless, it is not thought which makes each of them subsist; it is only because intelligence thought the divinity or movement, for instance, that the divinity or movement exists.[28] When we say that

thoughts are forms, we are mistaken if thereby we mean that the intelligible exists only because Intelligence thinks it. On the contrary, it is only because the intelligible exists, that Intelligence can think. Otherwise, how would Intelligence come to think the intelligible? It cannot meet the intelligible by chance, nor waste itself in fruitless efforts.

THOUGHT IS THE FORM, SHAPE THE ACTUALIZATION OF THE BEING.

8. Since the thought is something essentially one (?), the form, which is the object of thought, and the idea[29] are one and the same thing. Which is this thing? Intelligence and the intellectual "being," for no idea is foreign to intelligence; each form is intelligence, and the whole intelligence is all the forms; every particular form is a particular intelligence. Likewise science, taken in its totality, is all the notions it embraces; every notion is a part of the total science; it is not separated from the science locally, and exists potentially in the whole science.[30] Intelligence resides within itself, and by possessing itself calmly, is the eternal fulness of all things. If we conceived it as being prior to essence, we would have to say that it was the action and thought of Intelligence which produced and begat all beings. But as, on the contrary, it is certain that essence is prior to Intelligence, we should, within the thinking principle, first conceive the beings, then actualization and thought, just as (the nature) of fire is joined by the actualization of the fire, so that beings have innate intelligence (?[48]) as their actualization. Now essence is an actualization; therefore essence and intelligence are but a single actualization, or rather both of them fuse.[31] Consequently, they form but a single nature, as beings, the actualization of essence, and intelligence. In this case

the thought is the form, and the shape is the actualization of the being. When, however, in thought we separate essence from Intelligence, we must conceive one of these principles as prior to the other. The Intelligence which operates this separation is indeed different from the essence from which it separates;[82] but the Intelligence which is inseparable from essence and which does not separate thought from essence is itself essence and all things.

INTELLIGENCE CONTAINS THE UNIVERSAL ARCHETYPE.

9. What then are the things contained within the unity of Intelligence which we separate in thinking of them? They must be expressed without disturbing their rest, and we must contemplate the contents of Intelligence by a science that somehow remains within unity. Since this sense-world is an animal which embraces all animals, since it derives both its general and special existence from a principle different from itself,[83] a principle which, in turn, is derived from intelligence, therefore intelligence must itself contain the universal archetype, and must be that intelligible world of which Plato[84] (well) says; "Intelligence sees the ideas contained within the existing animal."[85] Since an animal, whose (seminal) reason exists with the matter fit to receive it, must of course be begotten, so the mere existence of a nature that is intellectual, all-powerful, and unhindered by any obstacle—since nothing can interpose between it and the (substance) capable of receiving the form—must necessarily be adorned (or, created) by intelligence, but only in a divided condition does it reveal the form it receives, so that, for instance, it shows us on one hand a man, and on the other the sun, while intelligence possesses everything in unity.

IN THE SENSE-WORLD ONLY THOSE THINGS THAT ARE FORMS PROCEED FROM INTELLIGENCE.

10. Therefore, in the sense-world, all the things that are forms proceed from intelligence; those which are not forms do not proceed therefrom. That is, in the intelligible world we do not find any of the things that are contrary to nature, any more than we find what is contrary to the arts in the arts themselves. Thus the seminal reason does not contain the defects, such as limping would be in a body. Congenital lameness is due to the reason's failure to dominate matter, while accidental lameness is due to deterioration of the form (idea?).

NATURAL CHARACTERISTICS ARE DERIVED FROM THE CATEGORIES IN THE INTELLIGIBLE.

The qualities that are natural, quantities, numbers, magnitudes, states, actions and natural experiences, movements and recuperations, either general or particular, are among the contents of the intelligible world, where time is replaced by eternity,[36] and space is replaced by the "telescoping" of intelligible entities (that are within each other). As all entities are together in the intelligible world, whatever entity you select (by itself) is intellectual and living "being," identity and difference, movement and rest;[37] it is what moves, and what is at rest; it is "being," and quality; that is, it is all. There every essence is in actualization, instead of merely being in potentiality; consequently it is not separated from quality.

THE INTELLIGIBLE WORLD FAILS TO CONTAIN EARTHLY IMPERFECTIONS.

Does the intelligible world contain only what is found in the sense-world, or does it contain anything additional? . . . . Let us consider the arts, in this respect. To begin with, the intelligible world does not contain any imperfection. Evils here below come from lack, privation, omission; it is a state of matter, or of anything similar to matter, which failed to be completely assimilated.[38]

SOME ARTS ARE PURELY EARTHLY; OTHERS, LIKE MUSIC, INTELLIGIBLE.

11. Let us therefore consider the arts and their products. Unless as represented within human reason, we cannot refer to the intelligible world arts of imitation such as painting, sculpture, dancing, or acting, because they are born here below, take sense-objects as models, representing their forms, motions, and visible proportions.[39] If, however, we possess a faculty which, by studying the beauties offered by the symmetry of animals, considers the general characteristics of this symmetry, it must form part of the intellectual power which, on high, contemplates universal symmetry. Music, however, which studies rhythm and harmony, is, so far as it studies what is intelligible in these things, the image of the music that deals with intelligible rhythm.

THERE ARE MANY AUXILIARY ARTS WHICH HELP THE PROGRESS OF NATURE.

The arts which produce sense-objects, such as architecture and carpentry, have their principles in the intelligible world, and participate in wisdom, so far as they make use of certain proportions. But as they apply these proportions to sense-objects, they cannot wholly be referred to the intelligible world, unless in so far as they are contained within human reason. The case is similar with agriculture, which assists the growth of plants; medicine, which increases health, and (gymnastics) which supplies the body with strength as well as vigor,[40] for on high there is another Power, another

Health, from which all living organisms derive their needed vigor.

OTHER ARTS ARE INTELLIGIBLE WHEN APPLIED TO THE INTELLIGIBLE.

Last, whenever rhetoric, strategy, private and public finance and politics weave beauty in their deeds, and they glance above, they (discover) that they have added to their science a contribution from the intelligible science.

The science of geometry, however, which deals (wholly) with intelligible entities, must be referred to the intelligible world. So also with philosophy, which occupies the first rank among sciences because it studies essence. This is all we have to say about arts and their products.

THE INTELLIGIBLE WORLD CONTAINS ONLY UNIVERSAL IDEAS; PARTICULARITIES ARE DERIVED FROM MATTER.

12. If the intelligible world contains the idea of Man, it must also contain that of the reasonable man, and of the artist; and consequently the idea of the arts that are begotten by Intelligence. We must therefore insist that the intelligible world contains the ideas of the universals, the idea of Man as such, and not, for instance, that of Socrates. Still we shall have to decide whether the intelligible world does not also contain the idea of the individual man, that is, of the man considered with the things that differ in each individual; for one may have a Roman nose and the other a pug nose. These differences are indeed implied within the idea of man, just as there are differences within the idea of animal. But the differences between a Roman or a snub nose are derived from matter. Likewise, amidst the varieties of colors, some are contained within the seminal reason, while others are derived from matter and space.

BESIDES IDEAS OF INDIVIDUAL SOULS AND INTELLIGENCE, THE INTELLIGIBLE WORLD CONTAINS THE SOUL ITSELF AND INTELLIGENCE ITSELF.

13. It remains for us to study whether the intelligible world contains only what is in the sense-world, or whether we should distinguish from the individual soul the Soul itself, from the particular intelligence, Intelligence itself, as we have above distinguished the particular man from Man himself. We should not consider all things here below as images of archetypes, for instance, the soul of a man as the image of the Soul herself. Only degrees of dignity differentiate souls; but these souls are not the Soul itself. As the Soul itself exists really, it must also contain a certain wisdom, justice and science, which are not images of wisdom, justice, and intelligible science, as sense-objects are images of intelligible entities, but which are these very entities located here below in entirely different conditions of existence; for they are not locally circumscribed. Therefore when the soul issues from the body, she preserves these things within herself; for the sense-world exists only in a determinate place, while the intelligible world exists everywhere; therefore all that the soul contains here below is also in the intelligible world. Consequently if, by "sense-objects" we really mean "visible" things, then indeed the intelligible world contains entities not present in this sense-world. If, on the contrary, we include within the "sense-world" the soul and all she implies, then all things that are above are present here below also.

THE SUPREME BEING ENTIRELY ONE DOES NOT EXPLAIN THE ORIGIN OF THE MANIFOLD.

14. Can we identify the nature that contains all the intelligibles (Intelligence) with the supreme Principle? Impossible, because the supreme Principle must

v.9] OF INTELLIGENCE, IDEAS, ESSENCE 117

be essentially one, and simple, while essences form a multitude. But as these essences form a multitude, we are forced to explain how this multitude, and all these essences can exist. How can (the single) Intelligence be all these things? Whence does it proceed? This we shall have to study elsewhere.[41]

THE SOUL RECEIVES ACCIDENTS FROM MATTER, BUT DEFECTS ARE NOT IN THE INTELLIGIBLE.

It may further be asked whether the intelligible world contains the ideas of objects which are derived from decay, which are harmful or disagreeable, such as, for instance, mud or excreta. We answer that all the things that universal Intelligence receives from the First are excellent. Among them are not found ideas of those dirty and vile objects mentioned above; Intelligence does not contain them. But though receiving from Intelligence ideas, the soul receives from matter other things, among which may be found the above-mentioned accidents. Besides, a more thorough answer to this question must be sought for in our book where we explain "How the Multitude of Ideas Proceeds from the One."[42]

NOT ALL EARTHLY ENTITIES HAVE CORRESPONDING IDEAS.

In conclusion, the accidental composites in which Intelligence does not share and which are formed by a fortuitous complex of sense-objects, have no ideas corresponding to them in the intelligible world. Things that proceed from decay are produced only because the Soul is unable to produce anything better in this case; otherwise she would have rather produced some object more agreeing with nature; she therefore produces what she can.

EVEN THE ARTS ARE DEPENDENT ON THE SOUL.

All the arts concerned with things natural to man are contained within the ideas of Man himself. The Art that is universal is prior to the other arts; but Art is posterior to the Soul herself, or rather, to the life that is in Intelligence before becoming soul, and which, on becoming soul, deserves to be called the Soul herself.

[1] As thought Plato, in the Phaedo, C81. [2] See i. 68 [3] See i. 3.1. [4] See i. 3. [5] See i. 6.2 [6] See i. 66 [7] See i 6.9, and the Philebus of Plato, C64. [8] As suggested in the Phaedo of Plato. [9] See ii 4.6. [10] The rational soul and intelligence, see iii. 9.5 [11] See ii. 9.12; iv. 4.14 [12] See ii 3.17. 18; ii. 9.2, 3; vi. 4.9. [13] A pun on "reason," or "logos," i. 6.2; ii 3.16; ii. 4.3, ii 6.2, ii. 7.3. [14] See iv. 4.10.12. [15] Far from the truth; see iii 8.3 7 [16] Stoics, see iv. 7.8. [17] Or Stoic form of inorganic objects. [18] The form of lower living beings. [19] The form of human nature. [20] See iv. 7.14. [21] Parmenides, see v. 1.8. [22] As Plato hints in his Cratylos, C50, by a pun between "soma" and "sozesthai." [23] The later theological "saved." [24] See Aristotle, de Gen. i. 18. [25] By Stoics [26] See iii. 8.1-3. [27] See v. 5.1. [28] See v. 1.4. [29] In Greek a pun on "eidos" and "idea." [30] See iv. 9.5. [31] See iii. 9.1. [32] See iii. 9.1. [33] The universal Soul. [34] Timaeus, C39 [35] See iii. 9.1. [36] See iii. 7.10 [37] See ii. 7.2. [38] To form, see i. 6.2 [39] As thought Plato, in his Republic, x [40] As thought Plato in Gorgias, C464. [41] vi. 7. [42] vi. 7.

DIFFICULT PASSAGES.

[29] This sentence might well be translated as follows: "When therefore thought (meets) the essentially one, the latter is the form, and the former the idea." While this version seems more literal, it makes no connected sense with what follows [43] Or, "so that it may contain the intelligence which is one, as its own actualization."

FOURTH ENNEAD, BOOK EIGHTH.

Of the Descent of the Soul Into the Body.[1]

THE EXPERIENCE OF ECSTASY LEADS TO QUESTIONS

1. On waking from the slumber of the body to return to myself, and on turning my attention from exterior things so as to concentrate it on myself, I often observe an alluring beauty, and I become conscious of an innate nobility. Then I live out a higher life, and I experience atonement with the divinity. Fortifying myself within it, I arrive at that actualization which raises me above the intelligible. But if, after this sojourn with the divinity, I descend once more from Intelligence to the exercise of my reasoning powers, I am wont to ask myself how I ever could actually again descend, and how my soul ever could have entered into a body, since, although she actually abides in the body, she still possesses within herself all the perfection I discover in her.

HERACLITUS, THE ORIGINATOR OF THESE QUESTIONS, ANSWERS THEM OBSCURELY.

Heraclitus, who recommends this research, asserts that "there are necessary changes of contraries into each other;" he speaks of "ascenscions" and of a "descent," says that it is "a rest to change, a fatigue to continue unremittingly in the same kinds of work, and to be overwrought. He thus reduces us to conjectures because he does not explain himself definitely; and he would even force us to ask how he himself came to discover what he propounds.

EMPEDOCLES, AS A POET, TELLS OF PYTHAGOREAN MYTHS.

Empedocles teaches that "it is a law for souls that have sinned to fall down here below;" and that "he himself, having withdrawn from the divinity, came down to the earth to become the slave of furious discord." It would seem that he limited himself to advancing the ideas that Pythagoras and his followers generally expressed by symbols, both on this and other subjects. Besides Empedocles is obscure because he uses the language of poetry.

PLATO SAYS MANY CONTRADICTORY THINGS THAT ARE BEAUTIFUL AND TRUE.

Last, we have the divine Plato, who has said so many beautiful things about the soul. In his dialogues he often spoke of the descent of the soul into the body, so that we have the right to expect from him something clearer. Unfortunately, he is not always sufficiently in agreement with himself to enable one to follow his thought. In general, he depreciates corporeal things; he deplores the dealings between the soul and the body; insists[2] that the soul is chained down to it, and that she is buried in it as in a tomb. He attaches much importance to the maxim taught in the mysteries that the soul here below is as in a prison.[3] What Plato calls the "cavern"[4] and Empedocles calls the "grotto," means no doubt the sense-world.[5] To break her chains, and to issue from the cavern, means the soul's[6] rising to the intelligible world. In the Phaedrus,[7] Plato asserts that the cause of the fall of the soul is the loss of her wings; that after having once more ascended on high, she is brought back here below by the periods;[8] that there are souls sent down into this world by judgments, fates, conditions, and necessity; still, at the same time, he finds fault with the "descent" of the soul into the body. But, speaking of the universe in the Timaeus,[9] he praises the world, and calls it a blissful divinity. He states that the demiurgic creator, being good, gave it a soul to make it intelligent, because without the soul, the universe could not have been as intelligent as it ought to have been.[10] Consequently, the purpose of the introduction of the universal Soul into the world, and similarly of each of our souls was only to achieve the perfection of the world; for it was necessary for the sense-world to contain animals equal in kind and numbers to those contained in the intelligible world.

QUESTIONS RAISED BY PLATO'S THEORIES.

2. Plato's theories about the soul lead us to ask how, in general, the soul has, by her nature, been led to enter into relations with the body. Other questions arise: What is the nature of the world where the soul lives thus, either voluntarily or necessarily, or in any other way? Does the Demiurge[11] act without meeting any obstacle, or is it with him as with our souls?

HUMAN BODIES ARE MORE DIFFICULT TO MANAGE THAN THE WORLD-BODY.

To begin with, our souls, charged with the administration of bodies less perfect than the world, had to penetrate within them profoundly in order to manage them; for the elements of these bodies tend to scatter, and to return to their original location, while, in the universe, all things are naturally distributed in their proper places.[12] Besides, our bodies demand an active and vigilant foresight, because, by the surrounding objects they are exposed to many accidents; for they always have a crowd of needs, as they demand continual protection against the dangers that threaten them.[18] But the body of the world is complete and perfect. It is self-sufficient; it has nothing to suffer contrary to its nature; and consequently, it (acts) on a mere order of the universal Soul. That is why the universal Soul can remain impassible, feeling no need, remaining in the disposition desired by her own nature. That is why Plato says that, when our soul dwells with this perfect Soul, she herself becomes perfect, soaring in the ethereal region, and governing the whole world.[14] So long as a human soul does not withdraw from the (universal) Soul to enter into a body, and to belong to some individual, she easily administers the world, in the same manner, and together with the universal Soul. Communicating to the body essence and perfection is therefore, for the soul, not an unmixed evil; because the providential care granted to an inferior nature does not hinder him who grants it from himself remaining in a state of perfection.

HOW THE TWO-FOLD SOUL EXERTS A TWO-FOLD PROVIDENCE.

In the universe there are, indeed, two kinds of providences.[15] The first Providence regulates everything in a royal manner, without performing any actions, or observing the details. The second, operating somewhat like an artisan, adjusts its creative power to the inferior nature of creatures by getting in contact with them.[16] Now as the divine Soul (or, the principal power,[17] always administers the whole world in the first or regal way, dominating the world by her superiority, and by injecting into the world her lowest power (nature), we could not accuse the divinity of having given a bad place to the universal Soul. Indeed, this universal Soul was never deprived of her natural power, possessing it always, because this power is not contrary to her being, possessing it uninterruptedly from all eternity.

STAR-SOULS, LIKE UNINCARNATE SOULS, GOVERN THE WORLD UNTROUBLEDLY.

(Plato) further states that the relation of the souls of the stars to their bodies is the same as that of the universal Soul to the universe,[18] where he makes the stars participate in the movements of the universal Soul. He thus grants to those souls the blessedness which is suitable to them. The intercourse of the soul with the body is usually blamed for two things: because it hinders the soul from busying herself with the conceptions of intelligence, and then because it exposes her to agreeable or painful sensations which fill her with desires. Now neither of these two results affect the soul that has not entered into a body, and which does not depend thereon by belonging to some particular individual. Then, on the contrary, she possesses the body of the universe, which has no fault, no need, which can cause her neither fears nor desires, because she has nothing to fear. Thus no anxiety ever forces her to descend to terrestrial objects, or to distract herself from her happy and sublime contemplation. Entirely devoted to divine things, she governs the world by a single power, whose exercise involves no anxiety.

DIFFERENCES BETWEEN HUMAN AND COSMIC INCARNATION.

3. Consider now the human soul which[19] undergoes numberless ills while in the body, eking out a miserable existence, a prey to griefs, desires, fears, sufferings of all kinds, for whom the body is a tomb, and the sense-world a "cave" or "grotto." This dif-

ference of opinions about the condition of the universal Soul and the human soul is not contradictory, because these two souls do not have the same reasons for descent into a body. To begin with, the location of thought, that we call the intelligible world,[20] contains not only the entire universal Intelligence, but also the intellectual powers, and the particular intelligences comprised within the universal Intelligence; since there is not only a single intelligence, but a simultaneously single and plural intelligence. Consequently, it must also have contained a single Soul, and a plurality of souls; and it was from the single Soul, that the multiple particular and different souls had to be born, as from one and the same genus are derived species that are both superior and inferior, and more or less intellectual. Indeed, in the intelligible world, there is, on one hand, the (universal) Intelligence which, like some great animal, potentially contains the other intelligences. On the other hand, are the individual intelligences, each of which possess in actualization what the former contains potentially. We may illustrate by a living city that would contain other living cities. The soul of the universal City would be more perfect and powerful; but nothing would hinder the souls of the other cities from being of the same kind. Similarly, in the universal Fire, there is on one hand a great fire, and on the other small fires, while the universal Being is the being of the universal Fire, or rather, is the source from which the being of the universal Fire proceeds.

THE RATIONAL SOUL POSSESSES ALSO AN INDIVIDUALITY.

The function of the rational soul is to think, but she does not limit herself to thinking. Otherwise there would be no difference between her and intelligence. Besides her intellectual characteristics, the soul's char-

iv.8] DESCENT OF SOUL INTO BODY   125

acteristic nature, by virtue of which she does not remain mere intelligence, has a further individual function, such as is possessed by every other being. By raising her glance to what is superior to her, she thinks; by bringing them down to herself, she preserves herself; by lowering them to what is inferior to her, she adorns it, administers it, and governs it. All these things were not to remain immovable in the intelligible world, to permit of a successive issue of varied beings, which no doubt are less perfect than that which preceded them, but which, nevertheless, exist necessarily during the persistence of the Principle from which they proceed.

INCARNATE SOULS WEAKEN BECAUSE THEY CONTEMPLATE THE INDIVIDUAL.

4. There are individual souls which, in their conversion[21] towards the principle from which they proceed, aspire to the intelligible world, and which also exercise their power on inferior things, just as light, which does not disdain to throw its rays down to us though remaining suspended to the sun on high. These souls must remain sheltered from all suffering so long as in the intelligible world they remain together with the universal Soul. They must besides, in heaven, share with it the administration of the world; like kings who, being colleagues of the great King of the universe, share the government with Him, without themselves descending from their thrones, without ceasing to occupy a place as elevated as He. But when they pass from this state in which they live with the universal Soul to a particular and independent existence, when they seem weary of dwelling with another, then each of them returns to what belongs to her individually. Now when a soul has done that for a long while, when she withdraws from the universal Soul, and distinguishes herself therefrom, when she

ceases to keep her glances directed towards the intelligible world; then, isolating herself in her individual existence, she weakens, and finds herself overwhelmed with a crowd of cares, because she directs her glance at something individual. Having therefore separated herself from the universal Soul as well as from the other souls that remain united thereto, and having attached herself to an individual body, and concentrating herself exclusively on this object, which is subjected to the destructive action of all other beings, she ceases to govern the whole to administer more carefully a part, the care of which forces her to busy herself, and mingle with external things, to be not only present in the body, but also to interpenetrate it.

THIS PROCESS EXPLAINS THE CLASSIC EXPRESSIONS ABOUT HER CONDITION.

Thus, in the common expression, she has lost her wings, and is chained by the bonds of the body, because she gave up the calm existence she enjoyed when with the universal Soul she shared the administration of the world; for when she was above she spent a much happier life. The fallen soul is therefore chained or imprisoned, obliged to have recourse to the senses because she cannot first make use of intelligence. She is, as it is said, buried in a tomb, or cavern. But by her conversion towards thought, she breaks her bonds, she returns upwards towards higher regions, when, starting from the indications of reminiscence she rises to the contemplation of the essences;[22] for even after her fall she always preserves something superior to the body.

SOULS AS AMPHIBIANS.

Souls therefore are necessarily amphibians;[23] since they alternately live in the intelligible world, and in the sense-world; staying longer in the intelligible world when they can remain united to supreme Intelligence more permanently, or staying longer or preponderatingly here below when nature or destiny imposes on them a contrary fate. That is the secret meaning of Plato's words[24] to the effect that the divinity divides the seeds of the souls formed by a second mixture in the cup, and that He separates them into (two) parts. He also adds that they must necessarily fall into generation after having been divided into a definite number. Plato's statement that the divinity sowed the souls,[25] as well as the divinity's address to the other deities, must be taken figuratively. For, in reference to the things contained in the universe, this implies that they are begotten or produced; for successive enumeration and description implies an eternal begetting, and that those objects exist eternally in their present state.

SOULS DESCENDING TO HELP ARE SENT BY GOD.

5. Without any inherent contradiction it may therefore be asserted either,[26] that the souls are sowed into generation, that they descend here below for the perfection of the universe, or that they are shut up in a cavern as the result of a divine punishment, that their fall is simultaneously an effect of their will and of necessity—as necessity does not exclude voluntariness —and that they are in evil so long as they are incarnate in bodies. Again, as Empedocles says, they may have withdrawn from the divinity, and have lost their way, and have committed some fault that they are expiating; or, as says Heraclitus, that rest consists in flight (from heaven, and descent here below), and that the descent of souls is neither entirely voluntary, nor involuntary. Indeed, no being ever falls voluntarily; but as it is by his own motion that he descends to lower things, and reaches a less happy condition, it may be said that he bears the punishment of his

conduct. Besides, as it is by an eternal law of nature that this being acts and suffers in that manner, we may, without contradiction or violence to the truth, assert that the being who descends from his rank to assist some lower thing is sent by the divinity.[27] In spite of any number of intermediate parts (which separate) a principle from its lower part, the latter may still be ascribed to the former.[28]

THE TWO POSSIBLE FAULTS OF THE SOUL.

Here there are two possible faults for the soul. The first consists in the motive that determines her to descend. The second is the evil she commits after having descended here below. The first fault is expiated by the very condition of the soul after she has descended here below. The punishment of the latter fault, if not too serious, is to pass into other bodies more or less promptly according to the judgment delivered about her deserts—and we speak of a "judgment" to show that it is the consequence of the divine law. If however the perversity of the soul passes all measure, she undergoes, under the charge of guardians in charge of her chastisement, the severe punishments she has incurred.

PROMPT FLIGHT HERE BELOW LEAVES THE SOUL
UNHARMED BY HER STAY HERE.

Thus, although the soul have a divine nature (or "being"), though she originate in the intelligible world, she enters into a body. Being a lower divinity, she descends here below by a voluntary inclination, for the purpose of developing her power, and to adorn what is below her. If she flee promptly from here below, she does not need to regret having become acquainted with evil, and knowing the nature of vice,[29] nor having had the opportunity of manifesting her faculties, and to manifest her activities and deeds. Indeed, the faculties of the soul would be useless if they slumbered continuously in incorporeal being without ever becoming actualized. The soul herself would ignore what she possesses if her faculties did not manifest by procession, for everywhere it is the actualization that manifests the potentiality. Otherwise, the latter would be completely hidden and obscured; or rather, it would not really exist, and would not possess any reality. It is the variety of sense-effects which illustrates the greatness of the intelligible principle, whose nature publishes itself by the beauty of its works.

CONTINUOUS PROCESSION NECESSARY TO THE SUPREME.

6. Unity was not to exist alone; for if unity remained self-enclosed, all things would remain hidden in unity without having any form, and no beings would achieve existence. Consequently, even if constituted by beings born of unity, plurality would not exist, unless the inferior natures, by their rank destined to be souls, issued from those beings by the way of procession. Likewise, it was not sufficient for souls to exist, they also had to reveal what they were capable of begetting. It is likewise natural for each essence to produce something beneath it, to draw it out from itself by a development similar to that of a seed, a development in which an indivisible principle proceeds to the production of a sense-object, and where that which precedes remains in its own place at the same time as it begets that which follows by an inexpressible power, which is essential to intelligible natures. Now as this power was not to be stopped or circumscribed in its actions by jealousy, there was need of a continuous procession until, from degree to degree, all things had descended to the extreme limits of what was possible;[30] for it is the characteristic of an inex-

haustible power to communicate all its gifts to everything, and not to permit any of them to be disinherited, since there is nothing which hinders any of them from participating in the nature of the Good in the measure that it is capable of doing so. Since matter has existed from all eternity, it was impossible that from the time since it existed, it should not participate in that which communicates goodness to all things according to their receptivity thereof.[31] If the generation of matter were the necessary consequence of anterior principles, still it must not be entirely deprived of the good by its primitive impotence, when the cause which gratuitously communicated "being" to it remained self-enclosed.

SENSE-OBJECTS ARE NECESSARY AS REVEALERS OF THE ETERNAL.

The excellence, power and goodness of intelligible (essences) are therefore revealed by sense-objects; and there is an eternal connection between intelligible (entities) that are self-existent, and sense-objects, which eternally derive their existence therefrom by participation, and which imitate intelligible nature to the extent of their ability.

THE SOUL'S NATURE IS OF AN INTERMEDIATE KIND

7. As there are two kinds of being (or, existence), one of sensation, and the other intelligible, it is preferable for the soul to live in the intelligible world; nevertheless, as a result of her nature, it is necessary for her also to participate in sense-affairs.[32] Since she occupies only an intermediate rank, she must not feel wronged at not being the best of beings.[33] Though on one hand her condition be divine, on the other she is located on the limits of the intelligible world, because of her affinity for sense-nature. She causes this nature to participate in her powers, and she even receives something therefrom, when, instead of managing

the body without compromising her own security, she permits herself to be carried away by her own inclination to penetrate profoundly within it, ceasing her complete union with the universal Soul. Besides, the soul can rise above the body after having learned to feel how happy one is to dwell on high, by the experience of things seen and suffered here below, and after having appreciated the true Good by the comparison of contraries. Indeed the knowledge of the good becomes clearer by the experience of evil, especially among souls which are not strong enough to know evil before having experienced it.[34]

THE PROCESSION OF INTELLIGENCE IS AN EXCURSION DOWNWARDS AND UPWARDS.

The procession of intelligence consists in descending to things that occupy the lowest rank, and which have an inferior nature,[35] for Intelligence could not rise to the superior Nature. Obliged to act outside of itself, and not being able to remain self-enclosed, by a necessity and by a law of its nature, intelligence must advance unto the soul where it stops; then, after having communicated of itself to that which immediately follows it, intelligence must return to the intelligible world. Likewise, the soul has a double action in her double relation with what is below and above her. By her first action, the soul manages the body to which she is united; by the second, she contemplates the intelligible entities. These alternatives work out, for individual souls, with the course of time; and finally there occurs a conversion which brings them back from the lower to the higher natures.

THE UNIVERSAL SOUL, HOWEVER, IS NOT DISTURBED BY THE URGENCIES BELOW HER.

The universal Soul, however, does not need to busy herself with troublesome functions, and remains out of the reach of evils. She considers what is below her in a purely contemplative manner, while at the same time remaining related to what is above her. She is therefore enabled simultaneously on one side to receive, and on the other to give, since her nature compels her to relate herself closely with the objects of sense.[36]

THE SOUL DOES NOT ENTIRELY ENTER INTO THE BODY.

8. Though I should set myself in opposition to popular views, I shall set down clearly what seems to me the true state of affairs. Not the whole soul enters into the body. By her higher part, she ever remains united to the intelligible world; as, by her lower part, she remains united to the sense-world. If this lower part dominates, or rather, if it be dominated (by sensation) and troubled, it hinders us from being conscious of what the higher part of the soul contemplates. Indeed that which is thought impinges on our consciousness only in case it descends to us, and is felt. In general, we are conscious of what goes on in every part of the soul only when it is felt by the entire soul. For instance, appetite, which is the actualization of lustful desire, is by us cognized only when we perceive it by the interior sense or by discursive reason, or by both simultaneously. Every soul has a lower part turned towards the body, and a higher part turned towards divine Intelligence. The universal Soul manages the universe by her lower part without any kind of trouble, because she governs her body not as we do by any reasoning, but by intelligence, and consequently in a manner entirely different from that adopted by art. The individual souls, each of whom administers a part of the universe,[37] also have a part that rises above their body; but they are distracted from thought by sensation, and by a perception of a

number of things which are contrary to nature, and which come to trouble them, and afflict them. Indeed, the body that they take care of constitutes but a part of the universe, is incomplete, and is surrounded by exterior objects. That is why it has so many needs, why it desires luxuriousness, and why it is deceived thereby. On the contrary, the higher part of the soul is insensible to the attraction of these transitory pleasures, and leads an undisturbed life.

[1] See iv. 3.9-17. [2] In the Cratylus, C400. [3] As in the Phaedo, C62 [4] Republic, vii, C514. [5] See Jamblichus, Cave of the Nymphs, 8. [6] Procession, or rising. [7] C246. [8] Of the universe. [9] C34 [10] Timaeus, C30. [11] The Creator, who is the universal Soul. [12] See iv. 3.9-11. [13] See iv 3.17. [14] As thought Plato in his Phaedrus, C246. [15] The First belongs to the principal power of the universal Soul, the second to its natural and plant power, see iii, 8.1 and iv. 4.13 [16] See iv. 4.13. [17] See ii. 3.18. [18] As in the Timaeus, C42. [19] iv. 8.1. [20] See iv. 2.2. [21] See iv. 3.6.7. [22] As thought Plato in his Phaedrus, C249 and Phaedo, C72. [23] That lead an alternate or double life. [24] In his Timaeus, C42, 69. [25] In the stars. [26] As does Plato, see iv. 8.1. [27] As a messenger, see iv. 3.12.13. [28] See ii. 9.2. [29] Without having given herself up to it. [30] See i. 8.7. [31] That is, of form, ii. 4.4 [32] See iv. 6.3. [33] See iii. 2.8. [34] See iv. 8.5 [35] See iv. 3.18. [36] See ii. 9.2. [37] That is, the body to which she is united.

FIFTH ENNEAD, BOOK FOUR.

How What is After the First Proceeds Therefrom; of the One.

NECESSITY OF THE EXISTENCE OF THE FIRST.

1. Everything that exists after the First is derived therefrom, either directly or mediately, and constitutes a series of different orders such that the second can be traced back to the First, the third to the second, and so forth. Above all beings there must be Something simple and different from all the rest which would exist in itself, and which, without ever mingling with anything else, might nevertheless preside over everything, which might really be the One, and not that deceptive unity which is only the attribute of essence, and which would be a principle superior even to being, unreachable by speech, reason, or science. For if it be not completely simple, foreign to all complexity and composition, and be not really one, it could not be a principle. It is sovereignly absolute only because it is simple and first. For what is not first, is in need of superior things; what is not simple has need of being constituted by simple things. The Principle of everything must therefore be one and only. If it were admitted that there was a second principle of that kind, both would constitute but a single one. For we do not say that they are bodies, nor that the One and First is a body; for every body is composite and begotten, and consequently is not a principle; for a principle cannot be begotten.[1] Therefore, since the

principle of everything cannot be corporeal, because it must be essentially one, it must be the First.

THE FIRST NECESSARILY BEGETS A SECOND, WHICH MUST BE PERFECT.

If something after the One exist, it is no more the simple One, but the multiple One. Whence is this derived? Evidently from the First, for it could not be supposed that it came from chance; that would be to admit that the First is not the principle of everything. How then is the multiple One derived from the First? If the First be not only perfect, but the most perfect, if it be the first Power, it must surely, in respect to power, be superior to all the rest, and the other powers must merely imitate it to the limit of their ability. Now we see that all that arrives to perfection cannot unfruitfully remain in itself, but begets and produces. Not only do beings capable of choice, but even those lacking reflection or soul have a tendency to impart to other beings, what is in them; as, for instance, fire emits heat, snow emits cold; and plant-juices (dye and soak) into whatever they happen to touch. All things in nature imitate the First principle by seeking to achieve immortality by procreation, and by manifestation of their qualities. How then would He who is sovereignly perfect, who is the supreme Good, remain absorbed in Himself, as if a sentiment of jealousy hindered Him from communicating Himself, or as if He were powerless, though He is the power of everything? How then would He remain principle of everything? He must therefore beget something, just as what He begets must in turn beget. There must therefore be something beneath the First. Now this thing (which is immediately beneath the First), must be very venerable, first because it begets everything else, then because it is begotten by the First, and because it must, as being the Second, rank and surpass everything else.

INTELLIGENCE CANNOT BE THE FIRST, AND RANKS ALL ELSE.

2. If the generating principle were intelligence, what it begot would have to be inferior to intelligence, and nevertheless approximate it, and resemble it more than anything else. Now as the generating principle is superior to intelligence, the first begotten thing is necessarily intelligence. Why, however, is the generating principle not intelligence? Because the act of intelligence is thought, and thought consists in seeing the intelligible; for it is only by its conversion towards it that intelligence achieves a complete and perfect existence. In itself, intelligence is only an indeterminate power to see; only by contemplation of the intelligible does it achieve the state of being determined. This is the reason of the saying, "The ideas and numbers, that is, intelligence, are born from the indefinite doubleness, and the One." Consequently, instead of being simple, intelligence is multiple. It is composed of several elements; these are doubtless intelligible, but what intelligence sees is none the less multiple. In any case, intelligence is simultaneously the object thought, and the thinking subject; it is therefore already double.

THE FIRST AND SECOND AS HIGHER AND LOWER INTELLIGIBLE ENTITIES.

But besides this intelligible (entity, namely, intelligence), there is another (higher) intelligible (the supreme Intelligible, the First). In what way does the intelligence, thus determined, proceed from the (First) Intelligible? The Intelligible abides in itself, and has need of nothing else, while there is a need of something else in that which sees and thinks (that is, that which thinks has need of contemplating the supreme Intelligible). But even while remaining within Himself, the Intelligible (One) is not devoid of sentiment; all things belong to Him, are in Him, and with Him. Consequently, He has the conception of Himself, a conception which implies consciousness, and which consists in eternal repose, and in a thought, but in a thought different from that of intelligence. If He begets something while remaining within Himself, He begets it precisely when He is at the highest point of individuality. It is therefore by remaining in His own state that He begets what He begets; He procreates by individualizing. Now as He remains intelligible, what He begets cannot be anything else than thought; therefore thought, by existing, and by thinking the Principle whence it is derived (for it could not think any other object), becomes simultaneously intelligence and intelligible; but this second intelligible differs from the first Intelligible from which it proceeds, and of which it is but the image and the reflection.

THE SECOND IS THE ACTUALIZATION OF THE POTENTIALITY OF THE FIRST.

But how is an actualization begotten from that self-limited (intelligible)? We shall have to draw a distinction between an actualization of being, and an actualization out of the being of each thing (actualized being, and actualization emanating from being). Actualized being cannot differ from being, for it is being itself. But the actualization emanating from being—and everything necessarily has an actualization of this kind—differs from what produces it. It is as if with fire: there is a difference between the heat which constitutes its being, and the heat which radiates exteriorly, while the fire interiorly realizes the actualization which constitutes its being, and which makes it preserve its nature. Here also, and far more so, the First remains in His proper state, and yet simultaneously, by His inherent perfection, by the actualization which resides in Him, has been begotten the actualization which, deriving its existence from so great a power, nay, from supreme Power, has arrived at, or achieved essence and being. As to the First, He was above being; for He was the potentiality of all things, already being all things.

HOW THE FIRST IS ABOVE ALL BEING.

If this (actualization begotten by the First, this external actualization) be all things, then that (One) is above all things, and consequently above being. If then (this external actualization) be all things, and be before all things, it does not occupy the same rank as the remainder (of all other things); and must, in this respect also, be superior to being, and consequently also to intelligence; for there is Something superior to intelligence. Essence is not, as you might say, dead; it is not devoid of life or thought; for intelligence and essence are identical. Intelligible entities do not exist before the intelligence that thinks them, as sense-objects exist before the sensation which perceives them. Intelligence itself is the things that it thinks, since their forms are not introduced to them from without. From where indeed would intelligence receive these forms? Intelligence exists with the intelligible things; intelligence is identical with them, is one with them. Reciprocally, intelligible entities do not exist without their matter (that is, Intelligence).

---

[1] As thought Plato in his Parmenides, C154.

FOURTH ENNEAD, BOOK NINE.

Whether All Souls Form a Single One?

IF ALL SOULS BE ONE IN THE WORLD-SOUL, WHY SHOULD THEY NOT TOGETHER FORM ONE?

1. Just as the soul of each animal is one, because she is entirely present in the whole body, and because she is thus really one, because she does not have one part in one organ, and some other part in another; and just as the sense-soul is equally one in all the beings which feel, and just as the vegetative soul is everywhere entirely one in each part of the growing plants; why then should your soul and mine not form a single unity? Why should not all souls form but a single one? Why should not the universal (Soul) which is present in all beings, be one because she is not divided in the manner of a body, being everywhere the same? Why indeed should the soul in myself form but one, and the universal (Soul) likewise not be one, similarly, since no more than my own is this universal (Soul) either material extension, or a body? If both my soul and yours proceed from the universal (Soul), and if the latter be one, then should my soul and yours together form but a single one. Or again, on the supposition that the universal (Soul) and mine proceed from a single soul, even on this hypothesis would all souls form but a single one. We shall have to examine in what (this Soul which is but) one consists.

SOULS MAY NOT FORM A NUMERIC UNITY, BUT MAY FORM A GENERIC UNITY.

Let us first consider if it may be affirmed that all souls form but one in the sense in which it is said that the soul of each individual is one. It seems absurd to pretend that my soul and yours form but one in this (numerical) sense; for then you would be feeling simultaneously with my feeling, and you would be virtuous when I was, and you would have the same desires as I, and not only would we both have the same sentiments, but even the identical sentiments of the universal (Soul), so that every sensation felt by me would have been felt by the entire universe. If in this manner all the souls form but one, why is one soul reasonable, and the other unreasonable, why is the one in an animal, and the other in a plant? On the other hand, if we do not admit that there is a single Soul, we will not be able to explain the unity of the universe, nor find a single principle for (human) souls.

THE UNITY OF THE PRINCIPLE OF SEVERAL SOULS NEED NOT IMPLY THEIR BEING IDENTICAL.

2. In the first place, if the souls of myself and of another man form but one soul, this does not necessarily imply their being identical with their principle. Granting the existence of different beings, the same principle need not experience in each the same affections. Thus, humanity may equally reside in me, who am in motion, as in you, who may be at rest, although in me it moves, and it rests in you. Nevertheless, it is neither absurd nor paradoxical to insist that the same principle is both in you and in me; and this does not necessarily make us feel the identical affections. Consider a single body: it is not the left hand which feels what the right one does, but the soul which is present in the whole body. To make you feel the same as I

do, our two bodies would have to constitute but a single one; then, being thus united, our souls would perceive the same affections. Consider also that the All remains deaf to a multitude of impressions experienced by the parts of a single and same organism, and that so much the more as the body is larger. This is the state of affairs, for instance, with the large whales which do not feel the impression received in some one part of their body, because of the smallness of the movement.

SYMPATHY DOES NOT FORCE IDENTITY OF SENSATION

It is therefore by no means necessary that when one member of the universe experiences an affection, the latter be clearly felt by the All. The existence of sympathy is natural enough, and it could not be denied; but this does not imply identity of sensation. Nor is it absurd that our souls, while forming a single one should be virtuous and vicious, just as it would be possible that the same essence be at motion in me, but at rest in you. Indeed, the unity that we attribute to the universal (Soul) does not exclude all multiplicity, such a unity as befits intelligence. We may however say that (the soul) is simultaneously unity and plurality, because she participates not only in divisible essence in the bodies, but also in the indivisible, which consequently is one. Now, just as the impression perceived by one of my parts is not necessarily felt all over my body, while that which happens to the principal organ is felt by all the other parts, likewise, the impressions that the universe communicates to the individual are clearer, because usually the parts perceive the same affections as the All, while it is not evident that the particular affections that we feel would be also experienced by the Whole.

UNITY OF ALL BEINGS IMPLIED BY SYMPATHY, LOVE, AND MAGIC ENCHANTMENT.

3. On the other hand, observation teaches us that we sympathize with each other, that we cannot see the suffering of another man without sharing it, that we are naturally inclined to confide in each other, and to love; for love is a fact whose origin is connected with the question that occupies us. Further, if enchantments and magic charms mutually attract individuals, leading distant persons to sympathize, these effects can only be explained by the unity of soul. (It is well known that) words pronounced in a low tone of voice (telepathically?) affect a distant person, and make him hear what is going on at a great distance. Hence appears the unity of all beings, which demands the unity of the Soul.

WHAT OF THE DIFFERENCES OF RATIONALITY, IF THE SOUL BE ONE?

If, however, the Soul be one, why is some one soul reasonable, another irrational, or some other one merely vegetative? The indivisible part of the soul consists in reason, which is not divided in the bodies, while the part of the divisible soul in the bodies (which, though being one in herself, nevertheless divides herself in the bodies, because she sheds sentiment everywhere), must be regarded as another power of the soul (the sensitive power); likewise, the part which fashions and produces the bodies is still another power (the vegetative power); nevertheless, this plurality of powers does not destroy the unity of the soul. For instance, in a grain of seed there are also several powers; nevertheless this grain of seed is one, and from this unity is born a multiplicity which forms a unity.

HOW SOULS FORM A SINGLE SOUL

THE POWERS OF THE SOUL ARE NOT EXERCISED EVERYWHERE BECAUSE THEY DIFFER.

But why do not all the powers of the soul act everywhere? Now if we consider the Soul which is one everywhere, we find that sensation is not similar in all its parts (that is, in all the individual souls); that reason is not in all (but in certain souls exclusively); and that the vegetative power is granted to those beings who do not possess sensation, and that all these powers return to unity when they separate from the body.

THE BODY'S POWER OF GROWTH IS DERIVED FROM THE WHOLE, AND THE SOUL; BUT NOT FROM OUR SOUL.

If, however, the body derive its vegetative power from the Whole and from this (universal) Soul which is one, why should it not derive it also from our soul? Because that which is nourished by this power forms a part of the universe, which possesses sensation only at the price of "suffering." As to the sense-power which rises as far as the judgment, and which is united to every intelligence, there was no need for it to form what had already been formed by the Whole, but it could have given its forms if these forms were not parts of the Whole which produces them.

THE UNITY OF THE SOULS IS A CONDITION OF THEIR MULTIPLICITY.

4. Such justifications will preclude surprise at our deriving all souls from unity. But completeness of treatment demands explanation how all souls are but a single one. Is this due to their proceeding from a single Soul, or because they all form a single one? If all proceed from a single one, did this one divide

herself, or did she remain whole, while begetting the multitude of souls? In this case, how could an essence beget a multitude like her, while herself remaining undiminished? We shall invoke the help of the divinity (in solving this problem); and say that the existence of the one single Soul is the condition of the existence of the multitude of souls, and that this multitude must proceed from the Soul that is one.

THE SOUL CAN BEGET MANY BECAUSE SHE IS AN INCORPOREAL ESSENCE.

If the Soul were a body, then would the division of this body necessarily produce the multitude of souls, and this essence would be different in its different parts. Nevertheless, as this essence would be homogeneous, the souls (between which it would divide itself) would be similar to each other, because they would possess a single identical form in its totality, but they would differ by their body. If the essence of these souls consisted in the bodies which would serve them as subjects, they would be different from each other. If the essence of these souls consisted in their form, they would, in form, be but one single form; in other terms, there would be but one same single soul in a mulittude of bodies. Besides, above this soul which would be one, but which would be spread abroad in the multitude of bodies, there would be another Soul which would not be spread abroad in the multitude of bodies; it would be from her that would proceed the soul which would be the unity in plurality, the multiple image of the single Soul in a single body, like a single seal, by impressing the same figure to a multitude of pieces of wax, would be distributing this figure in a multitude of impressions. In this case (if the essence of the soul consisted in her form) the soul would be

iv.9] HOW SOULS FORM A SINGLE SOUL 145

something incorporeal, and as she would consist in an affection of the body, there would be nothing astonishing in that a single quality, emanating from a single principle, might be in a multitude of subjects simultaneously. Last, if the essence of the soul consisted in being both things (being simultaneously a part of a homogeneous body and an affection of the body), there would be nothing surprising (if there were a unity of essence in a multitude of subjects). We have thus shown that the soul is incorporeal, and an essence; we must now consider the results of this view.

HOW AN ESSENCE CAN BE ONE IN A MULTITUDE OF SOULS IS ILLUSTRATED BY SEED.

5. How can an essence be single in a multitude of souls? Either this one essence is entire in all souls, or this one and entire essence begets all souls while remaining (undiminished) in itself. In either case, the essence is single. It is the unity to which the individual souls are related; the essence gives itself to this multitude, and yet simultaneously the essence does not give itself; it can give of itself to all individual souls, and neverthless remain single; it is powerful enough to pass into all simultaneously, and to be separated from none; thus its essence remains identical, while being present in a multitude of souls. This is nothing astonishing; all of science is entirely in each of its parts, and it begets them without itself ceasing to remain entire within itself. Likewise, a grain of seed is entire in each of its parts in which it naturally divides itself; each of its parts has the same properties as the whole seed; nevertheless the seed remains entire, without diminution; and if the matter (in which the seed resides) offer it any cause of division, all the parts will not any the less form a single unity.

THIS MIRACLE IS EXPLAINED BY THE USE OF THE CONCEPTION OF POTENTIALITY.

It may be objected that in science a part is not the total science. Doubtless, the notion which is actualized, and which is studied to the exclusion of others, because there is special need of it, is only partially an actualization. Nevertheless, in a latent manner it potentially comprises all the other notions it implies. Thus, all the notions are contained in each part of the science, and in this respect each part is the total science; for what is only partially actualized (potentially) comprises all the notions of science. Each notion that one wishes to render explicit is at one's disposition; and this in every part of the science that is considered; but if it be compared with the whole science, it seems to be there only potentially. It must not, however, be thought that the particular notion does not contain anything of the other notions; in this case, there would be nothing systematic or scientific about it; it would be nothing more than a sterile conception. Being a really scientific notion, it potentially contains all the notions of the science; and the genuine scientist knows how to discover all its notions in a single one, and how to develop its consequences. The geometical expert shows in his demonstrations how each theorem contains all the preceding ones, to which he harks back by analysis, and how each theorem leads to all the following ones, by deduction.

DIFFICULT AS THESE EXPLANATIONS ARE, THEY ARE CLEAR INTELLIGIBLY.

These truths excite our incredulity, because here below our reason is weak, and it is confused by the body. In the intelligible world, however, all the verities are clear, and each is evident, by itself.

SIXTH ENNEAD, BOOK NINE.

Of the Good and the One.

UNITY NECESSARY TO EXISTENCE OF ALL BEINGS.

1. All beings, both primary, as well as those who are so called on any pretext soever, are beings only because of their unity. What, indeed would they be without it? Deprived of their unity, they would cease to be what they are said to be. No army can exist unless it be one. So with a choric ballet or a flock. Neither a house nor a ship can exist without unity; by losing it they would cease to be what they are.[1] So also with continuous quantities which would not exist without unity. On being divided by losing their unity, they simultaneously lose their nature. Consider farther the bodies of plants and animals, of which each is a unity. On losing their unity by being broken up into several parts, they simultaneously lose their nature. They are no more what they were, they have become new beings, which themselves exist only so long as they are one. What effects health in us, is that the parts of our bodies are co-ordinated in unity. Beauty is formed by the unity of our members. Virtue is our soul's tendency to unity, and becoming one through the harmony of her faculties.

THE SOUL MAY IMPART UNITY, BUT IS NOT UNITY.

The soul imparts unity to all things when producing them, fashioning them, and forming them. Should we, therefore, after rising to the Soul, say that she not only imparts unity, but herself is unity in itself? Certainly not. The soul that imparts form and figure to bodies is not identical with form, and figure. Therefore the soul imparts unity without being unity. She unifies each of her productions only by contemplation of the One, just as she produces man only by comtemplating Man-in-himself, although adding to that idea the implied unity. Each of the things that are called "one" have a unity proportionate to their nature ("being"); so that they participate in unity more or less according as they share essence[2] (being). Thus the soul is something different from unity; nevertheless, as she exists in a degree higher (than the body), she participates more in unity, without being unity itself; indeed she is one, but the unity in her is no more than contingent. There is a difference between the soul and unity, just as between the body and unity. A discrete quantity such as a company of dancers, or choric ballet, is very far from being unity; a continuous quantity approximates that further; the soul gets still nearer to it, and participates therein still more. Thus from the fact that the soul could not exist without being one, the identity between the soul and unity is suggested. But this may be answered in two ways. First, other things also possess individual existence because they possess unity, and nevertheless are not unity itself; as, though the body is not identical with unity, it also participates in unity. Further, the soul is manifold as well as one, though she be not composed of parts. She possesses several faculties, discursive reason, desire, and perception—all of them faculties joined together by unity as a bond. Doubtless the soul imparts unity to something else (the body), because she herself possesses unity; but this unity is by her received from some other principle (namely, from unity itself).

BEING AND ESSENCE IDENTICAL WITH UNITY.

2. (Aristotle[3]) suggests that in each of the individual beings which are one, being is identical with unity. Are not being and essence identical with unity, in every being and in every essence, in a manner such that on discovering essence, unity also is discovered? Is not being in itself unity in itself, so that if being be intelligence, unity also must be intelligence, as intelligence which, being essence in the highest degree, is also unity in the first degree, and which, imparting essence to other things, also imparts unity to them? What indeed could unity be, apart from essence and being? As "man," and "a man" are equivalent,[4] essence must be identical with unity; or, unity is the number of everything considered individually; and as one object joined to another is spoken of as two, so an object alone is referred to as one.

UNITY IS NOT A NUMBERING DEVICE, BUT IS IDENTICAL WITH EXISTENCE.

If number belongs to the class of beings, evidently the latter must include unity also; and we shall have to discover what kind of a being it is. If unity be no more than a numbering device invented by the soul, then unity would possess no real existence. But we have above observed that each object, on losing unity, loses existence also. We are therefore compelled to investigate whether essence and unity be identical either when considered in themselves, or in each individual object.

EVEN UNIVERSAL ESSENCE CONTAINS MANIFOLDNESS.

If the essence of each thing be manifoldness, and as unity cannot be manifoldness, unity must differ from essence. Now man, being both animal and rational, contains a manifoldness of elements of which unity is the bond. There is therefore a difference between man and unity; man is divisible, while unity is indivisible. Besides, universal Essence, containing all essences, is still more manifold. Therefore it differs from unity; though it does possess unity by participation. Essence possesses life and intelligence, for it cannot be considered lifeless; it must therefore be manifold. Besides, if essence be intelligence, it must in this respect also be manifold, and must be much more so if it contain forms; for the idea[5] is not genuinely one. Both as individual and general it is rather a number; it is one only as the world is one.

BESIDES, ABSOLUTE UNITY IS THE FIRST, WHICH INTELLIGENCE IS NOT.

Besides, Unity in itself is the first of all; but intelligence, forms and essence are not primary. Every form is manifold and composite, and consequently must be something posterior; for parts are prior to the composite they constitute. Nor is intelligence primary, as appears from the following considerations. For intelligence existence is necessarily thought and the best intelligence which does not contemplate exterior objects, must think what is above it; for, on turning towards itself, it turns towards its principle. On the one hand, if intelligence be both thinker and thought, it implies duality, and is not simple or unitary. On the other hand, if intelligence contemplate some object other than itself, this might be nothing more than some object better than itself, placed above it. Even if intelligence contemplate itself simultaneously with what is better than it, even so intelligence is only of secondary rank. We may indeed admit that the intelligence which has such a nature enjoys the presence of the Good, of the First, and that intelligence contemplates the First; but nevertheless at the same time intelligence is present to itself, and thinks itself as being all things. Containing such a diversity, intelligence is far from unity.

UNITY AS ABOVE ALL THINGS, INTELLIGENCE AND ESSENCE.

Thus Unity is not all things, for if so, it would no longer be unity. Nor is it Intelligence, for since intelligence is all things, unity too would be all things. Nor is it essence, since essence also is all things.

UNITY IS DIFFICULT TO ASCERTAIN BECAUSE THE SOUL IS FEARFUL OF SUCH ABSTRUSE RESEARCHES.

3. What then is unity? What is its nature? It is not surprising that it is so difficult to say so, when it is difficult to explain of what even essence or form consist. But, nevertheless, forms are the basis of our knowledge. Everything that the soul advances towards what is formless, not being able to understand it because it is indeterminate, and so to speak has not received the impression of a distinctive type, the soul withdraws therefrom, fearing she will meet nonentity. That is why, in the presence of such things she grows troubled, and descends with pleasure. Then, withdrawing therefrom, she, so to speak, lets herself fall till she meets some sense-object, on which she pauses, and recovers; just as the eye which, fatigued by the contemplation of small objects, gladly turns back to large ones. When the soul wishes to see by herself, then seeing only because she is the object that she sees, and, further, being one because she forms but one with this object, she imagines that what she sought has escaped, because she herself is not distinct from the object that she thinks.

THE PATH OF SIMPLIFICATION TO UNITY.

Nevertheless a philosophical study of unity will follow the following course. Since it is Unity that we seek, since it is the principle of all things, the Good, the First that we consider, those who will wish to reach it must not withdraw from that which is of primary rank to decline to what occupies the last, but they must withdraw their souls from sense-objects, which occupy the last degree in the scale of existence, to those entities that occupy the first rank. Such a man will have to free himself from all evil, since he aspires to rise to the Good. He will rise to the principle that he possesses within himself. From the manifold that he was he will again become one. Only under these conditions will he contemplate the supreme principle, Unity. Thus having become intelligence, having trusted his soul to intelligence, educating and establishing her therein, so that with vigilant attention she may grasp all that intelligence sees, he will, by intelligence, contemplate unity, without the use of any senses, without mingling any of their perceptions with the flashes of intelligence. He will contemplate the purest Principle, through the highest degree of the purest Intelligence. So when a man applies himself to the contemplation of such a principle and represents it to himself as a magnitude, or a figure, or even a form, it is not his intelligence that guides him in this contemplation for intelligence is not destined to see such things; it is sensation, or opinion, the associate of sensation, which is active in him. Intelligence is only capable of informing us about things within its sphere.

UNITY AS THE UNIFORM IN ITSELF AND FORMLESS SUPERFORM.

Intelligence can see both the things that are above it, those which belong to it, and the things that proceed from it. The things that belong to intelligence are

OF THE GOOD AND THE ONE

pure; but they are still less pure and less simple than the things that are above Intelligence, or rather than what is above it; this is not Intelligence, and is superior to Intelligence. Intelligence indeed is essence, while the principle above it is not essence, but is superior to all beings. Nor is it essence, for essence has a special form, that of essence, and the One is shapeless, even intelligible. As Unity is the nature that begts all things, Unity cannot be any of them. It is therefore neither any particular thing, nor quantity, nor quality, nor intelligence, nor soul, nor what is movable, nor what is stable; it is neither in place nor time; but it is the uniform in itself, or rather it is formless, as it is above all form, above movement and stability. These are my views about essence and what makes it manifold.[6]

WHY IT IS NOT STABLE, THOUGH IT DOES NOT MOVE.

But if it does not move, why does it not possess stability? Because either of these things, or both together, are suitable to nothing but essence. Besides, that which possesses stability is stable through stability, and is not identical with stability itself; consequently it possesses stability only by accident, and would no longer remain simple.

BEING A PRIMARY CAUSE, UNITY IS NOTHING CONTINGENT.

Nor let anybody object that something contingent is attributed to Unity when we call it the primary cause. It is to ourselves that we are then attributing contingency, since it is we who are receiving something from Unity, while Unity remains within itself.

UNITY CANNOT BE DEFINED; WE CAN ONLY REFER TO IT BY OUR FEELINGS OF IT.

Speaking strictly, we should say that the One is this or that (that is, we should not apply any name to it). We can do no more than turn around it, so to speak, trying to express what we feel (in regard to it); for at times we approach Unity, and at times withdraw from it as a result of our uncertainty about it.

WE CANNOT COMPREHEND UNITY, WHICH WE APPROACH ONLY BY A PRESENCE.

4. The principal cause of our uncertainty is that our comprehension of the One comes to us neither by scientific knowledge, nor by thought, as the knowledge of other intelligible things, but by a presence which is superior to science. When the soul acquires the scientific knowledge of something, she withdraws from unity and ceases being entirely one; for science implies discursive reason and discursive reason implies manifoldness. (To attain Unity) we must therefore rise above science, and never withdraw from what is essentially One; we must therefore renounce science, the objects of science, and every other right (except that of the One); even to that of beauty; for beauty is posterior to unity, and is derived therefrom, as the day-light comes from the sun. That is why Plato[7] says of (Unity) that it is unspeakable and undescribable. Nevertheless we speak of it, we write about it, but only to excite our souls by our discussions, and to direct them towards this divine spectacle, just as one might point out the road to somebody who desired to see some object. Instruction, indeed, goes as far as showing the road, and guiding us in the way; but to obtain the vision (of the divinity), is the work suitable to him who has desired to obtain it.

OF THE GOOD AND THE ONE

THOSE WHO SEE GOD WITHOUT EMOTION HAVE FAILED TO RID THEMSELVES OF PHYSICAL HINDRANCES, AND HAVE NOT BECOME UNIFIED.

If your soul does not succeed in enjoying this spectacle, if she does not have the intuition of the divine light, if she remains cold and does not, within herself, feel a rapture such as that of a lover who sees the beloved object, and who rests within it, a rapture felt by him who has seen the true light, and whose soul has been overwhelmed with brilliance on approaching this light, then you have tried to rise to the divinity without having freed yourself from the hindrances which arrest your progress, and hinder your contemplation. You did not rise alone, and you retained within yourself something that separated you from Him; or rather, you were not yet unified. Though He be absent from all beings, He is absent from none, so that He is present (to all) without being present (to them). He is present only for those who are able to receive Him, and who are prepared for Him, and who are capable of harmonizing themselves with Him, to reach Him, and as it were to touch Him by virtue of the conformity they have with Him, and also by virtue of an innate power analogous to that which flows from Him, when at last their souls find themselves in the state where they were after having communicated with Him; then they can see Him so far as his nature is visible. I repeat: if you have not yet risen so far, the conclusion must be that you are still at a distance from Him, either by the obstacles of which we spoke above, or by the lack of such instruction as would have taught you the road to follow, and which would have imbued you with faith in things divine. In any case, you have no fault to find with any but yourself; for, to be alone, all you need to do is to detach yourself from everything. Lack of faith in arguments about it may be remedied by the following considerations.

HOW SUCH AS RISE AS FAR AS THE SOUL MAY ACHIEVE FAITH IN THE INTELLIGIBLE.

5. Such as imagine that beings are governed by luck or chance, and that they depend on material causes are far removed from the divinity, and from the conception of unity. It is not such men that we are addressing, but such as admit the existence of a nature different from the corporeal one, and who at least rise (to an acknowledgment of the existence of) the Soul. These should apply themselves to the study of the nature of the soul, learning, among other truths, that she proceeds from Intelligence, and that she can achieve virtue by participating in Intelligence through reason. They must then acknowledge the existence of an Intelligence superior to the intelligence that reasons, namely, to discursive reason. They must (also realize) that reasonings imply an interval (between notions), and a movement (by which the soul bridges this interval). They must be brought to see that scientific knowledge consists also of reasons of the same nature (namely, rational notions), reasons suitable to the soul, but which have become clear, because the soul has received the succession of intelligence which is the source of scientific knowledge. By intelligence (which belongs to her), the soul sees the divine Intellect, which to it seems sensual, in this sense that it is perceptible by intelligence, which dominates the soul, and is her father;[8] that is, the intelligible world, a calm intellect which vibrates without issuing from its tranquility, which contains everything, and which is all. It is both definite and indefinite manifoldness, for the ideas it contains are not distinct

like the reasons (the rational notions), which are conceived one by one. Nevertheless, they do not become confused. Each of them becomes distinct from the others, just as in a science all the notions, though forming an indivisible whole, yet each has its own separate individual existence.[9] This multitude of ideas taken together constitutes the intelligible world. This is the (entity) nearest to the First. Its existence is inevitably demonstrated by reason, as much as the necessity of the existence of the Soul herself; but though the intelligible world is something superior to the Soul, it is nevertheless not yet the First, because it is neither one, nor simple, while the one, the principle of all beings, is perfectly simple.

THE SUPREME IS ONE ONLY IN A FIGURATIVE SENSE.

The principle that is superior to what is highest among beings, to Intelligence (or intellect, or intelligible world) (may well be sought after). There must indeed be some principle above Intelligence; for intelligence does indeed aspire to become one, but it is not one, possessing only the form of unity. Considered in itself, Intelligence is not divided, but is genuinely present to itself. It does not dismember itself because it is next to the One, though it dared to withdraw therefrom. What is above Intelligence is Unity itself, an incomprehensible miracle, of which it cannot even be said that it is essence, lest we make of it the attribute of something else, and to whom no name is really suitable. If however He must be named, we may indeed call Him in general Unity, but only on the preliminary understanding that He was not first something else, and then only later became unity. That is why the One is so difficult to understand in Himself; He is rather known by His offspring;

that is, by Being, because Intelligence leads up to Being. The nature of the One, indeed, is the source of excellent things, the power which begets beings, while remaining within Himself, without undergoing any diminution, without passing into the beings to which He gives birth.[10] If we call this principle Unity, it is only for the mutual convenience of rising to some indivisible conception, and in unifying our soul. But when we say that this principle is one and indivisible, it is not in the same sense that we say it of the (geometric) point, and of the (arithmetical unity called the) monad. What is one in the sense of the unity of the point or the monad, is a principle of quantity, and would not exist unless preceded by being and the principle which precedes even that being. It is not of this kind of unity that we must think; still we believe that the point and the monad have analogy with the One by their simplicity as well as by the absence of all manifoldness and of all division.

THE ONE MAY BE CONCEIVED OF AS INDIVISIBLE AND INFINITE

6. In what sense do we use the name of unity, and how can we conceive of it? We shall have to insist that the One is a unity much more perfect than the point of the monad; for in these, abstracting (geometric) magnitude, and numerical plurality, we do indeed stop at that which is most minute, and we come to rest in something indivisible; but this existed already in a divisible being, in a subject other than itself, while the One is neither in a subject other than itself, nor in anything divisible. If it be indivisible, neither is it of the same kind as that which is most minute. On the contrary, it is that which is greatest, not by (geometric) magnitude, but by power; possessing no (geometric) magnitude, it is indivisible in

its power; for the beings beneath it are indivisible in their powers, and not in their mass (since they are incorporeal). We must also insist that the One is infinite, not as would be a mass of a magnitude which could be examined serially, but by the incommensurability of its power. Even though you should conceive of it as of intelligence or divinity, it is still higher. When by thought you consider it as the most perfect unity, it is still higher. You try to form for yourself an idea of a divinity by rising to what in your intelligence is most unitary (and yet He is still simpler); for He dwells within Himself, and contains nothing that is contingent.

THE ONE IS SELF-SUFFICIENT AND NEEDS NOTHING FOR ESTABLISHMENT.

His sovereign unity may best be understood by His being self-sufficient; for the most perfect principle is necessarily that which best suffices Himself, and which least needs anything else. Now anything that is not one, but manifold, needs something else. Not being one, but being composed of multiple elements, its being demands unification; but as the One is already one, He does not even need Himself. So much the more, the being that is manifold needs as many things as it contains; for each of the contained things exists only by its union with the others, and not in itself, and finds that it needs the others. Therefore such a being needs others, both for the things it contains, as for their totality. If then there must be something that fully suffices itself, it must surely be the One, which alone needs nothing either relatively to Himself, or to the other things. It needs nothing either to exist, or to be happy, or to be composed. To begin with, as He is the cause of the other beings, He does not owe His existence to them. Further, how could He derive

His happiness from outside Himself? Within Him, happiness is not something contingent, but is His very nature. Again, as He does not occupy any space, He does not need any foundation on which to be edified, as if He could not sustain Himself. All that needs compounding is inanimate; without support it is no more than a mass ready to fall. (Far from needing any support) the One is the foundation of the edification of all other things; by giving them existence, He has at the same time given them a location. However, that which needs a location is not (necessarily) self-sufficient.

THE SUPREME, AS SUPERGOODNESS, COULD NOT ASPIRE TO ANYTHING ELSE

A principle has no need of anything beneath it. The Principle of all things has no need of any of them. Every non-self-sufficient being is not self-sufficient chiefly because it aspires to its principle. If the One aspired to anything, His aspiration would evidently tend to destroy His unity, that is, to annihilate Himself. Anything that aspires evidently aspires to happiness and preservation. Thus, since for the One there is no good outside of Himself, there is nothing that He could wish. He is the super-good; He is the good, not for Himself, but for other beings, for those that can participate therein.

THE ONE IS NOT THINKER BUT THOUGHT ITSELF.

Within the One, therefore, is no thought, because there can be no difference within Him; nor could He contain any motion, because the One is prior to motion, as much as to thought. Besides, what would He think? Would He think Himself? In this case, He would be ignorant before thinking, and thought would be necessary to Him, who fully suffices to Himself. Neither should He be thought to contain ignorance, because He does not know Himself, and does not think Himself. Ignorance presupposes a relation, and consists in that one thing does not know another. But the One, being alone, can neither know nor be ignorant of anything. Being with Himself, He has no need of self-knowledge. We should not even predicate of Him presence with Himself, if we are to conceive of Him Unity in sheer purity. On the contrary, we should have to leave aside intelligence, consciousness, and knowledge of self and of other beings. We should not conceive of Him as being that which thinks, but rather as of thought. Thought does not think; but is the cause which makes some other being think; now the cause cannot be identical with that which is caused. So much the more reason is there then to say that that which is the cause of all these existing things cannot be any one of them. This Cause, therefore, must not be considered identical with the good He dispenses, but must be conceived as the Good in a higher sense, the Good which is above all other goods.

THE SOUL MUST BE STRIPPED OF FORM TO BE ILLUMINATED BY PRIMARY NATURE

7. Your mind remains in uncertainty because the divinity is none of these things (that you know). Apply it first to these things, and later fix it on the divinity. While doing so, do not let yourself be distracted by anything exterior for the divinity is not in any definite place, depriving the remainder of its presence, but it is present wherever there is any person who is capable of entering into contact therewith. It is absent only for those who cannot succeed therein. Just as, for other objects, one could not discover what one seeks by thinking of something else, and as one

should not add any alien thing to the object that is thought if one wishes to identify oneself therewith; likewise here one must be thoroughly convinced that it is impossible for any one whose soul contains any alien image to conceive of the divinity so long as such an image distracts the soul's attention. It is equally impossible that the soul, at the moment that she is attentive, and attached to other things, should assume the form of what is contrary to them. Just as it is said of matter that it must be absolutely deprived of all qualities to be susceptible of receiving all forms; likewise, and for a stronger reason, the soul must be stripped of all form, if she desire to be filled with and illuminated by the primary nature without any interior hindrance. Thus, having liberated herself from all exterior things, the soul will entirely turn to what is most intimate in her; she will not allow herself to be turned away by any of the surrounding objects and she will put aside all things, first by the very effect of the state in which she will find herself, and later by the absence of any conception of form. She will not even know that she is applying herself to the contemplation of the One, or that she is united thereto. Then, after having sufficiently dwelt with it, she will, if she can, come to reveal to others this heavenly communion. Doubtless it was enjoyment of this communion that was the basis of the traditional conversation of Minos with Jupiter.[11] Inspired with the memories of this interview, he made laws which represented it, because, while he was drawing them up, he was still under the influence of his union with the divinity. Perhaps even, in this state, the soul may look down on civil virtues as hardly worthy of her,[12] inasmuch as she desires to dwell on high; and this does indeed happen to such as have long contemplated the divinity.

ON SELF-KNOWLEDGE DEPENDS RECOGNITION OF DIVINE KINSHIP.

(In short), the divinity is not outside of any being. On the contrary, He is present to all beings, though these may be ignorant thereof. This happens because they are fugitives, wandering outside of Him or rather, outside of themselves. They cannot reach Him from whom they are fleeing, nor, having lost themselves, can they find another being. A son, if angry, and beside himself, is not likely to recognize his father. But he who will have learnt to know himself will at the same time discover from where he hails.[18]

TO BE ATTACHED TO THE CENTRE CONSTITUTES DIVINITY.

8. Self-knowledge reveals the fact that the soul's natural movement is not in a straight line, unless indeed it have undergone some deviation. On the contrary, it circles around something interior, around a centre. Now the centre is that from which proceeds the circle, that is, the soul.[14] The soul will therefore move around the centre, that is, around the principle from which she proceeds; and, trending towards it, she will attach herself to it, as indeed all souls should do. The souls of the divinities ever direct themselves towards it; and that is the secret of their divinity; for divinity consists in being attached to the Centre (of all souls). Anyone who withdraws much therefrom is a man who has remained manifold (that is, who has never become unified), or who is a brute.[15]

THE CELEBRATED SIMILE OF THE MAN WHOSE FEET ARE IN A BATH-TUB.

Is the centre of the soul then the principle that we are seeking? Or must we conceive some other principle towards which all centres radiate? To begin with, it is only by analogy that the words "centre" and "circle" are used. By saying that the soul is a circle, we do not mean that she is a geometrical figure, but that in her and around her subsists primordial nature.[16] (By saying that she has a centre, we mean that) the soul is suspended from the primary Principle (by the highest part of her being), especially when she is entirely separated (from the body). Now, however, as we have a part of our being contained in the the body, we resemble a man whose feet are plunged in water, with the rest of his body remaining above it. Raising ourselves above the body by the whole part which is not immerged, we are by our own centre reattaching ourselves to the Centre common to all beings, just in the same way as we make the centres of the great circles coincide with that of the sphere that surrounds them. If the circles of the soul were corporeal, the common centre would have to occupy a certain place for them to coincide with it, and for them to turn around it. But since the souls are of the order of intelligible (essences), and as the One is still above Intelligence, we shall have to assert that the intercourse of the soul with the One operates by means different from those by which Intelligence unites with the intelligible. This union, indeed, is much closer than that which is realized between Intelligence and the intelligible by resemblance or identity; it takes place by the intimate relationship that unites the soul with unity, without anything to separate them. Bodies cannot unite mutually;[17] but they could not hinder the mutual union of incorporeal (essences) because that which separates them from each other is not a local distance, but their distinction and difference. When there is no difference between them, they are present in each other.

THE FAMOUS ILLUSTRATION OF THE COSMIC CHORAL BALLET.

As the One does not contain any difference, He is always present; and we are ever present to Him as soon as we contain no more difference. It is not He who is aspiring to us, or who is moving around us; on the contrary, it is we who are aspiring to Him. Though we always move around Him, we do not always keep our glance fixed on Him. We resemble a chorus which always surrounds its leader, but (the members of) which do not always sing in time because they allow their attention to be distracted to some exterior object; while, if they turned towards the leader, they would sing well, and really be with him. Likewise, we always turn around the One, even when we detach ourselves from Him, and cease knowing Him. Our glance is not always fixed on the One; but when we contemplate Him, we attain the purpose of our desires, and enjoy the rest taught by Heraclitus.[18] Then we disagree no more, and really form a divine choric ballet around Him.

FOLLOWING NUMENIUS, PLOTINOS DESCRIBES THE SUPREME AS GIVER.

9. In this choric ballet, the soul sees the source of life, the source of intelligence, the principle of being, the cause of the good, and the root of love. All these entities are derived from the One without diminishing Him. He is indeed no corporeal mass; otherwise the things that are born of Him would be perishable. However, they are eternal, because their principle ever remains the same, because[19] He does not divide Himself to produce them, but remains entire. They persist, just as the light persists so long as the sun remains.[20] Nor are we separated from the One; we are not distant from Him, though corporeal nature,

by approaching us, has attracted us to it (thus drawing us away from the One).[21] But it is in the One that we breathe and have our being.[22] He gave us life not merely at a given moment, only to leave us later; but His giving is perpetual, so long as He remains what He is, or rather, so long as we turn towards Him. There it is that we find happiness, while to withdraw from Him is to fall. It is in Him that our soul rests; it is by rising to that place free from all evil that she is delivered from evils; there she really thinks, there she is impassible, there she really lives. Our present life, in which we are not united with the divinity, is only a trace or adumbration of real life. Real life (which is presence with the divinity) is the actualization of intelligence. It is this actualization of intelligence which begets the divinities by a sort of silent intercourse with the One; thereby begetting beauty, justice and virtue. These are begotten by the soul that is filled with divinity. In Him is her principle and goal; her principle, because it is from there that she proceeds; her goal, because there is the good to which she aspires, so that by returning thither she again becomes what she was. Life here below, in the midst of sense-objects, is for the soul a degradation, an exile, a loss of her wings.[23]

THE PARABLE OF CUPID AND PSYCHE, LEADING UP TO DIVINIZATION.

Another proof that our welfare resides up there is the love that is innate in our souls, as is taught in the descriptions and myths which represent love as the husband of the soul.[24] In fact, since the soul, which is different from the divinity, proceeds from Him, she must necessarily love Him; but when she is on high[25] her love is celestial; here below, her love is only commonplace; for it is on high that dwells the celestial

OF THE GOOD AND THE ONE

Venus (Urania); while here below resides the vulgar and adulterous Venus.[26] Now every soul is a Venus, as is indicated by the myth of the birth of Venus and Cupid, who is supposed to be born simultaneously with her.[27] So long as she remains faithful to her nature, the soul therefore loves the divinity, and desires to unite herself to Him, who seems like the noble father of a bride who has fallen in love with some handsome lover. When however the soul has descended into generation, deceived by the false promises of an adulterous lover, she has exchanged her divine love for a mortal one. Then, at a distance from her father, she yields to all kinds of excesses. Ultimately, however, she grows ashamed of these disorders; she purifies herself, she returns to her father, and finds true happiness with Him. How great her bliss then is can be conceived by such as have not tasted it only by comparing it somewhat to earthly love-unions, observing the joy felt by the lover who succeeds in obtaining her whom he loves. But such mortal and deceptive love is directed only to phantoms; it soon disappears because the real object of our love is not these sense-presentations, which are not the good we are really seeking. On high only is the real object of our love; the only one with which we could unite or identify ourselves, which we could intimately possess, because it is not separated from our soul by the covering of our flesh. This that I say will be acknowledged by any one who has experienced it; he will know that the soul then lives another life, that she advances towards the Divinity, that she reaches Him, possesses Him, and in his condition recognizes the presence of the Dispenser of the true life. Then she needs nothing more. On the contrary, she has to renounce everything else to fix herself in the Divinity alone, to identify herself with Him, and to cut off all that surrounds Him. We must therefore hasten to issue from here below, detaching ourselves so far as possible from the body to which we still have the regret of being chained, making the effort to embrace the Divinity by our whole being, without leaving in us any part that is not in contact with Him. Then the soul can see the Divinity and herself, so far as is possible to her nature. She sees herself shining brilliantly, filled with intelligible light; or rather, she sees herself as a pure light, that is subtle and weightless. She becomes divinity, or, rather, she is divinity. In this condition, the soul is a shining light. If later she falls back into the sense-world, she is plunged into darkness.

WHY DOES THE SOUL AFTER REACHING YONDER NOT STAY THERE?

10. Why does the soul which has risen on high not stay there? Because she has not yet entirely detached herself from things here below. But a time will come when she will uninterruptedly enjoy the vision of the divinity, that is, when she will no longer be troubled by the passions of the body. The part of the soul that sees the divinity is not the one that is troubled (the irrational soul), but the other part (the rational soul). Now she loses the sight of the divinity when she does not lose this knowledge which consists in demonstratings, conjectures and reasonings. In the vision of the divinity, indeed, that which sees is not the reason, but something prior and superior to reason; if that which sees be still united to reason, it then is as that which is seen. When he who sees himself sees, he will see himself as simple, being united to himself as simple, and will feel himself as simple. We should not even say that he will see, but only that he will be what he sees, in case that it would still here be possible to distinguish that which sees from that

which is seen, or to assert that these two things do not form a single one. This assertion, however, would be rash, for in this condition he who sees does not, in the strict sense of the word, see; nor does he imagine two things. He becomes other, he ceases to be himself, he retains nothing of himself. Absorbed in the divinity, he is one with it, like a centre that coincides with another centre. While they coincide, they form but one, though they form two in so far as they remain distinct. In this sense only do we here say that the soul is other than the divinity. Consequently this manner of vision is very difficult to describe. How indeed could we depict as different from us Him who, while we were contemplating Him, did not seem other than ourselves, having come into perfect at-one-ment with us?

ILLUSTRATION FROM THE SECRECY OF THE MYSTERY-RITES.

11. That, no doubt, is the meaning of the mystery-rites' injunction not to reveal their secrets to the uninitiated. As that which is divine is unspeakable, it is ordered that the initiate should not talk thereof to any (uninitiated person) who have not had the happiness of beholding it (the vision).

THE TRANCE OR ENTHEASM OF ECSTASY.

As (this vision of the divinity) did not imply (the existence of) two things, and as he who was identical to Him whom he saw, so that he did not see Him, but was united thereto, if anyone could preserve the memory of what he was while thus absorbed into the Divinity, he would within himself have a faithful image of the Divinity. Then indeed had he attained at-one-ment, containing no difference, neither in regard to himself, nor to other beings. While he was thus transported into the celestial region, there was within him no activity, no anger, nor appetite, nor reason, nor even thought. So much the more, if we dare say so, was he no longer himself, but sunk in trance or enthusiasm, tranquil and solitary with the divinity, he enjoyed an imperturable calm. Contained within his own "being," (or, essence), he did not incline to either side, he did not even turn towards himself, he was indeed in a state of perfect stability, having thus, so to speak, become stability itself.

ABOVE BEAUTY AND ABOVE VIRTUE THIS ECSTATIC SIMPLIFICATION IS A COMMUNION.

In this condition, indeed, the soul busies herself not even with the beautiful things, for she rises above beauty, and passes beyond even the (Stoic) "choir of virtues." Thus he who penetrates into the interior of a sanctuary leaves behind him the statues placed (at the entrance) of the temple. These indeed are the first objects that will strike his view on his exit from the sanctuary, after he shall have enjoyed the interior spectacle, after having entered into intimate communion, not indeed with an image or statue, which would be considered only when he comes out, but with the divinity. The very word "divine spectacle" does not, here, seem sufficient (to express the contemplation of the soul); it is rather an ecstasy, a simplification, a self-abandonment, a desire for intercourse, a perfect quietude, and last, a wish to become indistinguishable from what was contemplated in the sanctuary.[28] Any one who would seek to see the Divinity in any other way would be incapable of enjoying His presence.

THE SPIRITUAL TRUTH OF THE ANCIENT MYSTERIES.

By making use of these mysterious figures, wise interpreters wished to indicate how the divinity might be seen. But the wise hierophant, penetrating the mystery, may, when he has arrived thither, enjoy the veritable vision of what is in the sanctuary. If he have not yet arrived thither, he can at least conceive the invisibility (for physical sight) of That which is in the sanctuary; he can conceive the source and principle of everything, and he recognizes it as the one particular principle worthy of the name. (But when he has succeeded in entering into the sanctuary) he sees the Principle, enters into communication with it, unites like to like, leaving aside no divine thing the soul is capable of acquiring.

SUBSEQUENT ECSTATIC EXPERIENCES OF THE SOUL.

Before obtaining the vision of the divinity, the soul desires what yet remains to be seen. For him, however, who has risen above all things, what remains to be seen is He who is above all other things. Indeed, the nature of the soul will never reach absolute nonentity. Consequently, when she descends, she will fall into evil, that is, nonentity, but not into absolute nonentity. Following the contrary path, she will arrive at something different, namely, herself. From the fact that she then is not in anything different from herself, it does not result that she is within anything, for she remains in herself. That which, without being in essence, remains within itself, necessarily resides in the divinity. Then it ceases to be "being," and so far as it comes into communion with the Divinity it grows superior to "being" (it becomes supra-being). Now he who sees himself as having become divinity, possesses within himself an image of the divinity. If he rise above himself, he will achieve the limit of his ascension, becoming as it were an image that becomes indistinguishable from its model. Then, when he shall have lost sight of the divinity, he may still, by arousing the virtue preserved within himself, and by considering the perfections that adorn his soul, reascend to the celestial region, by virtue rising to Intelligence, and by wisdom to the Divinity Himself.

THE SOUL'S ULTIMATE FATE IS DETACHMENT AND FLIGHT.

Such is the life of the divinities; such is also that of divine and blessed men; detachment from all things here below, scorn of all earthly pleasures, and flight of the soul towards the Divinity that she shall see face to face (that is, "alone with the alone, as thought Numenius).[29]

---

[1] See vi. 6 13 [2] "Being" It has been found impossible, in order to preserve good English idiom, to translate "ousia" by "being," and "to on" by "essence," with uniformity. Where the change has been made, the proper word has been added in parentheses, as here [3] In his Methaphysics, iv. 2. [4] Aristotle, Met. iv. 2. [5] Evidently a pun on forms and ideas. [6] See vi. 27 [7] In the Timaeus not accurately quoted. [8] As Plato said in the Timaeus, 37. [9] See iv. 9 5. [10] See vi 8 11. [11] Odyss xix. 178. [12] See i, 2.2. [13] See iv. 3.1. [14] See ii. 2 2. [15] See the beginning of Plato's Republic, ix. [16] See i 87. [17] Because they do not allow of mutual penetration. [18] See iv. 8 5. [19] As thought Numenius 29. [20] See ii. 3. [21] See i. 8 14. [22] See Acts, xvii. 25, 27, 28. [23] See iv. 3.7, following the Phaedrus of Plato. [24] Cupid and Psyche, as interpreted by Apuleius [25] See iii. 5 2. [26] See iii. 5 4 [27] See iii. 5 7-9. [28] See v 5 11; i 67, 8; v 8 4; vi. 9 11 It has been contended that this was a description of the Isiac temple in Rome. [29] Num. 10.

FIFTH ENNEAD, BOOK ONE.

The Three Principal Hypostases, or Forms of Existence.

AUDACITY THE CAUSE OF HUMAN APOSTASY FROM THE DIVINITY.

1. How does it happen that souls forget their paternal divinity? Having a divine nature, and having originated from the divinity, how could they ever misconceive the divinity or themselves? The origin of their evil is "audacity,"[1] generation, the primary diversity, and the desire to belong to none but themselves.[2] As soon as they have enjoyed the pleasure of an independent life, and by largely making use of their power of self-direction, they advanced on the road that led them astray from their principle, and now they have arrived at such an "apostasy" (distance) from the Divinity, that they are even ignorant that they derive their life from Him. Like children that were separated from their family since birth, and that were long educated away from home finally lose knowledge of their parents and of themselves, so our souls, no longer seeing either the divinity or themselves, have become degraded by forgetfulness of their origin, have attached themselves to other objects, have admired anything rather than themselves, have like prodigals scattered their esteem and love on exterior objects, and have, by breaking the bond that united them to the divinities, disdainfully wandered away from it. Their ignorance of the divinity is therefore caused by excessive valuation of external objects, and their scorn

of themselves. The mere admiration and quest after what is foreign implies, on the soul's part, an acknowledgment of self-depreciation. As soon as a soul thinks that she is worth less than that which is born and which perishes, and considers herself as more despicable and perishable than the object she admires, she could no longer even conceive of the nature and power of the divinity.

CONVERSION IS EFFECTED BY DEPRECIATION OF EXTERNALITIES, AND APPRECIATION OF THE SOUL HERSELF.

Souls in such conditions may be converted to the Divinity, and raised to the supreme Principle, to the One, to the First, by being reasoned with in two ways. First, they may be led to see the worthlessness of the objects they at present esteem;[3] then they must be reminded of the origin and dignity of the soul. The demonstration of the latter point logically precedes that of the former; and if clearly done, should support it.

KINSHIP OF THE HUMAN SOUL WITH THE DIVINE.

It is the second point, therefore, that we shall here discuss. It is related to the study of the object we desire to know; for it is the soul that desires to know that object. Now the soul must first examine her own nature in order to know whether she possess the faculty of contemplating the divinity, if this study be suited to her, and if she may hope for success therein. For indeed if the soul be foreign to divine things, the soul has no business to ferret out their nature. If however a close kinship obtains between them, she both can and should seek to know them.

SOULS ARE DIVINE BECAUSE THE WORLD WAS CREATED BY THE UNIVERSAL SOUL.

2. This is the first reflection of every soul.[4] By an influx of the spirit of life, the universal Soul produced all the animals upon earth, in the air and in the sea, as well as the divine stars, the sun, and the immense heaven. It was the universal Soul that gave form to the heavens, and which presides over their regular revolutions; and she effects all that without mingling with the being to whom she communicates form, movement and life. The universal Soul is far superior to all created things. While the latter are born or die in the measure that she imparts to them, or withdraws from them their life, she herself is "being" and eternal life, because she could not cease being herself. To understand how life can simultaneously be imparted to the universe and to each individual, we must contemplate the universal Soul. To rise to this contemplation, the soul must be worthy of it by nobility, must have liberated herself from error, and must have withdrawn from the objects that fascinate the glances of worldly souls, must have immersed herself in a profound meditation, and she must have succeeded in effecting the silence not only of the agitations of the body that enfolds her, and the tumult of sensations, but also of all that surrounds her. Therefore let silence be kept by all—namely, earth, air, sea, and even heaven. Then let the soul represent to herself the great Soul which, from all sides, overflows into this immovable mass, spreading within it, penetrating into it intimately, illuminating it as the rays of the sun light and gild a dark cloud. Thus the universal Soul, by descending into this world redeemed this great body from the inertia in which it lay, imparting to it movement, life and immortality. Eternally moved by an intelligent power, heaven be-

came a being full of life and felicity. The presence
of the Soul made an admirable whole from what before was no more than in inert corpse, water and
earth, or rather, darkness of matter, which, as Homer[5]
says, was an "object of horror for the divinities."

SOUL-POWER REVEALED IN THE SIMULTANEITY OF CONTROL OVER THE WORLD.

The nature and power of the Soul reveal themselves
still more gloriously in the way she embraces and
governs the world at will. She is present in every
point of this immense body, she animates all its parts,
great and small. Though these may be located in
different parts, she does not divide as they do, she
does not split up to vivify each individual. She vivifies all things simultaneously, ever remaining whole
and indivisible, resembling the intelligence from which
she was begotten by her unity and universality.[6] It
is her power which contains this world of infinite magnitude and variety within the bonds of unity. Only
because of the presence of the Soul are heaven, sun,
and stars divinities; only because of her are we anything; for "a corpse is viler than the vilest dung-hill."[7]

AS LIFE TRANSFIGURES MATTER, SO THE UNIVERSAL SOUL GLORIFIES US.

But if the deities owe their divinity to the universal
Soul, she herself must be a divinity still more venerable. Now our soul is similar to the universal Soul.
Strip her of all coverings, consider her in her pristine
purity, and you will see how precious is the nature of
the soul, how superior she is to everything that is
body.[8] Without the soul, no body is anything but
earth. Even if you add to earth fire, water and air,
still there is nothing that need claim your veneration.
If it be the Soul that imparts beauty to the body, why

should we forget the souls within ourselves, while prostituting our admiration on other objects? If 't be the soul that you admire in them, why do you not admire her within yourselves?

THE SOUL AS THE HYPOSTATIC ACTUALIZATION OF INTELLIGENCE.

3. Since the nature of the Soul is so divine and precious, you may be assured of being able to reach the divinity through her; with her you can ascend to Him. You will not need to search for Him far from yourself; nor will there be several intermediaries between yourself and Him. To reach Him, take as guide the divinest and highest part of the Soul, the power from which she proceeds, and by which she impinges on the intelligible world. Indeed, in spite of the divinity which we have attributed to her, the Soul is no more than an image of Intelligence. As the exterior word (speech) is the image of the (interior) word (of thought?) of the soul, the Soul herself is the word and actualization of Intelligence.[9] She is the life which escapes from Intelligence to form another hypostatic form of existence, just as the fire contains the latent heat which constitutes its essence ("being"), and also the heat that radiates from it outside. Nevertheless, the Soul does not entirely issue from within Intelligence; she does partly reside therein, but also forms (a nature) distinct therefrom. As the Soul proceeds from Intelligence, she is intelligible; and the manifestation of her intellectual power is discursive reason. From Intelligence the Soul derives her perfection, as well as her existence; only in comparison with Intelligence does the Soul seem imperfect. The Soul, therefore, is the hypostatic substance that proceeds from Intelligence, and when the Soul contemplates Intelligence the soul is reason actual-

ized. Indeed, while the soul contemplates Intelligence, the Soul intimately possesses the things she thinks; from her own resources she draws the actualizations she produces; these intellectual and pure actualizations are indeed the Soul's only characteristic activities. Those of an inferior nature really proceed from a foreign principle; they are passions.

THE SOUL'S RELATION TO INTELLIGENCE IS THAT OF MATTER TO FORM.

Intelligence therefore, makes the Soul diviner, because Intelligence (as a father) begets the Soul, and grants its (helpful) presence to the Soul. Nothing intervenes between them but the distinction between their natures. The Soul is to Intelligence in the same relation as that obtaining between form and matter.[10] Now the very matter of Intelligence is beautiful, because it has an intellectual form, and is simple. How great then, must Intelligence be, if it be still greater than the Soul.

THE INTELLIGIBLE WORLD IS THE ARCHETYPE OF OURS.

4. The dignity of Intelligence may be appreciated in still another way. After having admired the magnitude and beauty of the sense-world, the eternal regularity of its movement, the visible or hidden divinities, the animals and plants it contains, we may (taking our direction from all this), rise to this world's archetype, a more real World. There we may contemplate all the intelligible entities which are as eternal as the intelligible world, and which there subsist within perfect knowledge and life. There preside pure intelligence and ineffable wisdom; there is located the real Saturnian realm,[11] which is nothing else than pure intelligence. This indeed embraces every immortal essence, every intelligence, every divinity, every soul;

everything there is eternal and immutable. Since its condition is blissful, why should Intelligence change? Since it contains everything, why should it aspire to anything? Since it is sovereignly perfect, what need of development would it have? Its perfection is so much completer, since it contains nothing but perfect things, and since it thinks them; it thinks them, not because it seeks to know them, but because it possesses them.[12] Its felicity is not in any way contingent on anything else; itself is true eternity, of which time furnishes a moving image of the sphere of the soul. Indeed, the soul's action is successive, and divided by the different objects that attract its attention. Now it thinks Socrates, and then it thinks a horse; never does it grasp but one part of reality, while intelligence always embraces all things simultaneously. Intelligence, therefore, possesses all things immovable in identity. It is; it never has anything but the present;[13] it has no future, for it already is all it could ever later become; it has no past, for no intelligible entity ever passes away; all of them subsist in an eternal present, all remain identical, satisfied with their present condition. Each one is both intelligence and existence; all together, they are universal Intelligence, universal Existence.

ABOVE INTELLIGENCE AND EXISTENCE IS THEIR SIMULTANEOUS PRINCIPLE.

Intelligence exists (as intelligence) because it thinks existence. Existence exists (as existence) because, on being thought, it makes intelligence exist and thinks.[14] There must therefore exist something else which makes intelligence think, and existence exist, and which consequently is their common principle. In existence they are contemporaneous and substantial, and can never fail each other. As intelligence and existence constitute a duality, their common principle in this consubstantial unity that they form, and which is simultaneously existence and intelligence, the thinking subject and the object thought; intelligence as thinking subject, and existence as object thought; for thought simultaneously implies difference and identity.

THE SIX CATEGORIES FROM WHICH ALL THINGS ARE DERIVED.

The first principles, therefore, are existence and intelligence, identity and difference, movement and rest.[15] Rest is the condition of identity; movement is the condition of thought, since the latter presupposes the differences of the thinking subject and of the object thought, and because it is silent if reduced to unity. The elements of thought (subject and object) must thus stand in the relation of differences, but also in that of unity, because they form a consubstantial unity, and because there is a common element in all that is derived therefrom. Besides, here difference is nothing else than distinction. The plurality formed by elements of thought constitutes quantity and number;[16] and the characteristic of every element, quality.[17] From these first principles (the categories, that are the genera of being) all things are derived.

THE SOUL AS NUMBER CONNECTED WITH INTELLIGENCE.

5. Thus the human soul is full of this divinity (of Intelligence); she is connected therewith by these (categories), unless the soul (purposely) withdraws from (that intelligence). The Soul approaches Intelligence, and thus having been unified, the Soul wonders, 'Who has begotten this unity?' It must be He who is simple, who is prior to all multiplicity, who imparts to Intelligence its existence and manifoldness, and who consequently produces number. Number, indeed, is not something primitive; for the One is prior to the

"pair." The latter ranks only second, being begotten and defined by unity, by itself being indefinite. As soon as it is defined, it is a number in so far as it is a "being"; for these are the grounds on which the Soul also is a number.[18]

THOUGHT IS ACTUALIZATION OF SIGHT, AND BOTH FORM BUT ONE THING.

Besides everything that is a mass or a magnitude could not occupy the first rank in nature; those gross objects which are by sensation considered beings must be ranked as inferior. In seeds, it is not the moist element that should be valued, but the invisible principle, number, and the (seminal) reason. Number and "pair" are only names for the reasons (ideas) and intelligence. The "pair" is indeterminate so far as it plays the part of substrate (in respect to unity). The number that is derived from the pair, and the one, constitute every kind of form, so that Intelligence has a shape which is determined by the ideas[19] begotten within it. Its shape is derived in one respect from the one, and in another respect, from itself, just like actualized sight. Thought, indeed, is actualized sight, and both these entities (the faculty and the actualization) form but one.

MYSTERY OR DERIVATION OF SECOND FROM FIRST.

6. How does Intelligence see, and what does it see? How did the Second issue from the First, how was it born from the First, so as that the Second might see the First? For the soul now understands that these principles must necessarily exist. She seeks to solve the problem often mooted by ancient philosophers. "If the nature of the One be such as we have outlined, how does everything derive its hypostatic substance (or, form of existence), manifoldness, duality, and

number from the First? Why did the First not remain within Himself, why did He allow the leakage of manifoldness seen in all beings, and which we are seeking to trace back to the First?" We shall tell it. But we must, to begin with, invoke the Divinity, not by the utterance of words, but by raising our souls to Him in prayer. Now the only way to pray is (for a person), when alone, to advance towards the One, who is entirely alone. To contemplate Unity, we must retire to our inner sanctuary, and there remain tranquil above all things (in ecstasy); then we must observe the statues which as it were are situated outside of (soul and intelligence), and in front of everything, the statue that shines in the front rank (Unity), contemplating it in a manner suitable to its nature (in the mysteries).[20]

GENERATION IS THE RADIATION OF AN IMAGE.

All that is moved must have a direction towards which it is moved; we must therefore conclude that that which has no direction towards which it is moved must be at a stand-still, and that anything born of this principle must be born without causing this principle to cease being turned towards itself. We must, however, remove from our mind the idea of a generation operated within time, for we are here treating of eternal things. When we apply to them the conception of generation, we mean only a relation of causality and effect. What is begotten by the One must be begotten by Him without any motion on the part of the One; if He were moved, that which was begotten from Him would, because of this movement, be ranked third, instead of second.[21] Therefore, since the One is immovable, He produces the hypostatic (form of existence) which is ranked second, without volition, consent, or any kind of movement. What conception are we then to form of this generation of Intelligence by this immovable Cause? It is a radiation of light which escapes without disturbing its quietness, like the splendor which emanates perpetually from the sun, without affecting its quietness, which surrounds it without leaving it. Thus all things, in so far as they remain within existence, necessarily draw from their own essence ("being") and produce externally a certain nature that depends on their power, and that is the image of the archetype from which it is derived.[22] Thus does fire radiate heat; thus snow spreads cold. Perfumes also furnish a striking example of this process; so long as they last, they emit exhalations in which everything that surrounds them participates. Everything that has arrived to its point of perfection begets something. That which is eternally perfect begets eternally; and that which it begets is eternal though inferior to the generating principle. What then should we think of Him who is supremely perfect? Does He not beget? On the contrary, He begets that which, after Him, is the greatest. Now that which, after Him, is the most perfect, is the second rank principle, Intelligence. Intelligence contemplates Unity, and needs none but Him; but the Unity has no need of Intelligence. That which is begotten by the Principle superior to Intelligence can be nothing if not Intelligence; for it is the best after the One, since it is superior to all other beings. The Soul, indeed, is the word and actualization of Intelligence, just as Intelligence is word and actualization of the One. But the Soul is an obscure word. Being an image of Intelligence, she must contemplate Intelligence, just as the latter, to subsist, must contemplate the One. Intelligence contemplates the One, not because of any separation therefrom, but only because it is after the One. There is no intermediary between the One and Intelligence, any more than between Intelligence and the Soul. Every begotten being desires to unite with the principle that begets it, and loves it, especially when the begetter and the begotten are alone. Now when the begetter is supremely perfect, the begotten must be so intimately united to Him as to be separated from Him only in that it is distinct from Him.

INTELLIGIBLE REST IS THE DETERMINATION AND FORM BY WHICH THEY SUBSIST.

7. We call Intelligence the image of the One. Let us explain this. It is His image because Intelligence is, in a certain respect, begotten by Unity, because Intelligence possesses much of the nature of its father, and because Intelligence resembles Him as light resembles the sun. But the One is not Intelligence; how then can the hypostatic (form of existence) begotten by the One be Intelligence? By its conversion towards the One, Intelligence sees Him; now it is this vision[23] which constitutes Intelligence. Every faculty that perceives another being is sensation or intelligence; but sensation is similar to a straight line, while intelligence resembles a circle.[24] Nevertheless, the circle is divisible, while Intelligence is indivisible; it is one, but, while being one, it also is the power of all things. Now thought considers all these things (of which Intelligence is the power), by separating itself, so to speak, from this power; otherwise, Intelligence would not exist. Indeed, Intelligence has a consciousness of the reach of its power, and this consciousness constitutes its nature. Consequently, Intelligence determines its own nature by the means of the power it derived from the One; and at the same time Intelligence sees that its nature ("being") is a part of the entities which belong to the One, and that proceed from Him. Intelligence sees that it owes all its force to the One, and that it is due to Him that Intelligence has the privilege of being a "being" (or, essence). Intelligence sees that, as it itself is divisible, it derives from the One, which is indivisible, all the entities it possesses, life and

thought; because the One is not any of these things. Everything indeed is derived from the One, because it is not contained in a determinate form; it simply is the One, while in the order of beings Intelligence is all things. Consequently the One is not any of the things that Intelligence contains; it is only the principle from which all of them are derived. That is why they are "being," for they are already determined, and each has a kind of shape. Existence should be comtemplated, not in indetermination, but on the contrary in determination and rest. Now, for Intelligible entities, rest consists in determination, and shape by which they subsist.

MYTHS OF SATURN, JUPITER AND RHEA

The Intelligence that deserves to be called the purest intelligence, therefore, cannot have been born from any source, other than the first Principle. It must, from its birth, have begotten all beings, all the beauty of ideas, all the intelligible deities; for it is full of the things it has begotten; it devours them in the sense that it itself retains all of them, that it does not allow them to fall into matter, nor be born of Rhea.[25] That is the meaning of the mysteries and myths; "Saturn, the wisest of the divinities, was born before Jupiter, and devoured his children." Here Saturn represents intelligence, big with its conceptions, and perfectly pure.[26] They add, "Jupiter, as soon as he was grown, in his turn begat." As soon as Intelligence is perfect, it begets the Soul, by the mere fact of its being perfect, and because so great a power cannot remain sterile. Here again the begotten being had to be inferior to its principle, had to represent its image, had, by itself, to be indeterminate, and had later to be determined and formed by the principle that begat it. What Intelligence begets is a reason, a hypostatic form of existence whose nature it is to reason. The latter moves around Intelligence; is the light that surrounds it, the ray that springs from it. On the one hand it is bound to Intelligence, fills itself with it; enjoys it, participates in it, deriving its intellectual operations from it. On the other hand, it is in contact with inferior things, or rather, begets them. Being thus begotten by the Soul, these things are necessarily less good than the Soul, as we shall further explain. The sphere of divine things ends with the Soul.

PLATO TEACHES THREE SPHERES OF EXISTENCE.[47]

8. This is how Plato establishes three degrees in the hierarchy of being[27]: "Everything is around the king of all." He is here speaking of first rank entities. He adds, "What is of the second order is around the second principle; and what is of the third order is around the third principle." Plato[28] further says that "God is the father of the cause." By cause, he means Intelligence; for, in the system of Plato, it is Intelligence which plays the part of demiurgic creator. Plato adds that it is this power that forms the Soul in the cup.[29] As the cause is intelligence, Plato applies the name of father to the absolute Good, the principle superior to Intelligence and superior to "Being." In several passages he calls the Idea "existence and intelligence." He therefore really teaches that Intelligence is begotten from the Good, and the Soul from Intelligence. This teaching, indeed, is not new; it has been taught from the most ancient times, but without being brought out in technical terms. We claim to be no more than the interpreters of the earlier philosophers, and to show by the very testimony of Plato that they held the same views as we do.

THIS DOCTRINE TAUGHT BY PARMENIDES.

The first philosopher who taught this was Parmenides, who identified Existence and Intelligence, and who does not place existence among sense-objects, "for, thought is the same thing as existence."[30] He adds[31] that existence is immovable, although being thought. Parmenides thus denies all corporeal movement in existence, so as that it might always remain the same. Further, Parmenides[32] compares existence to a sphere, because it contains everything, drawing thought not from without, but from within itself. When Parmenides, in his writings, mentions the One, he means the cause, as if he recognized that this unity (of the intelligible being) implied manifoldness. In the dialogue of Plato he speaks with greater accuracy, and distinguishes three principles: the First, the absolute One; the second, the manifold one; the third, the one and the manifold. He therefore, as we do, reaches three natures.

ANAXAGORAS TEACHES THE SAME THING.

9. Anaxagoras, who teaches a pure and unmingled Intelligence[33] also insists that the first Principle is simple, and that the One is separated from sense-objects. But, as he lived in times too ancient, he has not treated this matter in sufficient detail.

HERACLITUS ALSO TAUGHT THE SAME THING.

Heraclitus also taught the eternal and intelligible One; for Heraclitus holds that bodies are ceaselessly "becoming" (that is, developing), and that they are in a perpetual state of flux.[34]

EMPEDOCLES TAUGHT THE SAME THING.

In the system of Empedocles, discord divides, and concord unites; now this second principle is posited as incorporeal, and the elements play the part of matter.[35]

ARISTOTLE TAUGHT THE SAME THING.

Aristotle, who lived at a later period, says that the First Principle is separated from (sense-objects), and that it is intelligible.[36] But when Aristotle says that He thinks himself, Aristotle degrades Him from the first rank. Aristotle also asserts the existence of other intelligible entities in a number equal to the celestial spheres, so that each one of them might have a principle of motion. About the intelligible entities, therefore, Aristotle advances a teaching different from that of Plato, and as he has no plausible reason for this change, he alleges necessity. A well-grounded objection might here be taken against him. It seems more reasonable to suppose that all the spheres co-ordinated in a single system should, all of them, stand in relation to the One and the First. About Aristotle's views this question also might be raised: do the intelligible entities depend on the One and First, or are there several principles for the intelligible entities? If the intelligible entities depend on the One, they will no doubt be arranged symmetrically, as, in the sense-sphere, are the spheres, each of which contains another, and of which a single One, exterior to the others, contains them, and dominates them all. Thus, in this case, the first intelligible entity will contain all entities up there, and will be the intelligible world. Just as the spheres are not empty, as the first is full of stars, and as each of the others also is full of them, so above their motors will contain many entities, and everything will have a more real existence. On the other hand, if each of the intelligible entities is a principle, all will be contingent. How then will they unite their action, and will they, by agreement, contribute in producing a single effect, which is the harmony of heaven? Why should sense-objects, in heaven, equal in number their intelligible motors? Again, why are there several of these, since they are incorporeal, and since no matter separates them from each other?

WHAT THE PYTHAGOREANS TAUGHT ON THE SUBJECT.

Among ancient philosophers, those who most faithfully followed the doctrine of Pythagoras, of his disciples, and of Pherecydes, have specially dealt with the intelligible.[87] Some of them have committed their opinions to their written works; others have set them forth only in discussions that have not been preserved in writing. There are others of them, also, who have left us nothing on the subject.

TO THE THREE PRINCIPLES IN THE UNIVERSE MUST CORRESPOND THREE PRINCIPLES IN US.

10. Above existence, therefore, is the One. This has by us been proved as far as could reasonably be expected, and as far as such subjects admit of demonstration. In the second rank are Existence and Intelligence; in the third, the Soul. But if these three principles, the One, Intelligence, and the Soul, as we have said, obtain in nature, three principles must also obtain within us. I do not mean that these three principles are in sense-objects, for they are separate therefrom; they are outside of the sense-world, as the three divine principles are outside of the celestial sphere, and, according to Plato's expression,[88] they constitute the "the interior man." Our soul, therefore, is something divine; it has a nature different (from sense-nature), which conforms to that of the universal Soul. Now the perfect Soul possesses intelligence; but we must distinguish between the intelligence that reasons (the discursive reason), and the Intelligence that furnishes the principles of reasoning (pure intelligence). The discursive reason of the soul has no need, for operation, of any bodily organ;[89] in its operations, it

preserves all its purity, so that it is capable of reasoning purely. When separated from the body, it must, without any hesitation, be ranked with highest intellectual entities. There is no need of locating it in space; for, if it exist within itself, outside of body, in an immaterial condition, it is evidently not mingled with the body, and has none of its nature. Consequently Plato[40] says, "The divinity has spread the Soul around the world." What he here means is that a part of the Soul remains in the intelligible world. Speaking of our soul he also says, "she hides her head in heaven."[41] He also advises us to wean the soul from the body; and he does not refer to any local separation, which nature alone could establish. He means that the soul must not incline towards the body, must not abandon herself to the phantoms of imagination, and must not, thus, become alienated from reason. He means that the soul should try to elevate to the intelligible world her lower part which is established in the sense-world, and which is occupied in fashioning the body.[42]

THERE MUST BE AN OBJECTIVE JUSTICE AND BEAUTY TO WHICH WE ARE INTIMATELY UNITED.

11. Since the rational soul makes judgments about what is just or beautiful, and decides whether some object is beautiful, whether such an action be just, there must exist an immutable justice and beauty from which discursive reason draws its principles.[43] Otherwise, how could such reasonings take place? If the soul at times reasons about justice and beauty, but at times does not reason about them, we must possess within ourselves the intelligence which, instead of reasoning, ever possesses justice and beauty; further, we must within us possess the cause and Principle of Intelligence, the Divinity, which is not divisible, which sub-

sists, not in any place, but in Himself; who is contemplated by a multitude of beings, by each of the beings fitted to receive Him, but which remains distinct from these beings, just as the centre subsists within itself, while all the radii come from the circumference to centre themselves in it.[44] Thus we ourselves, by one of the parts of ourselves, touch the divinity, unite ourselves with Him and are, so to speak, suspended from Him; and we are founded upon Him (we are "edified" by Him) when we turn towards Him.

THESE PRINCIPLES LAST EVER, EVEN THOUGH WE ARE DISTRACTED FROM THEM.

12. How does it happen that we possess principles that are so elevated, almost in spite of ourselves, and for the most part without busying ourselves about them? For there are even men who never notice them. Nevertheless these principles, that is, intelligence, and the principle superior to intelligence, which ever remains within itself (that is, the One), these two principles are ever active. The case is similar with the soul. She is always in motion; but the operations that go on within her are not always perceived; they reach us only when they succeed in making themselves felt. When the faculty that is active within us does not transmit its action to the power that feels, this action is not communicated to the entire soul; however, we may not be conscious thereof because, although we possess sensibility, it is not this power, but the whole soul that constitutes the man.[45] So long as life lasts, each power of the soul exercises its proper function by itself; but we know it only when communication and perception occur. In order to perceive the things within us, we have to turn our perceptive faculties towards them, so that (our soul) may apply her whole attention thereto.[46] The person

that desires to hear one sound must neglect all others, and listen carefully on its approach. Thus we must here close our senses to all the noises that besiege us, unless necessity force us to hear them, and to preserve our perceptive faculty pure and ready to listen to the voices that come from above.

[1] By virtue of which, according to the Pythagoreans, the dyad "dared" to issue from the unity. [2] That is the desire which leads souls to separate themselves primitively from the divinity, and to unite themselves to bodies. [3] We have seen this elsewhere, i 31. [4] See ii 23. [5] Iliad xx. 65. [6] See vi. 44. [7] As said Heraclitus, Plutarch, Banquet, iv. 4. [8] See iv. 7.10. [9] See i. 23; iv 311. [10] See iii. 9.5. [11] As thought Plato in his Cratylus, C. xi 39, and Macrobins, in his Commentary on the Dream of Scipio, i. 11. [12] See i 8.2; ii. 92. [13] See iii. 72-4. [14] See v. 92, 7 [15] See vi. 2. [16] See vi 8 [17] See vi. 3. [18] See iii. 61. [19] Pun on "ideas" and "forms." [20] vi 9. 11. This seems to refer to the Roman temple of Isis in front of which stood the statues of the divinities, vi. 9.11. [21] Would be soul, instead of intelligence. [22] See v. 41. [23] See iii. 8.10. [24] As thought Plato, Laws, x; see ii. 23. [25] See iii 619 [26] As thought Plato, in the Cratylos, C. xi. 39. [27] See Plato's Second Letter, 312; in English, Burges, p. 482; i 82. [28] In Timaeus, 34. [29] In his Timaeus, C43. [30] As quoted by Clemens Al. Strom. vi. p. 627. [31] In Simplicius, Comm. in Phys Arist, 9. [32] See Plato's Sophists, C244. [33] See ii. 77. [34] See ii 12 [35] See ii 47. [36] See Metaph xii 78. [37] Referring to Numenius's work on "The Good," and on the "Immateriality of the Soul." [38] In the Acibiades, C36. [39] See i. 19. [40] In his Timaeus, C30. [41] In the Phaedrus. [42] See iii 65 [43] See v. 33. [44] From the circumference, see, iii. 87. [45] Cicero, Tusculans, i. 22. [46] See i 49. [47] This paragraph is founded on Numenius 36, 39.

FIFTH ENNEAD, BOOK TWO.

Of Generation, and of the Order of things that Rank Next After the First.

WHY FROM UNITY THIS MANIFOLD WORLD WAS
ABLE TO COME FORTH.

1. The One is all things, and is none of these things. The Principle of all things cannot be all things.[1] It is all things only in the sense that all things coexist within it. But in it, they "are" not yet, but only "will be."[2] How then could the manifoldness of all beings issue from the One, which is simple and identical, which contains no diversity or duality? It is just because nothing is contained within it, that everything can issue from it.[3] In order that essence might exist, the One could not be (merely) essence, but had to be the 'father' of essence, and essence had to be its first-begotten. As the One is perfect, and acquires nothing, and has no need or desire, He has, so to speak, superabounded, and this superabundance has produced a different nature.[4] This different nature of the One turned towards Him, and by its conversion, arrived at the fulness (of essence). Then it had the potentiality of contemplating itself, and thus determined itself as Intelligence. Therefore, by resting near the One, it became Essence; and by contemplating itself, became Intelligence. Then by fixing itself within itself to contemplate itself, it simultaneously became Essence-and-Intelligence.

BY SIMILAR EFFUSION OF SUPERABUNDANCE INTELLIGENCE CREATED THE SOUL.

Just like the One, it was by effusion of its power that Intelligence begat something similar to itself. Thus from Intelligence emanated an image, just as Intelligence emanated from the One. The actualization that proceeds from Essence (and Inelligence) is the universal Soul. She is born of Intelligence, and determines herself without Intelligence issuing from itself, just as Intelligence itself proceeded from the One without the One ceasing from His repose.

SIMILARLY THE UNIVERSAL SOUL, BY PROCESSION, BEGETS NATURE.

Nor does the universal Soul remain at rest, but enters in motion to beget an image of herself. On the one hand, it is by contemplation of the principle from which she proceeds that she achieves fulness; on the other hand, it is by advancing on a path different from, and opposed to (the contemplation of Intelligence), that she begets an image of herself, sensation, and the nature of growth.[6] Nevertheless, nothing is detached or separated from the superior principle which begets her. Thus the human soul seems to reach down to within that of (plant) growth.[7] She descends therein inasmuch as the plant derives growth from her. Nevertheless it is not the whole soul that passes into the plant. Her presence there is limited to her descent towards the lower region, and in so far as she produces another hypostatic substance, by virtue of her procession, which occurs by her condescension to care for the things below her. But the higher part of the Soul, that which depends on Intelligence, allows the Intelligence to remain within itself. . . .

What[8] then does the soul which is in the plant

do? Does she not beget anything? She begets the plant in which she resides. This we shall have to study from another standpoint.

PROCESSION IS UNIVERSAL FROM HIGHEST TO LOWEST.

2. We may say that there is a procession from the First to the last; and in this procession each occupies its proper place. The begotten (being) is subordinated to the begetting (being). On the other hand, it becomes similar to the thing to which it attaches, so long as it remains attached thereto. When the soul passes into the plant, there is one of her parts that unites thereto (the power of growth); but besides, it is only the most audacious[9] and the most senseless part of her that descends so low. When the soul passes into the brute, it is because she is drawn thereto by the predominance of the power of sensation.[10] When she passes into man, it is because she is led to do so by the exercise of discursive reason, either by the movement by which she proceeds from Intelligence, because the soul has a characteristic intellectual power, and consequently has the power to determine herself to think, and in general, to act.

THE SOUL IS NOWHERE BUT IN A PRINCIPLE THAT IS EVERYWHERE AND NOWHERE.

Now, let us retrace our steps. When we cut the twigs or the branches of a tree, where goes the plant-soul that was in them? She returns to her principle,[11] for no local difference separates her therefrom. If we cut or burn the root, whither goes the power of growth present therein? It returns to the plant-power of the universal Soul, which does not change place, and does not cease being where it was. It ceases to be where it was only when returning to its principle; otherwise, it passes into another plant; for it is not obliged to contract, or to retire within itself. If, on the contrary, it retire, it retires within the superior power.[12] Where, in her turn, does the latter reside? Within Intelligence, and without changing, location; for the Soul is not within any location, and Intelligence still less. Thus the Soul is nowhere; she is in a principle which, being nowhere, is everywhere.[13]

THE SOUL MAY REMAIN IN AN INTERMEDIATE LIFE.

If, while returning to superior regions, the soul stops before reaching the highest, she leads a life of intermediary nature.[14]

ALL THESE THINGS ARE IN INTELLIGENCE, WITHOUT CONSTITUTING IT.

All these entities (the universal Soul and her images) are Intelligence, though none of them constitutes Intelligence. They are Intelligence in this respect, that they proceed therefrom. They are not Intelligence in this respect that only by dwelling within itself Intelligence has given birth to them.[15]

THE WHOLE UNIVERSE IS ONE IMMENSE CONCATENATION OF ALL THINGS.

Thus, in the universe, life resembles an immense chain in which every being occupies a point, begetting the following being, and begotten by the preceding one, and ever distinct, but not separate from the (upper) generating Being, and the (lower) begotten being into which it passes without being absorbed.

---

[1] See iii. 9.9 [2] See iii. 8.9. [3] iii. 9.4 [4] iii. 8.9. [5] See v. 1.7. [6] See i 1.8; iv. 9.3. [7] See iii. 4.1, 2. [8] Fragment belonging here, apparently, but misplaced at end of next paragraph [9] See v. 1.1. [10] See iii 4.2. [11] See iv. 4.29; iv. 5.7. [12] That is, in the principal power of the universal soul, see ii. 3.18 [13] See vi. 5; that is, within intelligence. [14] Between celestial and terrestrial life; see iii. 4.6. [15] See iii. 8.7.

SECOND ENNEAD, BOOK FOUR.

Of Matter.

MATTER AS SUBSTRATE AND RESIDENCE OF FORMS.

1. Matter is a substrate (or subject) underlying nature, as thought Aristotle,[1] and a residence for forms. Thus much is agreed upon by all authors who have studied matter, and who have succeeded in forming a clear idea of this kind of nature; but further than this, there is no agreement. Opinions differ as to whether matter is an underlying nature (as thought Aristotle),[2] as to its receptivity, and to what it is receptive.

THE STOIC CONCEPTION OF MATTER.

(The Stoics, who condensed Aristotle's categories to four, substrate, quality-mode and relation),[3] who admit the existence of nothing else than bodies, acknowledge no existence other than that contained by bodies. They insist that there is but one kind of matter, which serves as substrate to the elements, and that it constitutes "being"; that all other things are only affections ("passions") of mattter, or modified matter: as are the elements. The teachers of this doctrine do not hesitate to introduce this matter into the (very nature of the) divinities, so that their supreme divinity is no more than modified matter.[4] Besides, of matter they make a body, calling it a "quantityless body," still attributing to it magnitude.

MATTER ACCORDING TO THE PYTHAGOREANS, PLATONISTS AND ARISTOTELIANS.

Others (Pythagoreans, Platonists and Aristotelians) insist that matter is incorporeal. Some even distinguish two kinds of matter, first, the (Stoic) substrate of bodies, mentioned above; the other matter being of a superior nature, the substrate of forms and incorporeal beings.

THE ARISTOTELIAN INTELLIGIBLE MATTER.

2. Let us first examine whether this (latter intelligible) matter exists, how it exists, and what it is. If (the nature) of matter be something indeterminate, and shapeless, and if in the perfect (intelligible beings) there must not be anything indeterminate or shapeless, it seems as if there could not be any matter in the intelligible world. As every (being) is simple, it could not have any need of matter which, by uniting with something else, constitutes something composite. Matter is necessary in begotten beings, which make one thing arise out of another; for it is such beings that have led to the conception of matter (as thought Aristotle).[5] It may however be objected that in unbegotten beings matter would seem useless. Whence could it have originated to enter in (among intelligible beings), and remain there? If it were begotten, it must have been so by some principle; if it be eternal, it must have had several principles; in which case the beings that occupy the first rank would seem to be contingent. Further, if (in those beings) form come to join matter, their union will constitute a body, so that the intelligible (entities) will be corporeal.

INTELLIGIBLE MATTER IS NOT SHAPELESS.

3. To this it may first be answered that the indeterminate should not be scorned everywhere, nor

that which is conceived of as shapeless, even if this be the substrate of the higher and better entities; for we might call even the soul indeterminate, in respect to intelligence and reason, which give it a better shape and nature. Besides, when we say that intelligible things are composite (of matter and form), this is not in the sense in which the word is used of bodies. Even reasons would thus be called composite, and by their actualization form another alleged composite, nature, which aspires to form. If, in the intelligible world, the composite tend toward some other principle, or depend thereon, the difference between this composite and bodies is still better marked. Besides, the matter of begotten things ceaselessly changes form, while the matter of the intelligible entities ever remains identical. Further, matter here below is subject to other conditions (than in the intelligible world). Here below, indeed, matter is all things only partly, and is all things only successively; consequently, amidst these perpetual changes nothing is identical, nothing is permanent. Above, on the contrary, matter is all things simultaneously, and possessing all things, could not transform itself. Consequently, matter is never shapeless above; for it is not even shapeless here below. Only the one (intelligible matter) is situated differently from the other (sense-matter). Whether, however, (intelligible matter) be begotten, or be eternal, is a question that cannot be determined until we know what it is.

THE NATURE OF IDEAS IMPLIES AN INDIVIDUAL FORM, WHICH AGAIN IMPLIES A SUBSTRATE.

4. Granting now the existence of ideas, whose reality has been demonstrated elsewhere,[6] we must draw their legitimate consequences. Necessarily ideas have something in common, inasmuch as they are manifold; and since they differ from each other, they

must also have something individual. Now the individuality of any idea, the difference that distinguishes it from any other, consists of its particular shape. But form, to be received, implies a substrate, that might be determined by the difference. There is therefore always a matter that receives form, and there is always a substrate (even in ideas, whose matter is genus, and whose form is its difference).

RELYING ON THE PUN BETWEEN WORLD AND ADORNMENT, PLOTINOS CONCLUDES THAT IF THE INTELLIGIBLE WORLD BE THE IMAGE OF THIS, IT MUST ALSO BE A COMPOSITE OF FORM AND MATTER.

Besides, our world is an image of the intelligible world. Now as our world is a composite of matter (and form), there must be matter also on high (that is, in the intelligible world). Otherwise, how could we call the intelligible world "kosmos" (that is, either world, or adornment), unless we see matter (receiving) form therein? How could we find form there, without (a residence) that should receive it? That world is indivisible, taken in an absolute sense; but in a relative sense, is it divisible? Now if its parts be distinct from each other, their division or distinction is a passive modification of matter; for what can be divided, must be matter. If the multitude of ideals constitute an indivisible being, this multitude, which resides in a single being, has this single being as substrate, that is, as matter and is its shapes. This single, yet varied substrate conceives of itself as shapeless, before conceiving of itself as varied. If then by thought you abstract from it variety, forms, reasons, and intelligible characteristics, that which is prior is indeterminate and shapeless; then there will remain in this (subject) none of the things that are in it and with it.

OF MATTER

THE BOTTOM OF EVERYTHING IS MATTER, WHICH IS RELATIVE DARKNESS.

5. If, we were to conclude that there were no matter in intelligible entities, because they were immutable, and because, in them, matter is always combined with (shape), we would be logically compelled to deny the existence of matter in bodies; for the matter of bodies always has a form, and every body is always complete (containing a form and a matter). Each body, however, is none the less composite, and intelligence observes its doubleness; for it splits until it arrives to simplicity, namely, to that which can no longer be decomposed; it does not stop until it reaches the bottom things. Now the bottom of each thing is matter. Every matter is dark, because the reason (the form) is the light, and because intelligence is the reason.[7] When, in an object, intelligence considers the reason, it considers as dark that which is below reason, or light. Likewise, the eye, being luminous, and directing its gaze on light and on the colors which are kinds of light, considers what is beneath, and hidden by the colors, as dark and material.

INTELLIGIBLE MATTER CONSISTS OF REAL BEING, ESPECIALLY AS SHAPED.

Besides, there is a great difference between the dark bottom of intelligible things and that of sense-objects; there is as much difference between the matter of the former and of the latter as there is between their form. The divine matter, on receiving the form that determines it, possesses an intellectual and determinate life. On the contrary, even when the matter of the bodies becomes something determinate, it is neither alive nor thinking; it is dead, in spite of its borrowed beauty.[8] As the shape (of sense-objects) is only an image, their substrate also is only an image. But as the shape (of intelligible entities) possesses veritable (reality), their substrate is of the same nature We have, therefore, full justification for calling matter "being," that is, when referring to intelligible matter; for the substrate of intelligible entities really is "being," especially if conceived of together with its inherent (form). For "being" is the luminous totality (or complex of matter and form). To question the eternity of intelligible matter is tantamount to questioning that of ideas; indeed, intelligible entities are begotten in the sense that they have a principle; but they are non-begotten in the sense that their existence had no beginning, and that, from all eternity, they derive their existence from their principle. Therefore they do not resemble the things that are always becoming, as our world; but, like the intelligible world, they ever exist.

THE CATEGORIES OF MOVEMENT AND DIFFERENCE APPLIED TO INTELLIGIBLES.

The difference that is in the intelligible world ever produces matter; for, in that world, it is the difference that is the principle of matter, as well as of primary motion. That is why the latter is also called difference, because difference and primary motion were born simultaneously.[9]

The movement and difference, that proceed from the First (the Good), are indeterminate, and need it, to be determinate. Now they determine each other when they turn towards it. Formerly, matter was as indeterminate as difference; it was not good because it was not yet illuminated by the radiance of the First. Since the First is the source of all light, the object that receives light from the First does not always possess light; this object differs from light, and possesses light as something alien, because it derives light from some other source. That is the nature of matter as contained in intelligible (entities). Perhaps this treatment of the subject is longer than necessary.

SUBSTRATE IS DEMANDED BY TRANSFORMATION OF ELEMENTS, BY THEIR DESTRUCTION AND DISSOLUTION.

6. Now let us speak of bodies. The mutual transformation of elements demonstrates that they must have a substrate. Their transformation is not a complete destruction; otherwise (a general) "being"[10] would perish in nonentity. Whereas, what is begotten would have passed from absolute non-entity to essence; and all change is no more than the passing of one form into another (as thought Aristotle).[11] It presupposes the existence of permanent (subject) which would receive the form of begotten things only after having lost the earlier form. This is demonstrated by destruction, which affects only something composite; therefore every dissolved object must have been a composite. Dissolution proves it also. For instance, where a vase is dissolved, the result is gold; on being dissolved, gold leaves water; and so analogy would suggest that the dissolution of water would result in something else, that is analogous to its nature. Finally, elements necessarily are either form, or primary matter, or the composites of form and matter. However, they cannot be form, because, without matter, they could not possess either mass nor magnitude. Nor can they be primary matter, because they are subject to destruction. They must therefore be composites of form and matter; form constituting their shape and quality, and matter a substrate that is indeterminate, because it is not a form.

THE VIEWS OF EMPEDOCLES AND ANAXAGORAS ON MATTER.

7. (Accoding to Aristotle),[12] Empedocles thinks matter consists of elements; but this opinion is refuted by the decay to which they are exposed. (According to Aristotle),[13] Anaxagoras supposes that matter is a mixture and, instead of saying that this (mixture) is capable of becoming all things, he insists that it contains all things in actualization. Thus he annihilates the intelligence that he had introduced into the world; for, according to him, it is not intelligence that endows all the rest with shape and form; it is contemporaneous with matter, instead of preceding it.[14] Now it is impossible for intelligence to be the contemporary of matter, for if mixture participate in essence, then must essence precede it; if, however, essence itself be the mixture, they will need some third principle. Therefore if the demiurgic creator necessarily precede, what need was there for the forms in miniature to exist in matter, for intelligence to unravel their inextricable confusion, when it is possible to predicate qualities of matter, because matter had none of its own, and thus to subject matter entirely to shape? Besides, how could (the demiurgic creator) then be in all?

REFUTATION OF ANAXIMANDER'S VIEWS ABOUT MATTER.

(Anaximander)[15] had better explain the consistence of the infinity by which he explains matter. Does he, by infinity, mean immensity? In reality this would be impossible. Infinity exists neither by itself, nor in any other nature, as, for instance, the accident of a body. The infinite does not exist by itself, because each of its parts would necessarily be infinite. Nor does the infinite exist as an accident, because that of which it would be an accident would, by itself, be neither infinite, nor simple; and consequently, would not be matter.

REFUTATION OF DEMOCRITUS'S ATOMS AS EXPLANATIONS OF MATTER.

(According to Aristotle's account of Democritus),[16] neither could the atoms fulfil the part of matter because they are nothing (as before thought Cicero).[17] Every body is divisible to infinity. (Against the system of the atoms) might further be alleged the continuity and humidity of bodies. Besides nothing can exist without intelligence and soul, which could not be composed of atoms. Nothing with a nature different from the atoms could produce anything with the atoms, because no demiurgic creator could produce something with a matter that lacked continuity. Many other objections against this system have and can be made; but further discussion is unnecessary.

MATTER IS NOTHING COMPOSITE, BUT BY NATURE SIMPLE AND ONE.

8. What then is this matter which is one, continuous, and without qualities? Evidently, it could not be a body, since it has no quality; if it were a body, it would have a quality. We say that it is the matter of all sense-objects, and not the matter of some, and the form of others, just as clay is matter, in respect to the potter, without being matter absolutely (as thought Aristotle).[18] As we are not considering the matter of any particular object, but the matter of all things, we would not attribute to its nature anything of what falls under our senses—no quality, color, heat, cold, lightness, weight, density, sparseness, figure or magnitude; for magnitude is something entirely different from being large, and figure from the figured object. Matter therefore is not anything composite, but something simple, and by nature one (according to the views of

Plato and Aristotle combined).[19] Only thus could matter be deprived of all properties (as it is).

MATTER AND THE INFORMING PRINCIPLE MUST BE CONTEMPORARIES TO ACCOUNT FOR THEIR MUTUAL RELATIONS.

The principle which informs matter will give it form as something foreign to its nature; it will also introduce magnitude and all the real properties. Otherwise, it would be enslaved to the magnitude of matter, and could not decide of the magnitude of matter, and magnitude would be dependent on the disposition of matter. A theory of a consultation between it and the magnitude of matter would be an absurd fiction. On the contrary, if the efficient cause precede matter, matter will be exactly as desired by the efficient cause, and be capable of docilely receiving any kind of form, including magnitude. If matter possessed magnitude, it would also possess figure, and would thus be rather difficult to fashion. Form therefore enters into matter by importing into it (what constitutes corporeal being); now every form contains a magnitude and a quantity which are determined by reason ("being"), and with reason. That is why in all kinds of beings, quantity is determined only along with form; for the quantity (the magnitude) of man is not the quantity of the bird. It would be absurd to insist on the difference between giving to matter the quantity of a bird, and impressing its quality on it, that quality is a reason, while quantity is not a form; for quantity is both measure and number.

ANTI-STOIC POLEMIC, AGAINST THE CORPOREITY OF MATTER AND QUANTITY.

9. It may be objected that it would be impossible to conceive of something without magnitude. The fact is that not everything is identical with quantity,

Essence is distinct from quantity; for many other things beside it exist. Consequently no incorporeal nature has any quantity. Matter, therefore, is incorporeal. Besides, even quantity itself is not quantative, which characterizes only what participates in quantity (in general); a further proof that quantity is a form, as an object becomes white by the presence of whiteness; and as that which, in the animal, produces whiteness and the different colors, is not a varied color, but a varied reason; likewise that which produces a quantity is not a definite quantity, but either quantity in itself, or quantity as such, or the reason of quantity. Does quantity, on entering into matter extend matter, so as to give it magnitude? By no means, for matter had not been condensed. Form therefore imparts to matter the magnitude which it did not possess, just as form impresses on matter the quality it lacked.[20]

BY ABSTRACTION, THE SOUL CAN FIND AND DESCRY THE QUALITY-LESS THING-IN-ITSELF. THIS PROCESS IS CALLED "BASTARD REASONING."

10. (Some objector) might ask how one could conceive of matter without quantity? This might be answered by a retort. How then do you (as you do) manage to conceive of it without quality? Do you again object, by what conception or intelligence could it be reached? By the very indetermination of the soul. Since that which knows must be similar to that which is known (as Aristotle[21] quotes from Empedocles), the indeterminate must be grasped by the indeterminate. Reason, indeed, may be determined in respect to the indeterminate; but the glance which reason directs on the indeterminate itself is indeterminate. If everything were known by reason and by intelligence, reason here tells us about matter what reason rightly should tell us about it. By wishing to conceive of matter in an intellectual manner, intelli-

gence arrives at a state which is the absence of intelligence, or rather, reason forms of matter a "bastard" or "illegitimate" image, which is derived from the other, which is not true, and which is composed of the other (deceptive material called) reason. That is why Plato[22] said that matter is perceived by a "bastard reasoning." In what does the indetermination of the soul consist? In an absolute ignorance, or in a complete absence of all knowledge? No: the indeterminate condition of the soul implies something positive (besides something negative). As for the eye, darkness is the matter of all invisible color, so the soul, by making abstraction in sense-objects of all things that somehow are luminous, cannot determine what then remains; and likewise, as the eye, in darkness (becomes assimilated to darkness), the soul becomes assimilated to what she sees. Does she then see anything else? Doubtless, she sees something without figure, without color, without light, or even without magnitude.[23] If this thing had any magnitude, the soul would lend it a form.

DIFFERENCE BETWEEN MENTAL BLANK AND IMPRESSION OF THE SHAPELESS.

(An objector might ask) whether there be identity of conditions between the soul's not thinking, and her experience while thinking of matter? By no means; when the soul is not thinking of anything, she neither asserts anything, nor experiences anything. When she thinks of matter, she experiences something, she receives the impression of the shapeless. When she presents to herself objects that possess shape and magnitude, she conceives of them as composite; for she sees them as distinct (or, colored?) and determined by qualities they contain. She conceives of both the totality and its two constituent elements. She also has a clear perception, a vivid sensation of properties inherent (in matter). On the contrary, the soul receives only an obscure perception of the shapeless subject, for there is no form there. Therefore, when the soul considers matter in general, in the composite, with the qualities inherent in this composite, she separates them, analyzes them, and what is left (after this analysis), the soul perceives it vaguely, and obscurely, because it is something vague and obscure; she thinks it, without really thinking it. On the other hand, as matter does not remain shapeless, as it is always shaped, within objects, the soul always imposes on matter the form of things, because only with difficulty does she support the indeterminate, since she seems to fear to fall out of the order of beings, and to remain long in nonentity.

THE COMPOSITION OF A BODY NEEDS A SUBSTRATE.

11. (Following the ideas of Aristotle,[24] Plotinos wonders whether some objector) will ask whether the composition of a body requires anything beyond extension and all the other qualities? Yes: it demands a substrate to receive them (as a residence). This substrate is not a mass; for in this case, it would be an extension. But if this substrate have no extension, how can it be a residence (for form)? Without extension, it could be of no service, contributing neither to form nor qualities, to magnitude nor extension. It seems that extension, wherever it be, is given to bodies by matter. Just as actions, effects, times and movements though they do not imply any matter, nevertheless are beings, it would seem that the elementary bodies do not necessarily imply matter (without extension), being individual beings, whose diverse substance is constituted by the mingling of several forms. Matter without extension, therefore, seems to be no more than a meaningless name.

MATTER AS THE IMAGE OF EXTENSION, CAN YET BE RESIDENCE OF FORM.

(Our answer to the above objection is this:) To begin with, not every residence is necessarily a mass, unless it have already received extension. The soul, which possesses all things, contains them all simultaneously. If it possessed extension, it would possess all things in extension. Consequently matter receives all it contains in extension, because it is capable thereof. Likewise in animals and plants there is a correspondence between the growth and diminution of their magnitude, with that of their quality. It would be wrong to claim that magnitude is necessary to matter because, in sense-objects, there exists a previous magnitude, on which is exerted the action of the forming principle; for the matter of these objects is not pure matter, but individual matter (as said Aristotle).[25] Matter pure and simple must receive its extension from some other principle. Therefore the residence of form could not be a mass; for in receiving extension, it would also receive the other qualities. Matter therefore, is the image of extension, because as it is primary matter, it possesses the ability to become extended. People often imagine matter as empty extension; consequently several philosophers have claimed that matter is identical with emptiness. I repeat: matter is the image of extension because the soul, when considering matter, is unable to determine anything, spreads into indetermination, without being able to circumscribe or mark anything; otherwise, matter would determine something. This substrate could not properly be called big or little; it is simultaneously big and little (as said Aristotle).[26] It is simultaneously extended and non-extended, because it is the matter of extension. If it were enlarged or made smaller, it would somehow move in extension. Its indetermination is an extension which consists in being the very residence of extension, but really in being only imaginary extension, as has been explained above. Other beings, that have no extension, but which are forms, are each of them determinate, and consequently imply no other idea of extension. On the contrary, matter, being indeterminate, and incapable of remaining within itself, being moved to receive all forms everywhere, ever being docile, by this very docility, and by the generation (to which it adapts itself), becomes manifold. It is in this way its nature seems to be extension.

POLEMIC AGAINST MODERATUS OF GADES. FORMS DEMAND A RESIDENCE, VASE, or LOCATION.

12. Extensions therefore contribute to the constitutions of bodies; for the forms of bodies are in extensions. These forms produce themselves not in extension (which is a form), but in the substrate that has received extension. If they occurred in extension, instead of occurring in matter, they would nevertheless have neither extension nor (hypostatic) substance; for they would be no more than reasons. Now as reasons reside in the soul, there would be no body. Therefore, in the sense-world, the multiplicity of forms must have a single substrate which has received extension, and therefore must be other than extension. All things that mingle form a mixture, because they contain matter; they have no need of any other substrate, because each of them brings its matter along with it. But (forms) need a receptacle (a residence), a "vase" (or stand), a location (this in answer to the objection at the beginning of the former section). Now location is posterior to matter and to bodies. Bodies, therefore, presuppose matter. Bodies are not necessarily immaterial, merely because actions and operations are. In the occurrence of an action, matter serves as substrate to the agent; it remains within him without itself entering into action; for that is not that which is

sought by the agent. One action does not change into another, and consequently has no need of containing matter; it is the agent who passes from one action to another, and who, consequently, serves as matter to the actions (as thought Aristotle).[27]

NOT EVEN CORPOREITY INHERES IN MATTER WHICH IS REACHED BY BASTARD REASONING.

Matter, therefore, is necessary to quality as well as to quantity, and consequently, to bodies. In this sense, matter is not an empty name, but a substrate, though it be neither visible nor extended. Otherwise, for the same reason, we would be obliged also to deny qualities and extension; for you might say that each of these things, taken in itself, is nothing real. If these things possess existence, though their existence be obscure, so much the more must matter possess existence, though its existence be neither clear nor evident to the senses. Indeed, matter cannot be perceived by sight, since it is colorless; nor by hearing, for it is soundless; nor by smell or taste, because it is neither volatile nor wet. It is not even perceived by touch, for it is not a body. Touch cognizes only body, recognizes that it is dense or sparse, hard or soft, wet or dry; now none of these attributes is characteristic of matter. The latter therefore can be perceived only by a reasoning which does not imply the presence of intelligence, which, on the contrary, implies the complete absence of matter; which (unintelligent reasoning therefore) deserves the name of "bastard" (or, illegitimate) reasoning.[28] Corporeity itself,[29] is not characteristic of matter. If corporeity be a reason (that is, by a pun, a 'form'), it certainly differs from matter, both being entirely distinct. If corporeity be considered when it has already modified matter and mingled with it, it is a body; it is no longer matter pure and simple.

THE SUBSTRATE IS NOT A QUALITY COMMON TO ALL ELEMENTS; FOR THUS IT WOULD NOT BE INDETERMINATE.

13. Those who insist that the substrate of things is a quality common to all elements are bound to explain first the nature of this quality; then, how a quality could serve as substrate; how an unextended, immaterial (?) quality could be perceived in something that lacked extension; further, how, if this quality be determinate, it can be matter; for if it be something indeterminate, it is no longer a quality, but matter itself that we seek.

EVEN THIS PRIVATION MIGHT BE CONSIDERED A QUALITY; BUT SUCH A USE OF THE TERM WOULD DESTROY ALL COHERENT REASONING.

Let us grant that matter has no quality, because, by virtue of its nature, it does not participate in a quality of any other thing. What, however, would hinder this property, because it is a qualification in matter, from participating in some quality? This would be a particular and distinctive characteristic, which consists of the privation of all other things (referring to Aristotle)?[30] In man, the privation of something may be considered a quality; as, for instance, the privation of sight is blindness. If the privation of certain things inhere in matter, this privation is also a qualification for matter. If further the privation in matter extend to all things, absolutely, our objection is still better grounded, for privation is a qualification. Such an objection, however, amounts to making qualities and qualified things of everything. In this case quantity, as well as "being," would be a quality. Every qualified thing must possess some quality. It is ridiculous to suppose that something qualified is qualified by what itself has no quality, being other than quality.

BY A PUN BETWEEN "DIFFERENCE" AND "OTHERNESS," PLOTINOS DEFINES THE CHARACTERISTIC OF MATTER AS BEING A DISPOSITION TO BECOME SOMETHING ELSE.

Some one may object that that is possible, because "being something else" is a quality. We would then have to ask whether the thing that is other be otherness-in-itself? If it be otherness-in-itself, it is so not because it is something qualified, because quality is not something qualified. If this thing be only other, it is not such by itself, it is so only by otherness, as a thing that is identical by identity. Privation, therefore, is not a quality, nor anything qualified, but the absence of quality or of something else, as silence is the absence of sound. Privation is something negative; qualification is something positive. The property of matter is not a form; for its property consists precisely in having neither qualification nor form. It is absurd to insist that it is qualified, just because it has no quality; this would be tantamount to saying that it possessed extension by the very fact of its possessing no extension. The individuality (or, property) of matter is to be what it is. Its characteristic is not an attribute; it consists in a disposition to become other things. Not only are these other things other than matter, but besides each of them possesses an individual form. The only name that suits matter is "other," or rather, "others," because the singular is too determinative, and the plural better expresses indetermination.

PRIVATION IS A FORM OF MATTER.

14. Let us now examine if matter be privation, or if privation be an attribute of matter. If you insist that privation and matter are though logically distinct, substantially one and the same thing, you will have to explain the nature of these two things, for instance, defining matter without defining privation, and con-

versely. Either, neither of these two things implies the other, or they imply each other reciprocally, or only one of them implies the other. If each of them can be defined separately, and if neither of them imply the other, both will form two distinct things, and matter will be different from privation, though privation be an accident of matter. But neither of the two must even potentially be present in the definition of the other. Is their mutual relation the same as that of a stub nose, and the man with the stub nose (as suggested by Aristotle)?[31] Then each of these is double, and there are two things. Is their relation that between fire and heat? Heat is in fire, but fire is not necessarily contained in heat; thus matter, having privation (as a quality), as fire has heat (as a quality), privation will be a form of matter, and has a substrate different from itself, which is matter.[32] Not in this sense, therefore, is there a unity (between them).

PRIVATION IS NONENTITY, AND ADDS NO NEW CONCEPT.

Are matter and privation substantially identical, yet logically distinct, in this sense that privation does not signify the presence of anything, but rather its absence? That it is the negation of beings, and is synonymous with nonentity? Negation adds no attribute; it limits itself to the assertion that something is not. In a certain sense, therefore, privation is nonentity.

BEING SUBSTANTIALLY IDENTICAL, BUT LOGICALLY DISTINCT IS NONSENSE.

If matter be called nonentity in this sense that it is not essence, but something else than essence, there is still room to draw up two definitions, of which one would apply to the substrate, and the other to the privation, merely to explain that it is a disposition to become something else? It would be better to acknowledge that matter, like the substrate, should be defined a disposition to become other things. If the definition of privation shows the indetermination of matter, it can at least indicate its nature. But we could not admit that matter and privation are one thing in respect to their substrate, though logically distinct; for how could there be a logical distinction into two things, if a thing be identical with matter as soon as it is indeterminate, indefinite, and lacking quality?

MATTER AS THE INFINITE IN ITSELF.

15. Let us further examine if the indeterminate, or infinite, be an accident, or an attribute of some other nature; how it comes to be an accident, and whether privation ever can become an accident. The things that are numbers and reasons are exempt from all indetermination, because they are determinations, orders, and principles of order for the rest. Now these principles do not order objects already ordered, nor do they order orders. The thing that receives an order is different from that which gives an order, and the principles from which the order is derived are determination, limitation and reason. In this case, that which receives the order and the determination must necessarily be the infinite (as thought Plato).[83] Now that which receives the order is matter, with all the things which, without being matter, participate therein, and play the part of matter. Therefore matter is the infinite itself.[84] Not accidentally is it the infinite; for the infinite is no accident. Indeed, every accident must be a reason; now of what being can the infinite be an accident? Of determination, or of that which is determined? Now matter is neither of these two. Further, the infinite could not unite with the determinate without destroying its nature. The infinite, therefore, is no accident of matter (but is its nature, or "being"). Matter is

the infinite itself. Even in the intelligible world, matter is the infinite.

THE INFINITE MAY BE EITHER IDEAL OR REAL, INFINITE OR INDEFINITE.

The infinite seems born of the infinity of the One, either of its power, or eternity; there is no infinity in the One, but the One is creator of the infinite. How can there be infinity simultaneously above and below (in the One and in matter)? Because there are two infinities (the infinite and the indefinite; the infinite in the One, the indefinite in matter). Between them obtains the same difference as the archetype and its image.[85] Is the infinite here below less infinite? On the contrary, it is more so. By the mere fact that the image is far from veritable "being," it is more infinite. Infinity is greater in that which is less determinate (as thought Aristotle).[86] Now that which is more distant from good is further in evil. Therefore the infinite on high, possessing the more essence, is the ideal infinite; here below, as the infinite possesses less essence, because it is far from essence and truth, it degenerates into the image of essence, and is the truer (indefinite) infinite.

MATTER AS THE INFINITE IN ITSELF.

Is the infinite identical with the essence of the infinite? There is a distinction between them where there is reason and matter; where however matter is alone, they must be considered identical; or, better, we may say absolutely that here below the infinite does not occur; otherwise it would be a reason, which is contrary to the nature of the infinite. Therefore matter in itself is the infinite, in opposition to reason. Just as reason, considered in itself, is called reason, so matter, which is opposed to reason by its infinity, and which is nothing else (than matter), must be called infinite.

MATTER IS NONESSENTIAL OTHERNESS.

16. Is there any identity between matter and otherness? Matter is not identical with otherness itself, but with that part of otherness which is opposed to real beings, and to reasons. It is in this sense that one can say of nonentity that it is something, that it is identical with privation, if only privation be the opposition to things that exist in reason. Will privation be destroyed by its union with the thing of which it is an attribute? By no means. That in which a (Stoic) "habit" occurs is not itself a "habit," but a privation. That in which determination occurs is neither determination, nor that which is determined, but the infinite, so far as it is infinite. How could determination unite with the infinite without destroying its nature, since this infinite is not such by accident? It would destroy this infinite, if it were infinite in quantity; but that is not the case. On the contrary, it preserves its "being" for it, realizes and completes its nature; as the earth which did not contain seeds (preserves its nature) when it receives some of them; or the female, when she is made pregnant by the male. The female, then, does not cease being a female; on the contrary she is so far more, for she realizes her nature ("being").

INDIGENCE IS NECESSARILY EVIL.

Does matter continue to be evil when it happens to participate in the good? Yes, because it was formerly deprived of good, and did not possess it. That which lacks something, and obtains it, holds the middle between good and evil, if it be in the middle between the two. But that which possesses nothing, that which is in indigence, or rather that which is indigence itself, must necessarily be evil; for it is not indigence of wealth, but indigence of wisdom, of virtue, of beauty, of vigor, of shape, of form, of quality. How, indeed, could such a thing not be shapeless, absolutely ugly and evil?

THE RELATION OF BOTH KINDS OF MATTER TO ESSENCE.

In the intelligible world, matter is essence; for what is above it (the One), is considered as superior to essence. In the sense-world, on the contrary, essence is above matter; therefore matter is nonentity, and thereby is the only thing foreign to the beauty of essence.

---

[1] Met. vii 3. [2] Met. v. 8. [3] Diog. Laertes vii 61. [4] See Cicero, de Nat. Deor. i. 15 [5] Met viii 1. [6] See vi. 7 [7] See i. 8.4. [8] See i. 8.15. [9] Plotinos's six categories are identity, difference, being, life, motion and rest See v. 1; v. 2; vi 2 [10] Not the absolute eternal existence, nor the totality of the constitutive qualities of a thing, as in ii 6. [11] Met. xii. 2. [12] Met i. 3. [13] Met. xi 6. [14] See v. 1 9. [15] As reported by Diog. Laert. ii. 2. [16] Met. i. 4; vii. 13. [17] de Nat. Deor. i. 24. [18] Met. viii 4. [19] In the Timaeus, C49-52, Met. vii 3 [20] See ii, 7 3. [21] In Met. iii. 4 and de Anima i 2 5, ii 5. [22] In the Timaeus. [23] See i. 8 9; ii. 4 12. [24] Met. vii. 3, see iii 6 7-19. [25] Met viii. 4. [26] Met. i 6 [27] Met. vii. 7. [28] See ii. 4 10. [29] See ii. 7 3. [30] Met xii 2. [31] Met vi. 1; vii. 5. [32] See i. 2 1. [33] In the Philebus, 252. [34] The same definition is given of "evil" in i 8 10-14. [35] See i. 8 8 [36] Physics. iii. 7.

THIRD ENNEAD, BOOK NINE.

Fragments About the Soul, the Intelligence, and the Good.

DIFFERENCE BETWEEN INTELLIGENCE AND THE EXISTING ANIMAL.

1. Plato says, "The intelligence sees the ideas comprised within the existing animal." He adds, "The demiurge conceived that this produced animal was to comprise beings similar and equally numerous to those that the intelligence sees in the existing animal." Does Plato mean that the ideas are anterior to intelligence, and that they already exist when intelligence thinks them? We shall first have to examine whether the animal is identical with intelligence, or is something different. Now that which observes is intelligence; so the Animal himself should then be called, not intelligence, but the intelligibile. Shall we therefrom conclude that the things contemplated by intelligence are outside of it? If so, intelligence possesses only images, instead of the realities themselves—that is, if we admit that the realities exist up there; for, according to Plato, the veritable reality is up there within the essence, in which everything exists in itself.

RELATION BETWEEN INTELLIGENCE AND THE INTELLIGIBLE.

(This consequence is not necessary). Doubtless Intelligence and the intelligible are different; they are nevertheless not separated. Nothing hinders us from saying that both form but one, and that they are separated only by thought; for essence is one, but it is partly that which is thought, and partly that which thinks. When Plato says that intelligence sees the ideas, he means that it contemplates the ideas, not in another principle, but in itself, because it possesses the intelligible within itself. The intelligible may also be the intelligence, but intelligence in the state of repose, of unity, of calm, while Intelligence, which perceives this Intelligence which has remained within itself, is the actuality born therefrom, and which contemplates it. By contemplating the intelligible, intelligence is assimilated thereto and is its intelligence, because Intelligence thinks the intelligible it itself becomes intelligible by becoming assimilated thereto, and on the other hand also something thought.

It is (intelligence), therefore, which conceived the design in producing in the universe the four kinds of living beings (or elements), which it beholds up there. Mysteriously, however, Plato here seems to present the conceiving-principle as different from the other two principles, while others think that these three principles, the animal itself (the universal Soul), Intelligence and the conceiving principle form but a single thing. Shall we here, as elsewhere, admit that opinions differ, and that everybody conceives the three principles in his own manner?

THE WORLD-SOUL IS THE CONCEIVING-PRINCIPLE.

We have already noticed two of these principles (namely, intelligence, and the intelligible, which is called the Animal-in-itself, or universal Soul). What is the third? It is he who has resolved to produce, to form, to divide the ideas that intelligence sees in the Animal. Is it possible that in one sense intelligence is the dividing principle, and that in another the dividing principle is not intelligence? As far as divided things proceed from intelligence, intelligence is the dividing principle. As far as intelligence itself remains undivided, and that the things proceeding from it (that is, the souls) are divided, the universal Soul is the principle of this division into several souls. That is why Plato says that division is the work of a third principle, and that it resides in a third principle that has conceived; now, to conceive is not the proper function of intelligence; it is that of the Soul which has a dividing action in a divisible nature.

HOW THE SOUL ASCENDS TO THE INTELLIGIBLE WORLD. THE INTELLIGIBLE IS POSSESSED BY TOUCHING IT WITH THE BEST PART OF ONESELF.

2. (As Nicholas of Damascus used to say) the totality of a science is divided into particular propositions, without, however, thereby being broken up into fragments, inasmuch as each proposition contains potentially the whole science, whose principle and goal coincide. Likewise, we should so manage ourselves that each of the faculties we possess within ourselves should also become a goal and a totality; and then so arrange all the faculties that they will be consummated in what is best in our nature (that is, intelligence). Success in this constitutes "dwelling on high" (living spiritually); for, when one posssesses the intelligible, one touches it by what is best in oneself.

OF THE DESCENT OF THE SOUL INTO THE BODY. THE SOUL IS NOT IN THE BODY; BUT THE BODY IS IN THE SOUL.

3. The universal Soul has not come into any place, nor gone into any; for no such place could have existed. However, the body, which was in its neighborhood, participated in her, consequently, she is not inside a body. Plato, indeed, does not say that the

soul is in a body; on the contrary, he locates the body in the soul.

INDIVIDUAL SOULS, HOWEVER, MAY BE SAID TO COME AND GO

As to individual souls, they come from somewhere, for they proceed from the universal Soul; they also have a place whither they may descend, or where they may pass from one body into another; they can likewise reascend thence to the intelligible world.

THE UNIVERSAL SOUL EVER REMAINS IN THE INTELLIGIBLE.

The universal Soul, on the contrary, ever resides in the elevated region where her nature retains her; and the universe located below her participates in her just as the object which receives the sun's rays participates therein.

HOW THE SOUL INCARNATES.

The individual soul is therefore illuminated when she turns towards what is above her; for then she meets the essence; on the contrary, when she turns towards what is below her, she meets non-being. This is what happens when she turns towards herself; on wishing to belong to herself, she somehow falls into emptiness, becomes indeterminate, and produces what is below her, namely, an image of herself which is non-being (the body). Now the image of this image (matter), is indeterminate, and quite obscure; for it is entirely unreasonable, unintelligible, and as far as possible from essence itself. (Between intelligence and the body) the soul occupies an intermediary region, which is her own proper domain; when she looks at the inferior region, throwing a second glance thither, she gives a form to her image (her body); and, charmed by this image, she enters therein.

BY ITS POWER, THE ONE IS EVERYWHERE.

4. How does manifoldness issue from Unity? Unity is everywhere; for there is no place where it is not; therefore it fills everything. By Him exists manifoldness; or rather, it is by Him that all things exist. If the One were only everywhere, He would simply be all things; but, as, besides, He is nowhere, all things exist by Him, because He is everywhere; but simultaneously all things are distinct from Him, because He is nowhere. Why then is Unity not only everywhere, but also nowhere? The reason is, that Unity must be above all things, He must fill everything, and produce everything, without being all that He produces.

THE SOUL RECEIVES HER FORM FROM INTELLIGENCE

5. The soul's relation to intelligence is the same as that of sight to the visible object; but it is the indeterminate sight which, before seeing, is nevertheless disposed to see and think; that is why the soul bears to intelligence the relation of matter to form.

WE THINK AN INTELLECTUAL NATURE BY THINKING OURSELVES.

6. When we think, and think ourselves, we see a thinking nature; otherwise, we would be dupes of an illusion in believing we were thinking. Consequently, if we think ourselves, we are, by thinking ourselves, thinking an intellectual nature. This thought presupposes an anterior thought which implies no movement. Now, as the objects of thought are being and life, there must be, anterior to this being, another being; and anterior to this life, another life. This is well-known to all who are actualized intelligences. If the intelligences be actualizations which consist in thinking themselves, we ourselves are the intelligible by the real

foundation of our essence, and the thought that we have of ourselves gives us its image.

THE ONE IS SUPERIOR TO REST AND MOTION.

7. The First (or One) is the potentiality of movement and of rest; consequently, He is superior to both things. The Second principle relates to the First by its motion and its rest; it is Intelligence, because, differing from the First, it directs its thought towards Him, while the First does not think (because He comprises both the thinking thing, and the thing thought); He thinks himself, and, by that very thing, He is defective, because His good consists in thinking, not in its "hypostasis" (or existence).

OF ACTUALITY AND POTENTIALITY.

8. What passes from potentiality to actuality, and always remains the same so long as it exists, approaches actuality. It is thus that the bodies such as fire may possess perfection. But what passes from potentiality to actuality cannot exist always, because it contains matter. On the contrary, what exists actually, and what is simple, exists always. Besides, what is actual may also in certain respects exist potentially.

THE GOOD IS SUPERIOR TO THOUGHT; THE HIGHEST DIVINITIES ARE NOT THE SUPREME.

9. The divinities which occupy the highest rank are nevertheless not the First; for Intelligence (from which proceed the divinities of the highest rank, that is, the perfect intelligences) is (or, is constituted by) all the intelligible essences, and, consequently, comprises both motion and rest. Nothing like this is in the First. He is related to nothing else, while the other things subsist in Him in their rest, and direct their motion towards Him. Motion is an aspiration, and the First aspires to nothing. Towards what would He, in

any case, aspire? He does not think himself; and they who say that He thinks Himself mean by it only that He possesses Himself. But when one says that a thing thinks, it is not because it possesses itself, it is because it contemplates the First; that is the first actuality, thought itself, the first thought, to which none other can be anterior; only, it is inferior to the principle from which it derives its existence, and occupies the second rank after it. Thought is therefore not the most sacred thing; consequently, not all thought is sacred; the only sacred thought is that of the Good, and this (Good) is superior to thought.

THE GOOD IS SUPERIOR EVEN TO SELF-CONSCIOUSNESS AND LIFE.

Will the Good not be self-conscious? It is claimed by some that the Good would be good only if it possessed self-consciousness. But if it be Goodness, it is goodness before having self-consciousness. If the Good be good only because it has self-consciousness, it was not good before having self-consciousness; but, on the other hand, if there be no goodness, no possible consciousness can therefore exist. (Likewise, someone may ask) does not the First live? He cannot be said to live, because He Himself gives life.

THE SUPREME IS THEREFORE ABOVE THOUGHT.

Thus the principle which is self-conscious, which thinks itself (that is, Intelligence), occupies only the second rank. Indeed, if this principle be self-conscious, it is only to unite itself to itself by this act of consciousness; but if it study itself, it is the result of ignoring itself, because its nature is defective, and it becomes perfect only by thought. Thought should therefore not be attributed to the First; for, to attribute something to Him would be to imply that He had been deprived thereof, and needed it.

SECOND ENNEAD, BOOK TWO.

About the Movement of the Heavens.

QUESTIONS ABOUT THE MOVEMENTS OF THE HEAVENS.

1. Why do the heavens move in a circle? Because they imitate Intelligence. But to what does this movement belong? To the Soul, or to the body? Does it occur because the Soul is within the celestial sphere, which tends to revolve about her? Is the Soul within this sphere without being touched thereby? Does she cause this sphere to move by her own motion? Perhaps the Soul which moves this sphere should not move it in the future, although she did so in the past; that is, the soul made it remain immovable, instead of ceaselessly imparting to it a circular movement. Perhaps the Soul herself might remain immovable; or, if she move at all, it will at least not be a local movement.

THREE KINDS OF MOVEMENT.

How can the Soul impart to the heavens a local movement, herself possessing a different kind of motion? Perhaps the circular movement, when considered by itself, may not seem a local movement. If then it be a local movement only by accident, what is its own nature, by itself? It is the reflection upon itself, the movement of consciousness, of reflection, of life; it withdraws nothing from the world, it changes the location of nothing, while embracing all. Indeed, the power which governs the universal Animal (or world) embraces everything, and unifies everything. If then it remained immovable, it would not embrace everything either vitally or locally; it would not preserve the life of the interior parts of the body it possesses, because the bodily life implies movement. On the contrary, if it be a local movement, the Soul will possess a movement only such as it admits of. She will move, not only as soul, but as an animated body, and as an animal; her movement will partake both of the movement proper to the soul, and proper to the body. Now the movement proper to the body is to mobilize in a straight line; the movement proper to the Soul, is to contain; while both of these movements result in a third, the circular movement which includes both transportation and permanence.

FIRE MOVES STRAIGHT ONLY PRELIMINARILY.

To the assertion that the circular movement is a corporeal movement, it might be objected that one can see that every body, even fire, moves in a straight line. However, the fire moves in a straight line only till it reaches the place assigned to it by the universal order (it constitutes the heavens, which are its proper place). By virtue of this order its nature is permanent, and it moves towards its assigned location. Why then does the fire as soon as it has arrived there, not abide there quiescently? Because its very nature is constant movement; if it went in a straight line, it would dissipate; consequently, it necessarily possesses a circular motion. That is surely a povidential arrangement. Providence placed fire within itself (because it constitutes the heavens, which are its location); so that, as soon as it finds itself in the sky it must spontaneously move in a circle.

WHY SOUL ASSUMES A CIRCULAR MOTION.

We might further say that, if the fire tended to move in a straight line, it must effect a return upon itself in the only place where it is possible (in the heavens), inasmuch as there is no place outside of the world where it could go. In fact there is no further place, beyond the celestial fire, for itself constitutes the last place in the universe; it therefore moves in a circle in the place at its disposal; it is its own place, but not to remain immovable, but to move. In a circle, the centre is naturally immovable; and were the circumference the same, it would be only an immense centre. It is therefore better that the fire should turn around the centre in this living and naturally organized body. Thus the fire will tend towards the centre, not in stopping, for it would lose its circular form, but in moving itself around it; thus only will it be able to satisfy its tendency (towards the universal Soul). However, if this power effect the movement of the body of the universe, it does not drag it like a burden, nor give it an impulsion contrary to its nature. For nature is constituted by nothing else than the order established by the universal Soul. Besides, as the whole Soul is everywhere, and is not divided into parts, it endows the sky with all the ubiquity it can assimilate, which can occur only by traversing all of it. If the Soul remained immovable in one place, she would remain immovable as soon as the heavens reached this place; but as the Soul is everywhere, they would seek to reach her everywhere. Can the heavens never reach the Soul? On the contrary, they reach her ceaselessly; for the Soul, in ceaselessly attracting them to herself, endues them with a continual motion by which she carries them, not towards some other place, but towards herself, and in the same place, not in a straight line, but in a circle, and thus permits them to possess her in all the places which she traverses.

WHY THE HEAVENS DO NOT REMAIN STILL.

The heavens would be immovable if the Soul rested, that is, if she remained only in the intelligible world, where everything remains immovable. But because the Soul is in no one determinate place, and because the whole of her is everywhere, the heavens move through the whole of space; and as they cannot go out of themselves, they must move in a circle.

HOW OTHER BEINGS MOVE.[1]

2. How do the other beings move? As none of them is the whole, but only a part, consequently, each finds itself situated in a particular place. On the contrary, the heavens are the whole; they constitute the place which excludes nothing, because it is the universe. As to the law according to which men move, each of them, considered in his dependence towards the universe, is a part of all; considered in himself, he is a whole.

WHY THE HEAVENS MOVE IN A CIRCLE.

Now, if the heavens possess the Soul, wherever they are, what urges them to move in a circle? Surely because the Soul is not exclusively in a determinate place (and the world does not exclusively in one place desire to possess her). Besides, if the power of the Soul revolve around the centre, it is once more evident that the heavens would move in a circle.

DIFFERENCE BETWEEN THE CENTRE OF THE SOUL AND THE BODY.

Besides, when we speak of the Soul, we must not understand the term "centre" in the same sense as when it is used of the body. For the Soul, the centre is the focus of (the intelligence) whence radiates a second life (that is, the Soul); as to the body, it is a locality (the centre of the world). Since, however, both soul and body need a centre, we are forced to use this word in an analogous meaning which may suit both of them. Speaking strictly, however, a centre can exist only for a spherical body, and the analogy consists in this, that the latter, like the Soul, effects a reflection upon itself. In this case, the Soul moves around the divinity, embraces Him, and clings to Him with all her might; for everything depends from Him. But, as she cannot unite herself to Him, she moves around Him.

THE ADDITION OF OUR BODIES INTRODUCES CONFLICTING MOTIONS.

Why do not all souls act like the universal Soul? They do act like her, but do so only in the place where they are. Why do our bodies not move in a circle, like the heavens? Because they include an element whose natural motion is rectilinear; because they trend towards other objects, because the spherical element[2] in us can no longer easily move in a circle, because it has become terrestrial, while in the celestial region is was light and movable enough. How indeed could it remain at rest, while the Soul was in motion, whatever this movement was? This spirit(ual body) which, within us, is spread around the soul, does the same thing as do the heavens. Indeed, if the divinity be in everything, the Soul, which desires to unite herself to Him, must move around Him, since He resides in no determinate place. Consequently, Plato attributes to the stars, besides the revolution which they perform in common with the universe, a particular movement of rotation around their own centre. Indeed, every star, in whatever place it may be, is transported with joy while embracing the divinity; and this occurs not by reason, but by a natural necessity.

HOW MOTION IS IMPARTED TO LOWER EXISTENCES.

3. One more subject remains to be considered. The lowest power of the universal Soul (the inferior soul),[3] rests on the earth, and thence radiates abroad throughout the universe. The (higher, or celestial) power (of the world-Soul) which, by nature, possesses sensation, opinion, and reasoning, resides in the celestial spheres, whence it dominates the inferior power, and communicates life to it. It thereby moves the inferior power, embracing it in a circle; and it presides over the universe as it returns (from the earth) to the celestial spheres. The inferior power, being circularly embraced by the superior power, reflects upon itself, and thus operates on itself a conversion by which it imparts a movement of rotation to the body within which it reacts. (This is how motion starts) in a sphere that is at rest: as soon as a part moves, the movement spreads to the rest of it, and the sphere begins to revolve. Not otherwise is our body; when our soul begins to move, as in joy, or in the expectation of welfare, although this movement be of a kind very different from that natural to a body, this soul-movement produces local motion in the body. Likewise the universal Soul, on high, while approaching the Good, and becoming more sensitive (to its proximity), thereby impresses the body with the motion proper to it, namely, the local movement. (Our own human) sense-(faculty), while receiving its good from above, and while enjoying the pleasures proper to its nature, pursues the Good, and, inasmuch as the Good is everywhere present, it is borne everywhere. The intelligence is moved likewise; it is simultaneously at rest and in motion, reflecting upon itself. Similarly the universe moves in a circle, though simultaneously standing still.

[1] This paragraph interrupts the argument. [2] Plato's spirit in the Timaeus, C79. [3] The inferior soul, see ii. 3 18.

THIRD ENNEAD, BOOK FOUR.

Of Our Individual Guardian.

OUTLINE OF NATURES IN THE UNIVERSE.

Other principles remain unmoved while producing and exhibiting their ("hypostases," substantial acts, or) forms of existence. The (universal) Soul, however, is in motion while producing and exhibiting her ("substantial act," or) forms of existence, namely, the functions of sensation and growth, reaching down as far as (the sphere of the) plants. In us also does the Soul function, but she does not dominate us, constituting only a part of our nature. She does, however, dominate in plants, having as it were remained alone there. Beyond that sphere, however, nature begets nothing; for beyond it exists no life, begotten (matter) being lifeless. All that was begotten prior to this was shapeless, and achieved form only by trending towards its begetting principle, as to its source of life. Consequently, that which is begotten cannot be a form of the Soul, being lifeless, but must be absolute in determination. The things anterior (to matter, namely, the sense-power and nature), are doubtless indeterminate, but only so within their form; the are not absolutely indeterminate; they are indeterminate only in respect of their perfection. On the contrary, that which exists at present, namely, (mattter), is absolutely indeterminate. When it achieves perfection, it becomes body, on receiving the form suited to its power. This (form) is the receptacle of the principle which has begotten it, and which nourishes it. It is the only trace of the higher things in the body, which occupies the last rank amidst the things below.

AFTER DEATH, MAN BECOMES WHAT HE HAS LIVED.

2. It is to this (universal) Soul especially that may be applied these words of Plato:[1] "The general Soul cares for all that is inanimate." The other (individual) souls are in different conditions. "The Soul (adds Plato), circulates around the heavens successively assuming divers forms"; that is, the forms of thought, sense or growth. The part which dominates in the soul fulfills its proper individual function; the others remain inactive, and somehow seem exterior to them. In man, it is not the lower powers of the soul that dominate. They do indeed co-exist with the others. Neither is it always the best power (reason), which always dominates; for the inferior powers equally have their place. Consequently, man (besides being a reasonable being) is also a sensitive being, because he possesses sense-organs. In many respects, he is also a vegetative being; for his body feeds and grows just like a plant. All these powers (reason, sensibility, growth), therefore act together in the man; but it is the best of them that characterizes the totality of the man (so that he is called a "reasonable being"). On leaving the body the soul becomes the power she had preponderatingly developed. Let us therefore flee from here below, and let us raise ourselves to the intelligible world, so as not to fall into the pure sense-life, by allowing ourselves to follow sense-images, or into the life of growth, by abandoning ourselves to the pleasures of physical love, and to gormandizing; rather, let us rise to the intelligible world, to the intelligence, to the divinity!

LAWS OF TRANSMIGRATION.

Those who have exercised their human faculties are re-born as men. Those who have made use of their senses only, pass into the bodies of brutes, and particularly into the bodies of wild animals, if they have yiedled themselves to the transports of anger; so that, even in this case, the difference of the bodies they animate is proportioned to the difference of their inclinations. Those whose only effort it was to satisfy their desires and appetites pass into the bodies of lascivious and gluttonous animals.[2] Last, those who instead of following their desires or their anger, have rather degraded their senses by their inertia, are reduced to vegetate in plants; for in their former existence they exercised nothing but their vegetative power, and they worked at nothing but to make trees of themselves.[3] Those who have loved too much the enjoyments of music, and who otherwise lived purely, pass into the bodies of melodious birds. Those who have reigned tyrannically, become eagles, if they have no other vice.[4] Last, those who spoke lightly of celestial things, having kept their glance directed upwards, are changed into birds which usually fly towards the high regions of the air.[5] He who has acquired civil virtues again becomes a man; but if he does not possess them to a sufficient degree, he is transformed into a sociable animal, such as the bee, or other animal of the kind.

OUR GUARDIAN IS THE NEXT HIGHER FACULTY OF OUR BEING.

3. What then is our guardian? It is one of the powers of our soul. What is our divinity? It is also one of the powers of our soul. (Is it the power which acts principally in us as some people think?). For the power which acts in us seems to be that which leads us, since it is the principle which dominates in us. Is

that the guardian to which we have been allotted during the course of our life?[7] No: our guardian is the power immediately superior to the one that we exercise, for it presides over our life without itself being active. The power which is active in us is inferior to the one that presides over our life, and it is the one which essentially constitutes us. If then we live on the plane of the sense-life, our guardian is reason; if we live on the rational plane, our guardian will be the principal superior to reason (namely, intelligence); it will preside over our life, but it itself does not act, leaving that to the inferior power. Plato truly said that "we choose our guardian"; for, by the kind of life that we prefer, we choose the guardian that presides over our life. Why then does He direct us? He directs us during the course of our mortal life (because he is given to us to help us to accomplish our (destiny); but he can no longer direct us when our destiny is accomplished, because the power over the exercise of which he presided allows another power to act in his place (which however is dead, since the life in which it acted is terminated). This other power wishes to act in its turn, and, after having established its preponderance, it exercises itself during the course of a new life, itself having another guardian. If then we should chance to degrade ourselves by letting an inferior power prevail in us, we are punished for it. Indeed, the evil man degenerates because the power which he has developed in his life makes him descend to the existence of the brute, by assimilating him to it by his morals. If we could follow the guardian who is superior to him, he himself would become superior by sharing his life. He would then take as guide a part of himself superior to the one that governs him, then another part, still more elevated until he had arrived at the highest. Indeed, the soul is several things, or rather, the soul is all things; she is things both inferior and superior; she contains all the degrees of life. Each of us, in a certain degree, is the intelligible world; by our inferior part we are related to the sense-world, and by our superior part, to the intelligible world; we remain there on high by what constitutes our intelligible essence; we are attached here below by the powers which occupy the lowest rank in the soul. Thus we cause an emanation, or rather an actualization which implies no loss to the intelligible, to pass from the intelligible into the sense-world.

THE INTELLIGIBLE DOES NOT DESCEND; IT IS THE SENSE-WORLD THAT RISES.

4. Is the power which is the act of the soul always united to a body? No; for when the soul turns towards the superior regions, she raises this power with her. Does the universal (Soul) also raise with herself to the intelligible world the inferior power which is her actualization (nature)? No: for she does not incline towards her low inferior portion, because she neither came nor descended into the world; but, while she remains in herself, the body of the world comes to unite with her, and to offer itself to receive her light's radiation; besides, her body does not cause her any anxiety, because it is not exposed to any peril. Does not the world, then, possess any senses? "It has no sight" (says Plato[8]) "for it has no eyes. Neither has it ears, nostrils, nor tongue." Does it, then, as we, possess the consciousness of what is going on within it? As, within the world, all things go on uniformly according to nature, it is, in this respect, in a kind of repose; consequently, it does not feel any pleasure. The power of growth exists within it without being present therein; and so also with the sense-power. Besides, we shall return to a study of the question. For the present, we have said all that relates to the question in hand.

THE GUIDANCE OF THE GUARDIAN DOES NOT INTERFERE WITH MORAL RESPONSIBILITY.

5. But if (before coming on to the earth) the soul chooses her life and her guardian, how do we still preserve our liberty? Because what is called "choice" designates in an allegorical manner the character of the soul, and her general disposition everywhere. Again, it is objected that if the character of the soul preponderate, if the soul be dominated by that part which her former life rendered predominantly active, it is no longer the body which is her cause of evil; for if the character of the soul be anterior to her union with the body; if she have the character she has chosen; if, as said (Plato), she do not change her guardian, it is not here below that a man may become good or evil. The answer to this is, that potentially man is equally good or evil. (By his choics) however he may actualize one or the other.

THE SOUL HAS THE POWER TO CONFORM TO HER CHARACTER THE DESTINY ALLOTED TO HER.

What then would happen if a virtuous man should have a body of evil nature, or a vicious man a body of a good nature? The goodness of the soul has more or less influence on the goodness of the body. Exterior circumstances cannot thus alter the character chosen by the soul. When (Plato) says that the lots are spread out before the souls, and that later the different kinds of conditions are displayed before them, and that the fortune of each results from the choice made amidst the different kinds of lives present—a choice evidently made according to her character— (Plato) evidently attributes to the soul the power of conforming to her character the condition allotted to her.

OUR GUARDIAN IS BOTH RELATED TO US, AND INDEPENDENT OF US

Besides, our guardian is not entirely exterior to us; and, on the other hand, he is not bound to us, and is not active in us; he is ours, in the sense that he has a certain relation with our soul; he is not ours, in the sense that we are such men, living such a life under his supervision. This is the meaning of the terms used (by Plato) in the Timaeus.[9] If these be taken in the above sense, all explains itself; if not, Plato contradicts himself.

OUR GUARDIAN HELPS US TO CARRY OUT THE DESTINY WE HAVE CHOSEN

One can still understand thus why he says that our guardian helps us to fulfil the destiny we have chosen. In fact, pesiding over our life, he does not permit us to descend very far below the condition we have chosen. But that which then is active is the principle below the guardian and which can neither transcend him, nor equal him; for he could not become different from what he is.

THAT MAN IS VIRTUOUS WHOSE HIGHEST PRINCIPLE IS ACTIVE WITHIN HIM

6. Who then is the virtuous man? He in whom is active the highest part of the soul. If his guardian contributed to his actions, he would not deserve being called virtuous. Now it is the Intelligence which is active in the virtuous man. It is the latter, then, who is a guardian, or lives according to one; besides, his guardian is the divinity. Is this guardian above Intelligence? Yes, if the guardian have, as guardian, the principle superior to Intelligence (the Good). But why does the virtuous man not enjoy this privilege since the beginning? Because of the trouble he felt in falling into generation. Even before the exercise of reason,

he has within him a desire which leads him to the things which are suitable to him. But does this desire direct with sovereign influence? No, not with sovereignty; for the soul is so disposed that, in such circumstances becoming such, she adopts such a life, and follows such an inclination.

BETWEEN INCARNATIONS IS THE TIME OF JUDGMENT AND EXPIATION.

(Plato) says that the guardian leads the soul to the hells,[10] and that he does not remain attached to the same soul, unless this soul should again choose the same condition. What does the guardian do before this choice? Plato teaches us that he leads the soul to judgment, that after the generation he assumes again the same form as before; and then as if another existence were then beginning, during the time between generations, the guardian presides over the chastisements of the souls, and this period is for them not so much a period of life, as a period of expiation.

EVEN THE SOULS ENTERING INTO ANIMAL BODIES HAVE A GUARDIAN.

Do the souls that enter into the bodies of brutes also have a guardian? Yes, doubtless, but an evil or stupid one.

CONDITION OF SOULS IN THE HIGHER REGIONS.

What is the condition of the souls that have raised themselves on high? Some are in the sensible world, others are outside of it. The souls that are in the sense-world dwell in the sun, or in some other planet, or in the firmament, according as they have more or less developed their reason. We must, indeed, remember that our soul contains in herself not only the intelligible world, but also a disposition conformable to the Soul of the world. Now as the latter is spread out in the movable spheres and in the immovable sphere by her various powers, our soul must possess powers conformable to these, each of which exercise their proper function. The souls which rise from here below into the heavens go to inhabit the star which harmonizes with their moral life, and with the power which they have developed; with their divinity, or their guardian. Then they will have either the same guardian, or the guardian which is superior to the power which they exert. This matter will have to be considered more minutely.

FATE OF THE DIVISIBLE HUMAN SOUL.

As to the souls which have left the sense-world, so long as they remain in the intelligible world, they are above the guardian condition, and the fatality of generation. Souls bring with them thither that part of their nature which is desirous of begetting, and which may reasonably be regarded as the essence which is divisible in the body, and which multiplies by dividing along with the bodies. Moreover, if a soul divide herself, it is not in respect to extension; because she is entirely in all the bodies. On the other hand, the Soul is one; and from a single animal are ceaselessly born many young. This generative element splits up like the vegetative nature in plants; for this nature is divisible in the bodies. When this divisible essence dwells in the same body, it vivifies the body, just as the vegetative power does for plants. When it retires, it has already communicated life, as is seen in cut trees, or in corpses where putrefation has caused the birth of several animals from a single one. Besides, the vegetative power of the human soul is assisted by the vegetative power that is derived from the universal (Soul), and which here below is the same (as on high).

FATE CONSISTS IN THE UNPREDICTABLE CIRCUMSTANCES WHICH ALTER THE LIFE-CURRENTS.

If the soul return here below, she possesses, according to the life which she is to lead, either the same guardian, or another. With her guardian she enters into this world as if in a skiff. Then she is subjected to the power (by Plato) called the Spindle of Necessity;[11] and, embarking in this world, she takes the place assigned to her by fortune. Then she is caught by the circular movement of the heavens, whose action, as if it were the wind, agitates the skiff in which the soul is seated; or rather, is borne along. Thence are born varied spectacles, transformations and divers incidents for the soul which is embarked in this skiff; whether because of the agitation of the sea which bears it, or because of the conduct of the passenger who is sailing in the bark, and who preserves her freedom of action therein. Indeed, not every soul placed in the same circumstances makes the same movements, wills the same volitions, or performs the same actions. For different beings, therefore, the differences arise from circumstances either similar or different, or even the same events may occur to them under different circumstances. It is this (uncertainty) that constitutes Providence.

[1] In his Phaedrus, C246.
[2] Plato, Phaedo, C. i. 242.
[3] Plato, Tim C77
[4] Plato, Rep. x p. 291.
[5] Plato, Tim 91.
[6] The text is very difficult.
[7] Plato, Rep x. p. 617-620
[8] In the Timaeus
[9] C90
[10] Phaedo, p 107, c i p. 300.
[11] Rep. x. 616, p. 234.

FIRST ENNEAD, BOOK NINE.

Of Suicide.

EVIL EFFECTS OF SUICIDE ON THE SOUL HERSELF.

1. (As says pseudo-Zoroaster, in his Magic Oracles), "The soul should not be expelled from the body by violence, lest she go out (dragging along with her something foreign," that is, corporeal). In this case, she will be burdened with this foreign element whithersoever she may emigrate. By "emigrating," I mean passing into the Beyond. On the contrary, one should wait until the entire body naturally detaches itself from the soul; in which case she no longer needs to pass into any other residence, being completely unburdened of the body.

HOW TO DETACH THE SOUL FROM THE BODY NATURALLY.

How will the body naturally detach itself from the soul? By the complete rupture of the bonds which keep the soul attached to the body, by the body's impotence to fetter the soul, on account of the complete destruction of the harmony which conferred this power on it.

VOLUNTARY SOUL-DETACHMENT IS FORBIDDEN.

One may not voluntarily disengage oneself from the fetters of the body. When violence is employed, it is not the body which disengages itself from the soul, it is the soul which makes an effort to snatch herself from the body, and that by an action which accomplishes itself not in the state of impassibility (which suits a sage), but as the result of grief, or suffering, or of anger. Now such an action is forbidden, or unworthy.

SUICIDE UNAVAILABLE EVEN TO AVOID INSANITY.

May one not forestall delirium or insanity, if one become aware of their approach? To begin with, insanity does not happen to a sage, and if it does, this accident should be considered one of those inevitable things which depend from fatality, and in which case one should direct one's path less according to his intrinsic quality than according to circumstances; for perhaps the poison one might select to eject the soul from the body might do nothing but injure the soul.

SUICIDE IS UNADVISABLE, FOR TWO REASONS.

If there be an appointed time for the life of each of us, it is not well to forestall the decree of Providence, unless, as we have said,[1] under absolute compulsion.

Last, if rank obtained above depend on the state obtaining at the time of exit from the body, no man should separate himself from it so long as he might still achieve progress.[2]

---

[1] In i. 2.8, 16. [2] See ii. 9.18.

SECOND ENNEAD, BOOK SIX.

Of Essence and Being.

DISTINCTION BETWEEN ESSENCE AND BEING.

1. Is "essence" something different from "being"? Does essence indicate an abstraction of the other (four categories), and is being, on the contrary, essence with the other (four categories), motion and rest, identity and difference? Are these the elements of being? Yes: "being" is the totality of these things, of which one is essence, the other is motion, and so forth. Motion, therefore, is accidental essence. Is it also accidental "being?" Or is it being completely? Motion is being, because all intelligible things are beings. But why is not each of the sense-things a being? The reason is, that on high all things form only a single group of totality, while here below they are distinct one from another because they are images that have been distinguished. Likewise, in a seminal (reason), all things are together, and each of them is all the others; the hand is not distinct from the head; while, on the contrary, in a body all the organs are separate, because thy are images instead of being genuine beings.

DISTINCTION BETWEEN COMPLEMENTS OF BEING, AND QUALITIES.

We may now say that, in the intelligible world, qualities are the characteristic differences in being or essence. These differences effect distinction between the beings; in short, they cause them to be beings. This definition seems reasonable. But it does not suit the qualities below (in the sense-world); some are differences of being, as biped, or quadruped (as thought Aristotle);[1] others are not differences, and on that very account are called qualities. Still, the same thing may appear a difference when it is a complement of the being, and again it may not seem a difference when it is not a complement of the being, but an accident: as, for instance, whiteness is a complement of being in a swan, or in white lead; but in a human being like you, it is only an accident (as thought Aristotle).[2] So long as the whiteness is in the ("seminal) reason," it is a complement of being, and not a quality; if it be on the surface of a being, it is a quality.

DISTINCTION BETWEEN ESSENTIAL AND MODAL QUALITIES.

Two kinds of qualities must be distinguished; the essential quality, which is a peculiarity of its being, and the mere quality, which affects the being's classification. The mere quality introduces no change in the essence, and causes none of its characteristics to disappear; but, when the being exists already, and is complete, this quality gives it a certain exterior disposition; and, whether in the case of a soul or body, adds something to it. Thus visible whiteness, which is of the very being of white lead, is not of the being of the swan, because a swan may be of some color other than white. Whiteness then completes the being of white lead, just as heat completes the being of fire. If igneousness is said to be the being of fire, whiteness is also the being of white lead. Nevertheless, the igneousness of the visible fire is heat, which constitutes the complement of its being; and whiteness plays the same part with respect to white lead. Therefore (differing according to the difference of various beings) the same things will be complements of being, and will not be qualities, or they will not be complements of being, and will be qualities; but it would not be reasonable to assert that these qualities are different according to whether or not they are complements of being, since their nature is the same.

DISTINCTION BETWEEN WHATNESS AND AFFECTIONS OF BEING.

We must acknowledge that the reasons which produce these things (as heat, and whiteness) are beings, if taken in their totality; but on considering their production, we see that what constitutes a whatness or quiddity (the Aristotelian "what it were to be") in the intelligible world, becomes a quality in the sense-world. Consequently, we always err on the subject of the quiddity, when we try to determine it, mistaking the simple quality for it (as thought Plato),[3] for, when we perceive a quality, the fire is not what we call fire, but a being. As to the things which arrest our gaze, we should distinguish them from the quiddity, and define them by the qualities of sense (objects); for they do not constitute the being, but the affections of being.

ACTUALIZED BEING LESS PERFECT THAN ESSENCE.

We are thus led to ask how a being can be composed of non-beings? It has already been pointed out that the things subject to generation could not be identical with the principles from which they proceed. Let us now add that they could not be beings. But still, how can one say that the intelligible being is constituted by a non-being? The reason is that in the intelligible world since being forms a purer and more refined essence, being really is somehow constituted by the differences of essence; or rather, we feel it ought to be called being from considering it together with its energies (or, actualizations). This being seems to be a perfecting of essence; but perhaps being is less perfect when it is thus considered together with its actualizations; for, being less simple, it veers away from essence.

SUCHNESS IS LATER THAN BEING AND QUIDDITY.

2. Let us now consider what quality in general is; for when we shall know this, our doubts will cease. First, must it be admitted that one and the same thing is now a quality, and then a complement of being? Can one say that quality is the complement of being, or rather of such a being? The suchness of being implies a previously existing being and quiddity.

BEING CANNOT PRECEDE SUCH BEING.

Taking the illustration of fire, is it "mere being" before it is "such being?" In this case, it would be a body. Consequently, the body will be a being; fire will be a hot body. Body and heat combined will not constitute being; but heat will exist in the body as in you exists the property of having a stub nose (as said Aristotle).[4] Consequently, if we abstract heat, shine and lightness, which seem to be qualities, and also impenetrability, nothing will remain but tridimensional extension, and matter will be "being." But this hypothesis does not seem likely; it is rather form which will be "being."

FORM IS NOT A QUALITY; BUT A REASON.

Is form a quality? No: form is a reason. Now what is constituted by (material) substance, and reason? (In the warm body) it is neither what burns, nor what is visible; it is quality. If, however, it be said that combustion is an act emanating from reason, that being hot and white are actualities, we could not find anything to explain quality.

QUALITIES ARE ACTS OF BEING, PROCEEDING FROM REASONS AND ESSENTIAL POTENTIALITIES.

What we call a complement of being should not be termed a quality, because they are actualizations of being, actualizations which proceed from the reasons and the essential potentialities. Qualities are therefore something outside of being; something which does not at times seem to be, and at other times does not seem not to be qualities; something which adds to being something that is not necessary; for example, virtues and vices, ugliness and beauty, health, and individual resemblance. Though triangle, and tetragon, each considered by itself, are not qualities; yet being "transformed into triangular appearance" is a quality; it is not therefore triangularity, but triangular formation, which is a quality. The same could be said of the arts and professions. Consequently, quality is a disposition, either adventitious or original, in already existing beings. Without it, however, being would exist just as much. It might be said that quality is either mutable or immutable; for it forms two kinds, according to whether it be permanent or changeable.

DIFFERENCE BETWEEN INTELLIGIBLE AND SENSE-QUALITY.

3. The whiteness that I see in you is not a quality, but an actualization of the potentiality of whitening. In the intelligible world all the things that we call qualities are actualizations. They are called qualities because they are properties, because they differentiate the beings from each other, because in respect to themselves they bear a particular character. But since quality in the sense-world is also an actualization, in what does it differ from the intelligible quality? The sense-quality does not show the essential quality of every being, nor the difference or character of sub-

stances, but simply the thing that we properly call quality, and which is an actualization in the intelligible world. When the property of something is to be a being, this thing is not a quality. But when reason separates beings from their properties, when it removes nothing from them, when it limits itself to conceiving and begetting different from these beings, it begets quality, which it conceives of as the superficial part of being. In this case, nothing hinders the heat of the fire, so far as it is natural to it, from constituting a form, an actualization, and not a quality of the fire; it is a quality when it exists in a substance where it no longer constitutes the form of being, but only a trace, an adumbration, an image of being, because it finds itself separated from the being whose actualization it is.

QUALITIES ARE ACCIDENTAL SHAPES OF BEING.

Qualities, therefore, are everything that, instead of being actualizations and forms of beings, are only its accidents, and only reveal its shapes. We will therefore call qualities the habituations and the dispositions which are not essential to substances. The archetypes (or models) of qualities are the actualizations of the beings, which are the principles of these qualities. It is impossible for the same thing at one time to be, and at another not to be a quality. What can be separated from being is quality; what remains united to being is being, form, and actualization. In fact, nothing can be the same in itself, and in some other condition where it has ceased to be form and an actualization. What, instead of being the form of a being, is always its accident, is purely and exclusively a quality.

---

[1] As thought Aristotle, Met v. 14. [2] As thought Aristotle, Met. v. 30. [3] As thought Plato, Letter 7, 343. [4] As said Aristotle, Met. vii. 5.

FIFTH ENNEAD, BOOK SEVEN.

Do Ideas of Individuals Exist?

TWO POSSIBLE HYPOTHESES OF IDEAS OF INDIVIDUALS

1. Do ideas of individuals (as well as of classes of individuals), exist? This means that if I, in company with some other man, were to trace ourselves back to the intelligible world, we would there find separate individual principles corresponding to each of us. (This might imply either of two theories.) Either, if the individual named Socrates be eternal, and if the soul of Socrates be Socrates himself, then the soul of each individual is contained in the intelligible world. Or if, on the contrary, the individual named Socrates be not eternal, if the same soul can belong successively to several individuals, such as Socrates or Pythagoras, then (as Alcinoous, e. g., and other Platonists insist), each individual does not have his idea in the intelligible world.

THE FIRST (NON-PLATONIC) HYPOTHESIS ALONE RIGHT.

If the particular soul of each man contains ("seminal) reasons" of all the things she does, then each individual corresponds to his idea in the intelligible world, for we admit that each soul contains as many ("seminal) reasons" as the entire world. In this case, the soul would contain not only the ("seminal) reasons" of men but also those of all animals, the number of these reasons will be infinite, unless (as the Stoics teach) the world does not re-commence the identical series of existences in fixed periods; for the only means of limiting the infinity of reasons, is that the same things should reproduce themselves.

DIFFERENCE OF THINGS DEPEND ON THEIR SEMINAL REASONS.

But, if produced things may be more numerous than their specimens, what would be the necessity for the "reasons" and specimens of all individuals begotten during some one period? It would seem that the (idea of) the "man himself" to explain the existence of all men, and that the souls of a finite number of them could successively animate men of an infinite number. (To this contention we demur: for) it is impossible for different things to have an identical ("seminal) reason." The (idea of) the man himself would not, as model, suffice (to account) for men who differ from each other not only by matter, but also by specific differences. They cannot be compared to the images of Socrates which reproduce their model. Only the difference of the ("seminal) reasons" could give rise to individual differences. (As Plato said),[1] the entire period contains all the ("seminal) reasons." When it recommences, the same things rearise through the same "reasons." We need not fear that, as a consequence, there would be an infinite (number or variety) of them in the intelligible world; for the multitude (of the seminal reasons) constitutes an indivisible principle from which each issues forth whenever active.

SEX ALONE WOULD NOT ACCOUNT FOR THIS DIVERSITY.

2. (First objection): The manner in which the ("seminal) reasons" of the male and female unite, in the act of generation, suffices to account for the divers-

ity of individuals, without implying that each of them possesses its own ("seminal) reason." The generating principle, the male, for eaxmple, will not propagate according to different ("seminal) reasons," since it possesses all of them, but only according to its own, or those of its father. Since it possesses all of the ("seminal) reasons," nothing would hinder it from begetting according to different "reasons," only, there are always some which are more disposed to act than are others.

EXPLANATION OF THE DIVERSITY FROM SAME PARENTS.

(Second objection): Please explain how differing individuals are born from the same parents. This diversity, if it be anything more than merely apparent, depends on the manner in which the two generating principles concur in the act of generation; at one time the male predominates, at other times, the female; again, they may both act equally. In either case, the ("seminal) reason" is given in its entirety, and dominates the matter furnished by either of the generating principles.

VARIETY MAY DEPEND ON THE LATENCY OF PART OF SEMINAL REASONS.

(Third objection): What then is the cause of the difference of the individuals conceived in some other place (than the womb, as in the mouth), (as Aristotle[2] and Sextus Empiricus[3] asked)? Would it arise from matter being penetrated by the ("seminal) reason" in differing degrees? In this case, all the individuals, except one, would be beings against nature (which, of course, is absurd). The varieties of the individuals are a principle of beauty; consequently, form cannot be one of them; ugliness alone should be attributed to the predominance of matter. In the intelligible world, the ("seminal) reasons" are perfect, and they are not given any less entirely for being hidden.

LEIBNITZ'S DOCTRINE OF THE INDISCERNIBLES.

(Fourth objection): Granting that the ("seminal) reasons" of the individuals are different, why should there be as many as there are individuals which achieve existence in any one period? It is possible that identical "reasons" might produce individuals differing in external appearance; and we have even granted that this may occur when the ("seminal) reasons" are given entirely. It is asked, is this possible when the same "reasons" are developed? We teach that absolutely similar things might be reproduced in different periods; but, within the same period, there is nothing absolutely identical.

THERE ARE DIFFERENT IDEAS FOR TWINS, BRETHREN, OR WORKS OF ART.

3. (Fifth objection): But how could ("seminal) reasons" be different in the conception of twins, and in the act of generation in the case of animals who procreate multiple offspring? Here it would seem that when the individuals are similar, there could be but one single "reason." No so; for in that case there would not be so many "reasons" as there are individuals; and, on the contrary, it will have to be granted that there are as many as there are individuals that differ by specific differences, and not by a mere lack of form. Nothing therefore hinders us from admitting that there are different "reasons," even for animal offspring which show no difference, if there were such. An artist who produces similar works cannot produce this resemblance without introducing in it some difference which depends on reasoning; so that every work he produces differs from the others, because he adds some difference to the similarity. In nature, where the difference does

not derive from reasoning, but only from differing ("seminal) reasons" the (individual) difference will have to be added to the specific form, even though we may not be able to discern it. The ("seminal) reason" would be different if generation admitted chance as to quantity (the number of offspring begotten). But if the number of things to be born is determinate, the quantity will be limited by the evolution and development of all the "reasons," so that, when the series of all things will be finished, another period may recommence. The quantity suitable to the world, and the number of beings who are to exist therein, are things regulated and contained in the principle which contains all the "reasons" (that is, the universal Soul), from the very beginning.

[1] Phaedros C1 217. [2] de Gen. An. 4.2. [3] Adv. Math. 5 102 p 355.

FIRST ENNEAD, BOOK TWO.

Concerning Virtue.

VIRTUE THE ROAD TO ESCAPE EVILS.

1. Man must flee from (this world) here below (for two reasons): because it is the nature of the soul to flee from evil, and because inevitable evil prevails and dominates this world here below. What is this flight (and how can we accomplish it)? (Plato),[1] tells us it consists in "being assimilated to divinity." This then can be accomplished by judiciously conforming to justice, and holiness; in short, by virtue.

CAN THESE VIRTUES BE ASCRIBED TO THE DIVINITY?

If then it be by virtue that we are assimilated (to divinity), does this divinity to whom we are trying to achieve assimilation, Himself possess virtue? Besides, what divinity is this? Surely it must be He who must most seem to possess virtue, the world-Soul, together with the principle predominating in her, whose wisdom is most admirable (supreme Intelligence)—for it is quite reasonable that we should be assimilated to Him. Nevertheless, one might, unreflectingly, question whether all virtues might suit this divinity; whether, for instance, moderation in his desires, or courage could be predicated of Him; for, as to courage, nothing can really harm Him, and He therefore has nothing to fear; and as to moderation, no pleasant object whose presence would excite His desires, or whose absence would in Him awaken regrets, could possibly exist. But inasmuch as the divinity, just as we ourselves, aspires to intelligible things, He is evidently the source of our gracious sanity and virtues. So we are forced to ask ourselves, "Does the divinity possess these virtues?"

HOMELY VIRTUES ASSIMILATE US TO DIVINITY ONLY PARTIALLY.

It would not be proper to attribute to Him the homely (or, civil) virtues, such as prudence, which "relates to the rational part of our nature"; courage, which "relates to our irascible part"; temperance, which consists of the harmonious consonance of our desires and our reason; last, of justice, which "consists in the accomplishment by all these faculties of the function proper to each of them," "whether to commnd, or to obey," (as said Plato[2]). But if we cannot become assimilated to the divinity by these homely virtues, that process must demand similarly named virtues of a superior order. However, these homely virtues would not be entirely useless to achieve that result, for one cannot say that while practising them one does not at all resemble the divinity as they who practise them are reputed to be godlike. These lower virtues do therefore yield some resemblance to the divinity, but complete assimilation can result only from virtues of a higher order.

THE DIVINE NEED NOT POSSESS THE LOWER VIRTUES BY WHICH WE ARE ASSIMILATED TO HIM.

Virtues, even if they be not homely, are therefore ultimately ascribed (to the divinity). Granting that the divinity does not possess the homely virtues, we may still become assimilated to Him by other virtues for with virtues of another order the case might differ. Therefore, without assimilating ourselves to the divinity by homely virtues we might nevertheless by means of virtues which still are ours, become assimilated to the Being which does not possess virtue.

This may be explained by an illustration. When a body is warmed by the presence of fire, the fire itself need not be heated by the presence of another fire. It might be argued that there was heat in the fire, but a heat that is innate. Reasoning by analogy, the virtue, which in the soul is only adventitious, is innate in Him from whom the soul derives it by imitation; (in other words, the cause need not necessarily possess the same qualities as the effect).

Our argument from heat might however be questioned, inasmuch as the divinity really does possess virtue, though it be of a higher nature. This observavation would be correct, if the virtue in which the soul participates were identical with the principle from which she derives it. But there is a complete opposition; for when we see a house, the sense-house is not identical with the intelligible House, though possessing resemblance thereto. Indeed, the sense-house participates in order and proportion, though neither order, proportion, nor symmetry could be attributed to the idea of the House. Likewise, we derived from the divinity order, proportion and harmony, which, here below, are conditions of virtue, without thereby implying that the divinity Himself need possess order, proportion, or harmony. Similarly, it is not necessary that He possess virtue, although we become assimilated to Him thereby.

Such is our demonstration that human assimilation to the divine Intelligence by virtue does not (necessarily imply) (in the divine Intelligence itself) possession of virtue. Mere logical demonstration thereof is not, however, sufficient; we must also convince.

THERE ARE TWO KINDS OF RESEMBLANCE.

2. Let us first examine the virtues by which we are assimilated to the divinity, and let us study the identity between our soul-image which constitutes virtue, and

supreme Intelligence's principle which, without being virtue, is its archetype. There are two kinds of resemblance: the first entails such identity of nature as exists when both similar things proceed from a same principle; the second is that of one thing to another which precedes it, as its principle. In the latter case, there is no reciprocity, and the principle does not resemble that which is inferior to it; or rather, the resemblance must be conceived entirely differently. It does not necessitate that the similar objects be of the same kind; it rather implies that they are of different kinds, inasmuch as they resemble each other differently.

HOW HOMELY VIRTUES MAY ASSIMILATE MAN TO THE SUPREME.

(It is difficult to define) what is virtue, in general or in particular. To clear up the matter, let us consider one particular kind of virtue: then it will be easy to determine the common essence underlying them all.

The above-mentioned homely virtues really render our souls gracious, and improve them, regulating and moderating our appetites, tempering our passions, delivering us from false opinions, limiting us within just bounds, and they themselves must be determined by some kind of measure. This measure given to our souls resembles the form given to matter, and the proportion of intelligible things; it is as it were a trace of what is most perfect above. What is unmeasured, being no more than formless matter, cannot in any way resemble divinity. The greater the participation in form, the greater the assimilation to the formless; and the closer we get to form, the greater the participation therein. Thus our soul, whose nature is nearer to divinity and more kindred to it than the body is, thereby participates the more in the divine, and increases that resemblance enough to make it seem that the divinity is all that she herself is. Thus arises the deception, which represents her as the divine divinity, as if her quality constituted that of the divinity. Thus are men of homely virtues assimilated to the divinity.

PLATO DISTINGUISHES BETWEEN THE HOMELY AND THE HIGHER VIRTUES.

3. We will now, following (Plato),[3] speak of another kind of assimilation as the privilege of a higher virtue. We will thus better understand the nature of homely virtues, and the higher virtues, and the difference between them. Plato is evidently distinguishing two kinds of virtues when he says that assimilation to the divinity consists in fleeing from (the world) here below; when he adds the qualification "homely" to the virtues relating to social life; and when in another place he asserts[4] that all virtues are processes of purification; and it is not to the homely virtues that he attributes the power of assimilating us to the divinity.

HOW VIRTUES PURIFY.

How then do the virtues purify? How does this process of purification bring us as near as possible to the divinity? So long as the soul is mingled with the body, sharing its passions and opinions, she is evil. She becomes better, that is, she acquires virtues, only when, instead of agreeing with the body, she thinks by herself (this is true thought, and constitutes prudence); when she ceases to share its passions (in other words, temperance); when she no longer fears separation from the body (a state called courage); and last, when reason and intelligence can enforce their command (or justice).

SELF-CONTROL IS ASSIMILATION TO THE DIVINITY.

We may therefore unhesitatingly state that the resemblance to the divinity lies in such regulation, in remaining impassible while thinking intelligible things; for what is pure is divine and the nature of the divine action is such that whatever imitates it thereby possesses wisdom. But it is not the divinity that possesses such a disposition, for dispositions are the property of souls only. Besides, the soul does not think intelligible objects in the same manner as the divinity; what is contained in the divinity is contained within us in a manner entirely different, or even perhaps is not at all contained. For instance, the divinity's thought is not at all identical with ours; the divinity's thought is a primary principle from which our thought is derived and differs. As the vocal word is only the image of the interior reason[5] of the soul, so also is the word of the soul only the image of the Word of a superior principle; and as the exterior word, when compared to the interior reason of the soul, seems discrete, or divided, so the reason of the soul, which is no more than the interpreter of the intelligible word, is discrete, in comparison with the latter. Thus does virtue belong to the soul without belonging either to absolute Intelligence, nor to the Principle superior to Intelligence.

PURIFICATION PRODUCES CONVERSION; AND VIRTUE MAKES USE OF THIS.

4. Purification may be either identical with the above-defined virtue, or virtue may be the result of purification. In this case, does virtue consist of the actual process of purification, or in the already purified condition? This is our problem here.

The process of purification is inferior to the already purified condition; for purity is the soul's destined goal. (Negative) purity is mere separation from extraneous things; it is not yet (positive) possession of its prize. If the soul had possessed goodness before losing her purity, mere purification would be sufficient; and even in this case the residuum of the purification would be the goodness, and not the purification. What is the residuum? Not goodness; otherwise, the soul would not have fallen into evil. The soul therefore possesses the form of goodness, without however being able to remain solidly attached thereto, because her nature permits her to turn either to the good, or the evil. The good of the soul is to remain united to her sister intelligence; her evil, is to abandon herself to the contrary things. After purifying the soul, therefore, she must be united to the divinity; but this implies turning her towards Him. Now this conversion does not begin to occur after the purification, but is its very result. The virtue of the soul, therefore, does not consist in her conversion, but in that which she thereby obtains. This is the intuition of her intelligible object; its image produced and realized within herself; an image similar to that in the eye, an image which represents the things seen. It is not necessary to conclude that the soul did not possess this image, nor had any reminiscence thereof; she no doubt possessed it, but inactively, latently, obscurely. To clarify it, to discover her possessions, the soul needs to approach the source of all clearness. As, however, the soul possesses only the images of the intelligibles, without possessing the intelligibles themselves, she will be compelled to compare with them her own image of them. Easily does the soul contemplate the intelligibles, because the intelligence is not foreign to her; when the soul wishes to enter in relations with them, all the soul needs to do is to turn her glance towards them. Otherwise, the intelligence, though present in the soul, will remain foreign to her. This explains how all our acquisitions of knowledge are foreign to us (as if non-existent), while we fail to recall them.

CONCERNING VIRTUE

THE LIMIT OF PURIFICATION IS THAT OF THE SOUL'S SELF-CONTROL.

5. The limit of purification decides to which (of the three hypostases of) divinity the soul may hope to assimilate and identify herself; therefore we shall have to consider that limit. To decide that would be to examine the limit of the soul's ability to repress anger, appetites, and passions of all kinds, to triumph over pain and similar feelings—in short, to separate her from the body. This occurs when, recollecting herself from the various localities over which she had, as it were, spread herself, she retires within herself; when she estranges herself entirely from the passions, when she allows the body only such pleasures as are necessary or suitable to cure her pains, to recuperate from its fatigues, and in avoiding its becoming importunate; when she becomes insensible to sufferings; or, if that be beyond her power, in supporting them patiently, and in diminishing them by refusing to share them; when she appeases anger as far as possible, even suppressing it entirely, if possible; or at least, if that be impossible, not participating therein; abandoning to the animal nature all unthinking impulses, and even so reducing to a minimum all reflex movements; when she is absolutely inaccessible to fear, having nothing left to risk; and when she represses all sudden movements, except nature's warning of dangers. Evidently, the purified soul will have to desire nothing shameful. In eating and drinking, she will seek only the satisfaction of a need, while remaining foreign to it; nor will she seek the pleasures of love; or, if she does, she will not go beyond the exactions of nature, resisting every unconsidered tendency, or even in remaining within the involuntary flights of fancy.

THE INFLUENCE OF REASON IS SUGGESTIVE.

In short, the soul will be pure from all these passions, and will even desire to purify our being's irrational part so as to preserve it from emotions, or at least to moderate their number and intensity, and to appease them promptly by her presence. So would a man, in the neighborhood of some sage, profit thereby, either by growing similar to him, or in refraining from doing anything of which the sage might disapprove. This (suggestive) influence of reason will exert itself without any struggle; its mere presence will suffice. The inferior principle will respect it to the point of growing resentful against itself, and reproaching itself for its weakness, if it feel any agitation which might disturb its master's repose.

THE GOAL OF PURIFICATION IS SECOND DIVINITY, INTELLIGENCE.

6 A man who has achieved such a state no longer commits such faults; for he has become corrected. But his desired goal is not to cease failing, but to be divine. In case he still allows within himself the occurrence of some of the above-mentioned unreflecting impulses, he will be simultaneously divinity and guardian, a double being; or rather, he will contain a principle of another nature (Intelligence), whose virtue will likewise differ from his. If, however, he be not troubled by any of those motions, he will be wholly divine; he will be one of those divinities "who (as Plato said)[6] form the attending escort of the First." It is a divinity of such a nature that has come down from above to dwell in us. To become again what one was originally, is to live in this superior world. He who has achieved that height dwells with pure Intelligence, and assimilates himself thereto as far as possible. Consequently, he feels none of those emotions, nor does he any more commit any actions, which

would be disapproved of by the superior principle who henceforth is his only master.

THE HIGHER VIRTUES MERGE INTO WISDOM.

For such a being the separate virtues merge. For him, wisdom consists in contemplating the (essences) possessed by Intelligence, and with which Intelligence is in contact. There are two kinds of wisdom, one being proper to intelligence, the other to the soul; only in the latter may we speak of virtue. In the Intelligence exists only the energy (of thought), and its essence. The image of this essence, seen here below in a being of another nature, is the virtue which emanates from it. In Intelligence, indeed, resides neither absolute justice, nor any of those genuinely so-called virtues; nothing is left but their type. Its derivative in the soul is virtue; for virtue is the attribute of an individual being. On the contrary, the intelligible belongs to itself only, and is the attribute of no particular being.

INCARNATE JUSTICE IS INDIVIDUAL; IF ABSOLUTE, IT IS INDIVISIBLE.

Must justice ever imply multiplicity if it consist in fulfilling its proper function? Surely, as long as it inheres in a principle with several parts (such as a human soul, in which several functions may be distinguished); but its essence lies in the accomplishment of the function proper to every being, even when inhering in a unitary principle (such as Intelligence). Absolute and veritable Justice consists in the self-directed action of an unitary Principle, in which no parts can be distinguished.

THE HIGHER FORMS OF THE VIRTUES.

In this higher realm, justice consists in directing the action of the soul towards intelligence; temperance is the intimate conversion of the soul towards intelligence; courage is the (suggestive fascination) or impassibility, by which the soul becomes similar to that which it contemplates; since it is natural for intelligence to be impassible. Now the soul derives this impassibility from the virtue which hinders her from sharing the passions of the lower principle with which she is associated.

EVEN THE LOWER VIRTUES ARE MUTUALLY RELATED.

7. Within the soul the virtues have the same interconnection obtaining within Intelligence between the types superior to virtue. For Intelligence, it is thought that constitutes wisdom and prudence; conversion towards oneself is temperance; the fulfillment of one's proper function is justice, and the intelligence's perseverance in remaining within itself, in maintaining itself pure and separated from matter, is analogous to courage. To contemplate intelligence will therefore, for the soul, constitute wisdom and prudence, which then become virtues, and no longer remain mere intellectual types. For the soul is not identical with the essences she thinks, as is intelligence. Similarly, the other soul-virtues will correspond to the superior types. It is not otherwise with purification, for since every virtue is a purification, virtue exacts preliminary purification; otherwise, it would not be perfect.

THE HIGHER VIRTUES IMPLY THE LOWER; BUT NOT CONVERSELY.

The possessor of the higher virtues necessarily possesses the potentiality for the inferior virtues; but the possessor of the lower does not, conversely, possess the higher. Such are the characteristics of the virtuous man.

PRUDENCE TO DECIDE WHETHER IT IS POSSIBLE TO POSSESS VIRTUES UNSYMMETRICALLY?

(Many interesting questions remain). Is it possible for a man to possess the higher or lower virtues in accomplished reality, or otherwise (merely theoretically)? To decide that, we would have individually to examine each, as, for example, prudence. How could such a virtue exist merely potentially, borrowing its principles from elsewhere? What would happen if one virtue advanced naturally to a certain degree, and another virtue to another? What would you think of a temperance which would moderate certain (impulses), while entirely suppressing others? Similar questions might be raised about other virtues, and the arbiter of the degree to which the virtues have attained would have to be prudence.

THE HOMELY VIRTUES MUST BE SUPPLEMENTED BY DIVINE DISCONTENT.

No doubt, under certain circumstances, the virtuous man, in his actions, will make use of some of the lower, or homely virtues; but even so he will supplement them by standards or ideas derived from higher virtues. For instance, he will not be satisfied with a temperance which would consist in mere moderation, but he will gradually seek to separate himself more and more from matter. Again, he will supplement the life of a respectable man, exacted by common-sense homely virtues; he will be continually aspiring higher, to the life of the divinities; for our effort at assimilation should be directed not at mere respectability, but to the gods themselves. To seek no more than to become assimilated to respectable individuals would be like trying to make an image by limiting oneself to copying another image, itself modelled after another image (but not copying the original). The assimilation here recommended results from taking as model a superior being.

---

[1] Theataetus, C2,132 [2] Rep. iv. E3,434. [3] Theataetus, 176. [4] Plato, Phaedo, 69. [5] Pun on the word "logos," which means both reason and word. [6] Plato, Phaedrus, 246.

FIRST ENNEAD, BOOK THREE.

Of Dialectic, or the Means of Raising the Soul to the Intelligible World.

SEARCH FOR A DEMONSTRATION OF DIVINITY SUCH THAT THE DEMONSTRATION ITSELF WILL DEIFY.

1. What method, art or study will lead us to the goal we are to attain, namely, the Good, the first Principle, the Divinity,[1] by a demonstration which itself can serve to raise the soul to the superior world?

METHODS DIFFER ACCORDING TO INDIVIDUALS; BUT THERE ARE CHIEFLY TWO.

He who is to be promoted to that world should know everything, or at least, as says (Plato),[2] he should be as learned as possible. In his first generation he should have descended here below to form a philosopher, a musician, a lover. That is the kind of men whose nature makes them most suitable to be raised to the intelligible world. But how are we going to raise them? Does a single method suffice for all? Does not each of them need a special method? Doubtless. There are two methods to follow: the one for those who rise to the intelligible world from here below, and the other for those who have already reached there. We shall start by the first of these two methods; then comes that of the men who have already achieved access to the intelligible world, and who have, so to speak, already taken root there. Even these must ceaselessly progress till they have reached the summit; for one must stop only when one has reached the supreme term.

RETURN OF THE SOUL OF THE PHILOSOPHER, MUSICIAN AND LOVER.

The latter road of progress must here be left aside (to be taken up later),[3] to discuss here fully the first, explaining the operation of the return of the soul to the intelligible world. Three kinds of men offer themselves to our examination: the philosopher, the musician, and the lover. These three must clearly be distinguished, beginning by determining the nature and character of the musician.

HOW THE MUSICIAN RISES TO THE INTELLIGIBLE WORLD.

The musician allows himself to be easily moved by beauty, and admires it greatly; but he is not able by himself to achieve the intuition of the beautiful. He needs the stimulation of external impressions. Just as some timorous being is awakened by the least noise, the musician is sensitive to the beauty of the voice and of harmonies. He avoids all that seems contrary to the laws of harmony and of unity, and enjoys rhythm and melodies in instrumental and vocal music. After these purely sensual intonations, rhythm and tunes, he will surely in them come to distinguish form from matter, and to contemplate the beauty existing in their proportions and relations. He will have to be taught that what excites his admiration in these things, is their intelligible harmony, the beauty it contains, and, in short, beauty absolute, and not particular. He will have to be introduced to philosophy by arguments that will lead him to recognize truths that he ignored, though he possessed them instinctively. Such arguments will be specified elsewhere.[4]

HOW THE LOVER RISES TO THE INTELLIGIBLE.

2. The musician can rise to the rank of the lover, and either remain there, or rise still higher. But the lover has some reminiscence of the beautiful; but as here below he is separated (from it, he is incapable of clearly knowing what it is). Charmed with the beautiful objects that meet his views, he falls into an ecstasy. He must therefore be taught not to content himself with thus admiring a single body, but, by reason, to embrace all bodies that reveal beauty; showing him what is identical in all, informing him that it is something alien to the bodies, which comes from elsewhere, and which exists even in a higher degree in the objects of another nature; citing, as examples, noble occupations, and beautiful laws. He will be shown that beauty is found in the arts, the sciences, the virtues, all of which are suitable means of familiarizing the lover with the taste of incorporeal things. He will then be made to see that beauty is one, and he will be shown the element which, in every object, constitutes beauty. From virtues he will be led to progress to intelligence and essence, while from there he will have nothing else to do but to progress towards the supreme goal.

HOW THE PHILOSOPHER RISES TO THE INTELLIGIBLE WORLD.

3. The philosopher is naturally disposed to rise to the intelligible world. Borne on by light wings, he rushes thither without needing to learn to disengage himself from sense-objects, as do the preceding men. His only uncertainty will concern the road to be followed, all he will need will be a guide. He must therefore be shown the road; he must be helped to detach himself entirely from sense-objects, himself already possessing, as he does, the desire, being since a long while already detached therefrom by his nature. For this purpose he will be invited to apply himself to

mathematics, so as to accustom him to think of incorporeal things, to believe in their existence. Being desirous of instruction, he will learn them easily; as, by his nature, he is already virtuous, he will need no more than promotion to the perfection of virtue. After mathematics, he will be taught dialectics, which will perfect him.

WHAT DIALECTICS IS.

4. What then is this dialectics, knowledge of which must be added to mathematics? It is a science which makes us capable of reasoning about each thing, to say what it is, in what it differs from the others, in what it resembles them, where it is, whether it be one of the beings, to determine how many veritable beings there are, and which are the objects that contain nonentity instead of veritable essence. This science treats also of good and evil; of everything that is subordinated to (being), the Good, and to its contrary; of the nature of what is eternal, and transitory. It treats of each matter scientifically, and not according to mere opinion. Instead of wandering around the sense-world, it establishes itself in the intelligible world; it concentrates its whole attention on this world, and after having saved our soul from deceit, dialectics "pastures our soul in the meadow of truth,"[5] (as thought Plato). Then it makes use of the Platonic method of division to discern ideas, to define each object, to rise to the several kinds of essences[6] (as thought Plato); then, by thought concatenating all that is thence derived, dialectics continues its deductions until it has gone through the whole domain of the intelligible. Then, by reversing, dialectics returns to the very Principle from which first it had started out.[7] Resting there, because it is only in the intelligible world that it can find rest, no longer needing to busy itself with a multitude of objects, because it has arrived at unity, dia-

lectics considers its logic, which treats of propositions and arguments. This logic is an art subordinate to dialectics just as writing is subordinate to thought. In logic, dialectics recognizes some principles as necessary, and others as constituting preparatory exercises. Then, along with everything else, subjecting these principles to its criticism, it declares some of them useful, and others superfluous, or merely technical.

DIALECTICS IS THE HIGHEST PART OF PHILOSOPHY.

5. ·Whence does this science derive its proper principles? Intelligence furnishes the soul with the clear principles she is capable of receiving. Having discovered and achieved these principles, dialectics puts their consequences in order. Dialectics composes, and divides, till it has arrived at a perfect intelligence of things; for according to (Plato),[8] dialectics is the purest application of intelligence and wisdom. In this case, if dialectics be the noblest exercise of our faculties, it must exercise itself with essence and the highest objects. Wisdom studies existence, as intelligence studies that which is still beyond existence (the One, or the Good). But is not philosophy also that which is most eminent? Surely. But there is no confusion between philosophy and dialectics, because dialectics is the highest part of philosophy. It is not (as Aristotle thought) merely an instrument for philosophy, nor (as Epicurus thought) made up of pure speculations and abstract rules. It studies things themselves, and its matter is the (real) beings. It reaches them by following a method which yields reality as well as the idea. Only accidentally does dialectics busy itself with error and sophisms. Dialectics considers them alien to its mission, and as produced by a foreign principle. Whenever anything contrary to the rule of truth is advanced, dialectics recognizes the error by the light of the truths it contains. Dialectics, however, does not care for

propositions, which, to it, seem only mere groupings of letters. Nevertheless, because it knows the truth, dialectics also understands propositions, and, in general, the operations of the soul. Dialectics knows what it is to affirm, to deny, and how to make contrary or contradictory assertions. Further, dialectics distinguishes differences from identities, grasping the truth by an intuition that is as instantaneous as is that of the senses; but dialectics leaves to another science, that enjoys those details, the care of treating them with exactness.

THE VARIOUS BRANCHES OF PHILOSOPHY CROWNED BY DIALECTICS.

6. Dialectics, therefore, is only one part of philosophy, but the most important. Indeed, philosophy has other branches. First, it studies nature (in physics), therein employing dialectics, as the other arts employ arithmetic, though philosophy owes far more to dialectics. Then philosophy treats of morals, and here again it is dialectics that ascertains the principles; ethics limits itself to building good habits thereon, and to propose the exercises that shall produce those good habits. The (Aristotelian) rational virtues also owe to dialectics the principles which seem to be their characteristics; for they chiefly deal with material things (because they moderate the passions). The other virtues[9] also imply the application of reason to the passions and actions which are characteristic of each of them. However, prudence applies reason to them in a superior manner. Prudence deals rather with the universal, considering whether the virtues concatenate, and whether an action should be done now, or be deferred, or be superseded by another[10] (as thought Aristotle). Now it is dialectics, or its resultant science of wisdom which, under a general and immaterial form, furnishes prudence with all the principles it needs.

WITHOUT DIALECTICS LOWER KNOWLEDGE WOULD BE IMPERFECT.

Could the lower knowledge not be possessed without dialectics or wisdom? They would, at least, be imperfect and mutilated. On the other hand, though the dialectician, that is, the true sage, no longer need these inferior things, he never would have become such without them; they must precede, and they increase with the progress made in dialectics. Virtues are in the same case. The possessor of natural virtues may, with the assistance of wisdom, rise to perfect virtues. Wisdom, therefore, only follows natural virtues. Then wisdom perfects the morals. Rather, the already existing natural virtues increase and grow perfect along with wisdom. Whichever of these two things precedes, complements the other. Natural virtues, however, yield only imperfect views and morals; and the best way to perfect them, is philosophic knowledge of the principles from which they depend.

[1] v 1 1. [2] In his Phaedrus, Et. 266 [3] In v. 1 1. [4] i 3. 4, 5, 6; i. 6. [5] In his Phaedrus, p. 248. [6] In his Politician, p. 262. [7] v 1 [8] In his Sophist, p 253 [9] See i 2 3-6 [10] Morals i. 34, 35; Nicom Eth., vi. 8, 11

FOURTH ENNEAD, BOOK TWO.

How the Soul Mediates Between Indivisible and Divisible Essence.

OUTLINE OF THE PSYCHOLOGICAL STUDY OF IV. 7.

1. While studying the nature ("being") of the soul, we have shown (against the Stoics) that she is not a body; that, among incorporeal entities, she is not a "harmony" (against the Pythagoreans); we have also shown that she is not an "entelechy" (against Aristotle), because this term, as its very etymology implies, does not express a true idea, and reveals nothing about the soul's (nature itself); last, we said that the soul has an intelligible nature, and is of divine condition; the "being" or nature of the soul we have also, it would seem, clearly enough set forth. Still, we have to go further. We have formerly established a distinction between intelligible and sense nature, assigning the soul to the intelligible world. Granting this, that the soul forms part of the intelligibe world, we must, in another manner, study what is suitable to her nature.

EXISTENCE OF DIVISIBLE BEINGS.

To begin with, there are (beings) which are quite divisible and naturally separable. No one part of any one of them is identical with any other part, nor with the whole, of which each part necessarily is smaller than the whole. Such are sense-magnitudes, or physical masses, of which each occupies a place apart, without being able to be in several places simultaneously.

DESCRIPTION OF INDIVISIBLE ESSENCE.

On the other hand, there exists another kind of essence ("being"), whose nature differs from the preceding (entirely divisible beings), which admits of no division, and is neither divided nor divisible. This has no extension, not even in thought. It does not need to be in any place, and is not either partially or wholly contained in any other being. If we dare say so, it hovers simultaneously over all beings, not that it needs to be built up on them,[1] but because it is indispensable to the existence of all. It is ever identical with itself, and is the common support of all that is below it. It is as in the circle, where the centre, remaining immovable in itself, nevertheless is the origin of all the radii originating there, and drawing their existence thence. The radii by thus participating in the existence of the centre, the radii's principle, depend on what is indivisible, remaining attached thereto, though separating in every direction.[2]

BETWEEN THEM IS AN INDIVISIBLE ESSENCE WHICH BECOMES DIVISIBLE WITHIN BODIES.

Now between entirely indivisible ("Being") which occupies the first rank amidst intelligible beings, and the (essence) which is entirely divisible in its sense-objects, there is, above the sense-world, near it, and within it, a "being" of another nature, which is not, like bodies, completely divisible, but which, nevertheless, becomes divisible within bodies. Consequently, when you separate bodies, the form within them also divides, but in such a way that it remains entire in each part. This identical (essence), thus becoming manifold, has parts that are completely separated from each other; for it then is a divisible form, such as colors, and all the qualities, like any form which can simultaneously remain entire in several things entirely separate, at a distance, and foreign to each other because of the different ways in which they are affected. We must therefore admit that this form (that resides in bodies) is also divisible.

BY PROCESSION THE SOUL CONNECTS THE TWO.

Thus the absolutely divisible (essence) does not exist alone; there is another one located immediately beneath it, and derived from it. On one hand, this inferior (essence) participates in the indivisibility of its principle; on the other, it descends towards another nature by its procession. Thereby it occupies a position intermediary between indivisible and primary (essence), (that is, intelligence), and the divisible (essence) which is in the bodies. Besides it is not in the same condition of existence as color and the other qualities; for though the latter be the same in all corporeal masses, nevertheless the quality in one body is completely separate from that in another, just as physical masses themselves are separate from each other. Although (by its essence) the magnitude of these bodies be one, nevertheless that which thus is identical in each part does not exert that community of affection which constitutes sympathy,[8] because to identity is added difference. This is the case because identity is only a simple modification of bodies, and not a "being." On the contrary, the nature that approaches the absolutely indivisible "Being" is a genuine "being" (such as is the soul). It is true that she unites with the bodies and consequently divides with them; but that hapens to her only when she communicates herself to the bodies. On the other hand, when she unites with the bodies, even with the greatest and most extended of all (the world), she does not cease to be one, although she yield herself up to it entirely.

DIVISION AS THE PROPERTY OF BODIES, BUT NOT THE CHARACTERISTIC OF SOUL.

In no way does the unity of this essence resemble that of the body; for the unity of the body consists in the unity of parts, of which each is different from the others, and occupies a different place. Nor does the unity of the soul bear any closer resemblance to the unity of the qualities. Thus this nature that is simultaneously divisible and indivisible, and that we call soul is not one in the sense of being continuous (of which each part is external to every other), it is divisible, because it animates all the parts of the body it occupies, but is indivisible because it entirely inheres in the whole body, and in each of its parts.[4] When we thus consider the nature of the soul, we see her magnitude and power, and we understand how admirable and divine are these and superior natures. Without any extension, the soul is present throughout the whole of extension; she is present in a location, though she be not present therein.[5] She is simultaneously divided and undivided, or rather, she is never really divided, and she never really divides; for she remains entire within herself. If she seem to divide, it is not in relation with the bodies, which, by virtue of their own divisibility, cannot receive her in an indivisible manner. Thus division is the property of the body, but not the characteristic of the soul.

SOUL AS BOTH ESSENTIALLY DIVISIBLE AND INDIVISIBLE.

2. Such then the nature of the soul had to be. She could not be either purely indivisible, nor purely divisible, but she necessarily had to be both indivisible

and divisible, as has just been set forth. This is further proved by the following considerations. If the soul, like the body, have several parts differing from each other, the sensation of one part would not involve a similar sensation in another part. Each part of the soul, for instance, that which inheres in the finger, would feel its individual affections, remaining foreign to all the rest, while remaining within itself. In short, in each one of us would inhere several managing souls (as said the Stoics).[6] Likewise, in this universe, there would be not one single soul (the universal Soul), but an infinite number of souls, separated from each other.

POLEMIC AGAINST THE STOIC PREDOMINATING
PART OF THE SOUL.

Shall we have recourse to the (Stoic) "continuity of parts"[7] to explain the sympathy which interrelates all the organs? This hypothesis, however, is useless, unless this continuity eventuate in unity. For we cannot admit, as do certain (Stoic) philosophers, who deceive themselves, that sensations focus in the "predominating principle" by "relayed transmission."[8] To begin with, it is a wild venture to predicate a "predominating principle" of the soul. How indeed could we divide the soul and distinguish several parts therein? By what superiority, quantity or quality are we going to distinguish the "predominating part" in a single continuous mass? Further, under this hypothesis, we may ask, Who is going to feel? Will it be the "predominating part" exclusively, or the other parts with it? If that part exclusively, it will feel only so long as the received impression will have been transmitted to itself, in its particular residence; but if the impression impinge on some other part of the soul, which happens to be incapable of sensation, this part will not be able to transmit the impression to the (predominating) part that directs, and sensation will not occur. Granting further that the impression does reach the predominating part itself, it might be received in a twofold manner; either by one of its (subdivided) parts, which, having perceived the sensation, will not trouble the other parts to feel it, which would be useless; or, by several parts simultaneously, and then we will have manifold, or even infinite sensations which will all differ from each other. For instance, the one might say, "It is I who first received the impression"; the other one might say, "I received the imression first received by another"; while each, except the first, will be in ignorance of the location of the impression; or again, each part will make a mistake, thinking that the impression occurred where itself is. Besides, if every part of the soul can feel as well as the predominating part, why at all speak of a "predominating part?" What need is there for the sensation to reach through to it? How indeed would the soul recognize as an unity the result of multiple sensations; for instance, of such as come from the ears or eyes?

THE SOUL HAS TO BE BOTH ONE AND MANIFOLD, EVEN ON THE STOIC HYPOTHESES.

On the other hand, if the soul were absolutely one, essentially indivisible and one within herself, if her nature were incompatible with manifoldness and division, she could not, when penetrating into the body, animate it in its entirety; she would place herself in its centre, leaving the rest of the mass of the animal lifeless. The soul, therefore, must be simultaneously one and manifold, divided and undivided, and we must not deny, as something impossible, that the soul, though one and identical, can be in several parts of the body simultaneously. If this truth be denied, this will destroy the "nature that contains and administers the universe" (as said the Stoics); which embraces everything at once, and directs everything with wisdom; a nature that is both manifold, because all beings are manifold; and single, because the principle that contains everything must be one. It is by her manifold unity that she vivifies all parts of the universe, while it is her indivisible unity that directs everything with wisdom. In the very things that have no wisdom, the unity that in it plays the predominating "part," imitates the unity of the universal Soul. That is what Plato wished to indicate allegorically by these divine words[9]: "From the "Being" that is indivisible and ever unchanging; and from the "being" which becomes divisible in the bodies, the divinity formed a mixture, a third kind of "being." The (universal) Soul, therefore, is (as we have just said) simultaneously one and manifold; the forms of the bodies are both manifold and one; the bodies are only manifold; while the supreme Principle (the One), is exclusively an unity.

[1] See iv. 1.22. [2] See iii 8.7.
[3] See iv. 2.2. [4] See iv. 3.19, 22, 23; iv. 4.28. [5] See iv. 3.20-22.
[6] Cicero, de Nat. Deor. ii. 31-33.
[7] See 4.7.6, 7. [8] Plutarch, de Plac. Phil. v. 21; Cicero, de Nat. Deor. ii. 11. The "predominating principle" had appeared in Plato's Timaeus, p. 41. [9] Of the Timaeus, p. 35.

Paragraph 3, of this book (iv 2,—21) will be found in its logical position—judging by the subject matter,—on pages 75 to 78, in the middle of iv. 7,—2.